RELEASED FROM CIRCULATION

AUG 1 4 2015

CENTRAL
GROSSE POINTE PUBLIC LIBRARY
GROSSE POINTE, MI 48236

# STICKS and STONES and BROKEN BONES

## What a Charmed Life I Lead

LINDA LEE KING

abbott press

Copyright © 2014 Linda Lee King.

All rights reserved. No part of this book may be used or reproduced by any means, graphic, electronic, or mechanical, including photocopying, recording, taping or by any information storage retrieval system without the written permission of the publisher except in the case of brief quotations embodied in critical articles and reviews.

Abbott Press books may be ordered through booksellers or by contacting:

Abbott Press
1663 Liberty Drive
Bloomington, IN 47403
www.abbottpress.com
Phone: 1-866-697-5310

Because of the dynamic nature of the Internet, any web addresses or links contained in this book may have changed since publication and may no longer be valid. The views expressed in this work are solely those of the author and do not necessarily reflect the views of the publisher, and the publisher hereby disclaims any responsibility for them.

Any people depicted in stock imagery provided by Thinkstock are models, and such images are being used for illustrative purposes only. Certain stock imagery © Thinkstock.

ISBN: 978-1-4582-1616-8 (sc)
ISBN: 978-1-4582-1618-2 (hc)
ISBN: 978-1-4582-1617-5 (e)

Library of Congress Control Number: 2014909329

Printed in the United States of America.

Abbott Press rev. date: 07/14/2014

# CONTENTS

Acknowledgments ..................................................................... ix
Prologue ................................................................................ xiii

PART 1: TRAUMATIZED ......................................................... 1
*Dedicated to trauma survivors*

1. Blood Money ................................................................... 3
   *Detroit, Michigan - April 1981*

2. Warning ........................................................................ 15
   *The road to recovery is in constant need of maintenance.*

3. "Vision is the art of seeing things what is invisible to others" ... 21
   *Jonathan Swift*

PART 2: THE HUMAN CONDITION ........................................ 31
*Dedicated to my children: Recognize destiny is a choice.*

4. A product of the 1950s ................................................... 33
   *Baby Boomers & Gypsies*

5. The Magyar life ............................................................. 39
   *Delray, Michigan, a.k.a. Hunkeytown - 1950*

6. Mother Superior ............................................................ 58
   *A lesson in abuse*

7. Nuns Don't Lie ......................................................................... 66
   *White lies only*

8. A Bogey in the House ............................................................ 83
   *Everybody needs an ally*

9. Welcome to the 60s ................................................................ 95
   *Ready, set, time to rock n' roll*

10. The 5:15 ............................................................................... 110
    *Be home in time for dinner*

11. Waiting for the Sun ............................................................. 115
    *Wild child on the run*

12. The Days of Linda Jones .................................................... 128
    *Run Amok*

13. My Man—My Life ............................................................. 134
    *Tommy, a ray of sunshine*

14. Another man—Another Life ............................................. 148
    *Leonard, my dark knight*

PART 3: STICKS & STONES ....................................................... 163
*Dedicated to Veronica - And the hits keep coming*

15. A Trail of Sorrows .............................................................. 165
    *An angry woman*

16. The Ghosts of Kenwood .................................................... 181
    *Can I get a witness?*

17. Kenwood Mansion ............................................................. 188
    *December 1983 Grosse Pointe, Michigan*

18. A Widow's Regret .................................................................. 199
    *Your wish is granted*

19. Roll the Dice ........................................................................ 212
    *Rolling in Crap*

20. In Spite of t All .................................................................... 217
    *Adjusting my moral compass*

21. Sticks & Stones .................................................................... 226
    *Broken people*

22. Ready or Not ....................................................................... 229
    *Here I come*

23. Linda's Last Chance Ranch ................................................. 233
    *Aromas, California - 2005*

24. The Road to Chaos ............................................................. 236
    *Welcome back*

25. Falling Apart ...................................................................... 239
    *A monstrous life*

26. The Universe Is Listening .................................................. 246
    *Invisible ears*

27. "The Book" ........................................................................ 253
    *A piece of work*

28. PTSD ................................................................................. 261
    *The next sleeping giant*

Epilogue .................................................................................... 267

# ACKNOWLEDGMENTS

If I were to thank every person who impacted my life in a positive way, this book would be nothing more than a list of names. If I forgot you, write your name down on the line: _____.

It goes without saying, but the obvious must be stated. My family roots are my strength, as they are my weakness. I am honored to be part of the Bodzsar-Bogard clan of characters I call *family*.

To my children, whom I especially acknowledge as my reason to carry on, to be more than a victim of circumstances, for you are the greatest gift of love that remains despite the hell I put you through.

Cousin Jeannine, a big thank-you. You were there for me in many ways. You provided sound advice. Admitted openly to others you "felt" (something) an urgency to call home because the family was in crisis. Most of all, I am grateful for a roof over my head when I was in transition.

To fellow classmates who were among the first to walk into St. Timothy's Catholic School that ominous September day in 1957, only to find the devil alive and well in the hearts of a few nuns, I dedicate this in your memory.

To Carol Stepanski, a classmate: You helped me figure out why I was mentally stuck in a "bathroom" for over fifty years. You unlocked that door, so please accept this recognition of friendship long overdue.

To Colleen Dolan, thank you for reminding us all to keep a watchful eye on those in charge of our spiritual well-being and never back down.

To Max Waagner, your personal story of intimidation is the common ground that many of our classmates share. Realize this: You helped connect the hard lessons learned as children: to accept abuse; tolerate the pain. It was the Catholic way to salvation.

Carol, Colleen, and I rebelled, but acquiring inner strength was not the intention—we reacted out of self-preservation to the nuns' false accusations. Max, we granted them no quarter because they reaped what they sowed and deserved to taste the bitter fruit from the seeds they planted in our hearts. The fact you remember us at all while dealing with your own troubles is "a bright light in those dark days."

Thank you, YAYAs from the class of '68: Veronica Stevens-Combs, Gloria Walden, Janice Schulte-Neubecker, and Jacki Masi–Razmus, for sending those good vibrations of love and encouragement, nudging me gently along to finish this piece of work. We did it!

To Tom Killian, thank you for your help editing of some very personal chapters and for being a friend all these years. You and Nikki are always a breath of fresh air flowing with logic and reason.

To all the people who impacted my life, though many are dead and gone, your memory lives in my heart and soul forever.

To Jim West, rest easy knowing that love, like fate, takes us by surprise, teaching us the most important lesson of all: Love comes in all shapes and sizes to anyone with a heartbeat, more than once if - you open your heart. Love is unconditional.

To the man in my life, Marc F. Dougherty, I share my heart. We are a couple of mismatched, star-crossed lovers. He calls me Moonbeam. Without Marc in my life, I would have been just fine—but now I'm a lot more than just fine.

During the tumultuous years, I never would have managed to thrive without the many wonderful people I have met. Bradley Dockery, you rock! You catered to our family's needs and shared your heart.

For twenty years, Pam and Steven Lucchesi, have supported my dreams. They too, have given me shelter in the past and a job in my time of need.

Linda Jane Tucker, Tom Robillard, the Morris family, without knowing it, you provided me more strength to pursue my dream and fulfill my childhood promise to do something for humanity.

A special thank you to Laurie O'Connell, your editing skills provided questions that needed answers to be effective and understood. To mankind, the best I can offer is my life story.

# PROLOGUE

Since childhood, I have written what I could not openly say for fear of stumbling over my words. Raised in the Catholic Church by a group of nuns who would beat me if I gave them an answer they didn't want to hear, I learned that I had to always be right or keep my mouth shut. So I wrote everything down on paper that troubled me, and my painful world was easier to live in.

I began my career as a professional writer in 1994 by writing profiles and conducting hundreds of interviews for *Bachelor Book* magazine in Coral Springs, Florida. During that year I assisted publisher Mindi Rudan with her book *Men, the Handbook* while raising my granddaughter. In a few short months, Mindi's book was published, and this book— well, it was still a work in progress. I didn't know what category to pick since I had many personal topics to choose from to write about: Widowhood, single parenting, homicide, abusive nuns and religion, the paranormal, sexual abuse, domestic violence, homelessness, mental illness, and addictions, just a few issues I have had to deal with or overcome. Indeed, I was overwhelmed.

As the years rolled by, I kept writing bits and pieces while telling myself "one day it will be finished," using every excuse in the world to tell myself why it wasn't. Truthfully, I didn't know why. It took another family crisis in 2009 to realize why I needed to publish this book. It is a desperate attempt to get through to my two oldest adult children before one of them dies feeding their demons. To say what I need to tell them without being interrupted by a barrage of questions.

Regardless of my efforts to shelter my young children from my personal trauma, there were repercussions. Today, they're broken adults I can't fix. The impact my life events had on me was transgenerational—I passed it on to my children. Realizing this in 2009, I began examining my own generational, social, and religious conditioning, and the significance it had in developing my odd behavior, and the way I dealt with issues.

By connecting my story to the social and moral issues we humans face on this planet, I realized, this story is about being human in any situation regardless how we are conditioned to fit in society because we all know, the rules change as we grow older. There lies the rub.

What our society in the 1950s believed to be legal, morally right, or the normal way to think and live just isn't true. When I was a young child, my mother wouldn't allow me to ride my bike in the street. Now it is illegal to ride a bike on the sidewalk. Homosexuals were immoral, and my lifestyle wasn't "normal." I live like a gypsy: never staying in one place too long, never knowing when the winds of change will throw me off course, but I keep smiling because I don't have time for tears. It's nonproductive. Currently, I struggle to finish this story, secretly fearing that when I do, my life will change before I'm ready. I shrug it off and find something else to do.

There is a way to cope with the harsh reality of major life events: Be productive. Think of the new you. Be the new you, even if you have to fake it for a while, until you believe it yourself. Reinventing my life and career has taught me that.

My two oldest children have not mended their emotional wounds. They deprive themselves of inner joy and peace of mind by refusing to seek help for their addictions and mental health issues. This particular lifestyle thrives on pain, and there is always a life-or-death crisis. In fact, probably every other person struggling with life in general would benefit from my human experiences except for my own children—the very reason I survived a life course set for self-destruction based on my religious conditioning.

So many changes to get where I am now... what's one more? I can reinvent myself to be an author. I have paid my dues with learned experiences. I earned it, fair and square.

In August of 1993, when I decided it was time to earn a living with my craft, I was forty-two years old, living back in Detroit, a new grandmother and confronted by an age-old question. "What are you going to do with the rest of your life?" A loud voice went off in my head. "Write!" My family had doubts when I called to say I was moving to Florida. It was a "little late" to start a new career, but despite my age, along with a few more family crises to resolve, this "late bloomer" blossomed. Less than a yearless than a year after I made this decision, I was working at *Bachelor Book* magazine, when Mindi promoted me to Senior Staff Writer and Traffic Manager. After a while, I was determined to pursue my writing career, but as a news reporter, and headed to California in Spring of 1998 to reinvent a new me.

Was it dumb luck? Fate? Or destiny that a month after I arrived in San Benito County, California, I had my first article as a freelance news reporter in the *Hollister Free Lance News*? It was destiny. I made a choice to do something with my life after my granddaughter went to live with her mother. My parenting responsibilities were no longer required. I would not be an "empty nest" victim and resort to self-pity just because I had no one to care for. I was "free."

The way I see it, pure "dumb luck," my first article in the *Hollister Free Lance[*, prompted Marvin Snow, editor-in-chief at the *Hollister Pinnacle* newspaper, to offer me an exclusive position as a freelance writer. Unfortunately, in December of 1998, Frank Klauer, the owner and publisher of the *Pinnacle*, died, and six months later I was let go due to a few controversial stories I wrote about construction defects that were discovered in new housing developments. Later, I learned that the attorney who handled the newspaper's legal business also worked with the developers of the homes I was reporting about—a conflict of interest that was swept under the rug. Snow was also let go, but eventually secured an editorial job with the *Atascadero Gazette* in

San Luis Obispo, California. In March 2000, Snow called me to fill in as a part-time reporter. I drove three counties away two to three times a week to cover stories. It was gruesome—driving 250 miles (round-trip) to make a few bucks and keep my writing career going in a hostile environment.

The owner of the Gazettes, David Weyrich was under fire for his ad policies. He would not print gay or abortion ads in any of his five weekly news publications. A slew of reporters and editors walked out in protest to this discriminatory policy. It was a perfect opportunity for me to expand my coverage to a regional audience. At the risk of failure, I had to forge ahead into the unknown territory if I wanted to grow as a writer and not retreat into my comfort zone.

As a freelance reporter without a contract, I could work on any project or cover any story I wanted, too. I took full advantage of this window of opportunity to earn a living as a writer.

Mid-summer of 2000, I was approached by a local candidate, Richard Place, who was running for district supervisor in San Benito County. He needed a writer to help with his campaign. My brain filled with ideas… a chance to show what I can do. Early morning on October 6, 2000, voters of San Benito County received in the mail the *San Benito County Gazette*, an eight-page tabloid with stories about the candidate and the issues the county faced.

During my self-employment I also peddled exclusive stories to the *Hollister Free Lance News* before they hired me on as a staff writer in the Fall of 2000—my first full-time position with benefits and a press pass. About a month after I was hired by the *Hollister Free Lance*, the *Pinnacle News* ran a story about Place's campaign expenditures with my name as the single most "biggest" expenditure. Seriously? I had to call my mother back in Michigan that day to share an inside joke she started when I was a child. After I told Mom I made the "news" again, she laughed a little bit harder.

Secretly, I wanted to be heard. I wanted to craft a column. I envisioned my byline underneath a column. Not many reporters get a lucky break like I did, but in less than two months, I had my column, my voice. I wrote about my human condition, our current issues that impacted families, the local community, and the world. In some alternate world, I viewed myself a crusader for weak-minded souls in need of a little human kindness to find their inner strength. I was proud of myself.

The next three years I spent developing my writing style. And then, in 2003, fate played its sneaky hand and the *Hollister Free Lance* changed ownership. The new management began firing writers along with other staff members who were over forty, me included. We sued for age discrimination and settled out of court in late spring of 2004. Ironically, the *Free Lance* was still running my weekly column when we filed our discrimination suit in 2003, and my unemployment was about to run out. I need to make an intentional change that would impact my career and improve my immediate world. If anything, my children should realize "I am the change I seek." Each day, I improve my world.

Very few people were aware of my career goals—for a very good reason. I didn't trust just anyone with something this important to me, *knowing* what I had to overcome to be a journalist, a columnist, and a professional writer. I did it. In spite of numerous hurdles coupled with the fact I didn't have a college degree or a high school diploma, I did what I set out to do. It was not an easy task. I believed in myself. I knew I could run a newspaper. What I lacked in degrees, I replaced with common sense, experience, contacts, and research. On April 1, 2004, the *Free Press News* ran its first edition. My harbored desire was a reality, but I couldn't do it without the help of my boyfriend, Jim West, who was also the newspaper's backer. He believed in me, too.

The *Free Press* was a weekly publication of Linda's Last Chance Ranch (The tagline of my weekly column) based in our home office in Aromas, California.

I printed stories on the good in the community and wrote for the underdog while helping want-to-be writers gain experience with a byline. As with any new business, the money was tight, but manageable. I had potential clients waiting for the newspaper's first year to run before their corporate offices would allow funds to advertise in any new publication.

On the brink of reaching the paper's first milestone, Jim decided to shut the paper down for a number of reasons. Basically, he couldn't handle the scrutiny "we" received as a couple after our recent engagement reached ears at the *Pinnacle News*. One reporter teased and speculated that a "strip miner" and a "reporter" were in bed together.

A few weeks later, Jim called off the engagement for his personal political agenda. He wanted a seat on the planning commission and the hospital board. I could understand, politics was a job he was born to do. I had a feeling a month earlier that he wanted to shut down the paper when he suggested Linda's Last Chance Ranch Publishing could do a monthly. I was thinking about it, but not ready. Why run a newspaper only to shut it down before its first year? An anniversary edition was in the planning stages. I declined. Was it his intention all along to shut it down if I said no? It didn't matter. I was on the road again.

After being dumped by Jim in the Spring of 2005, I headed to Pennsylvania, unaware this road trip would trigger an emotional and mental breakdown that would bring back years of pain, abuse, and grave losses back into my life. I would come to discover I had Post Traumatic Stress Disorder (PTSD).

Devastated by the loss of a personal relationship and no longer employed, I drove across the country towards Pennsylvania. "What will I do now?" I felt abandoned, emotionally betrayed. I told myself, "Oh, well. I'll get over it. Nothing lasts forever." When you've a few thousand miles to go, with no radio reception, there is nothing to do but think. Everything I lost in life flooded my mind with memories until I could hold it in no more. Tears blinded my vision. I had to pull the car over. All I thought about was what I left behind in Aromas, California: My home, my community, my rescued critters, and a dream. I had to start over again. "Do I have the strength to pick myself up again?"

Over and over while I drove back east, I thought about the lie Jim told the *Pinnacle News* and *Free Lance*, that I was "leaving the state to attend to family matters in Pennsylvania."

As I drove across country, the angrier I became. What will I do now? For the first time in my adult life, I had been living a so-called "normal" life with a man I loved and a job I was passionate about while fulfilling a childhood promise to help others. Every week, a "child in need" was featured. I also ran a weekly photo of homeless pets. Helping at a community level died every mile I drove away from a lifestyle I had become accustomed to. I was facing a new world— one of conflict, the past.

Tragic life events began to catch up with my thoughts as the miles went by. My parents were dead, and my younger siblings, though compassionate, never understood the underlying problems of my formative years. For one reason or another, one too many dead bodies have crossed my path since the age of four, when I saw a little girl get killed in front of me. She was on my mind when I pulled over somewhere in Kansas to get gas. Whenever something tragic happens to change my life, I think of her and I need to write. I jotted down a few thoughts, then went inside to pay for gas and a cup of coffee.

While the Caddy filled up, I sat in the front seat, sipping hot coffee. It was overcast. It was going to rain. I looked down at the newspaper on the passenger seat and saw that it was still folded to the page with the article that ran a day earlier.

As I read the quote again. I was angry enough to cry. It must be true—it was printed in black ink for all to read that I was leaving the state to take care of "family matters." That lie in print sent me on a collision course with my unresolved nun issues that I had buried. I was also reminded what my mother said.

"Don't believe everything you read in the newspapers, Linda."

In 2005, when I arrived at my daughter's house I was in crisis. What I didn't know then is that that little lie unlocked a door in my mind, allowing old ghosts from the past to come out after years of suppressing many sorrows and grievances for the sake of appearances. Time was catching up. I was tired of being "'the strong one" in a crisis. "Where's my shoulder to cry on? Where do I go for support?"

When I arrived in Pennsylvania, I thought I would bounce back as usual. Unfortunately, it would be two more years fighting with myself and lashing out in angry tears at my family while struggling with nightmares and flashbacks before a doctor explained I had PTSD. Knowing my demon by name, I turned on the light in every dark corner of my mind, calling it out, exposing this enemy that had been keeping me prisoner for over forty years. The physical and verbal abuse I was burdened with by a few nuns. What the nuns did to my classmates and me was criminal. They taught me to accept pain and abuse, a lifestyle I was accustomed to.

The most traumatic moment in my life was a day in 1974, when my husband was shot and killed. What I endured from my childhood experiences fueled my will to beat this PTSD demon down and tame it because for me, it will never go away. I have spent the last nine years learning about the effects of what happened to me as a child; how I was conditioned to think by nuns who used corporal punishment as a weapon to make us afraid of making mistakes when learning. I still stumble with my words when I talk, but I don't care. I understand *why*. I do not practice any religion. but live by my own constitutional beliefs, which are subject to change in light of any new discovery I may find to be more useful in my world.

The last four years, I have devoted my time to healing old wounds and becoming a new me, a new author. With this said, may this book inspire my children to seek the help they need. It is never too late to save yourself. Welcome to my world.

# PART I

# Traumatized

## Dedicated to trauma survivors

**V**iolence breeds broken people: war, racism, rape, and murder traumatize the soul. Society's next generation of children are growing up damaged. Violent experiences impact the way we live. For people of all ages, especially with children, early detection and counseling can prevent mental health problems from compounding into a life of torment, poverty, and addiction.

Based on my peculiar history, I'm one of fifty million reasons why early mental health intervention services are necessary for children and their parents in the event of unexpected tragedy.

Read this story with an open mind, because sooner or later everyone is traumatized by the experience of living.

# BLOOD MONEY

## Detroit, Michigan - April 1981

As I sat waiting with my attorney on a bench outside the Wayne County courtroom, no one would have recognized me. The attorneys did their job preparing me for the wrongful death civil case to go to trial, right down to the last detail with a conservative hairstyle and wardrobe. Though Tommy had been dead nearly eight years, I still, had to look the part of a grieving widow.

When it was time to start the jury selection process, an attorney from the other side made a hand motion for Joe to follow him into a room. In a matter of a few minutes, a final offer was made. Their $100,000 offer jumped to $1.3 million to walk away. I expected nothing less than my day in court. "No."

For most people, civil lawsuits are about money. Imagine turning down a million bucks. Imagine the price you pay if you settle for anything less than the truth. This is what I was waiting for: to tell the truth. I was going to let 'em have it for killing my husband, twenty-four-year old Thomas Eugene Holstin. Killed by a Grosse Pointe Park police officer.

History is written by the perception of those in power, the world's political winners. Our family's history would not be determined by lies and misinformation. It was my duty to be Tommy's champion, as he done for me in the past. I would clear his name from any fault for the record. Unarmed, Tommy was gunned down in front of me by a Grosse Pointe Park police officer. I was out for justice.

It doesn't matter what type of lawsuit is filed, whether or not it involves a defective product or a wrongful death suit—people sue because an injustice needs to be corrected. Most civilians don't have a clue how the process works, or the length of time you will live in limbo. It was seven years after Tommy's death when this civil case was finally brought to trial.

Seven years living in fear, living lies of omission to protect my family. I learned to live a lie in my daily life to tell the truth in court. I was more than ready to have my day in court. The lawyers had their own agenda to settle.

Most times, it is easier and profitable to settle out of court. Attorneys have their payday and the insurance companies love it. No public record. However, settling has restrictions. The facts may never be discussed. The records are sealed, along with the mouths of witnesses; something I could not live with. My state of mind depended on it. Too many times over the years I was told to keep my mouth shut about the case for fear of retaliation. I needed my day in court to free me. Turning down the million-dollar offer surprised everyone, including the judge.

Visibly caught off guard, my attorney asked me to "seriously consider" the offer on the table. "Guaranteed," he emphasized, "that's an awful lot of money to turn down."

Seven years living for this day to come, just to be forever silenced by settling out of court for the sake of a "sure thing?" Hell, no! How could I heal? How could I move forward, reliving that day over and over without seeing it through to the end? No one understood this wasn't a healthy situation for any of us.

Thomas Eugene Holstin's death wasn't going to be dismissed. His children's tears would not be ignored, and they needed to know their father did not deserved to be gunned down. Tommy was worth more than any amount of material wealth.

Everyone behind the scene believed I would call it quits and settle. Instead, I challenged the powers that be, including Judge Michael Stacey. All of them believed I would take the money and run. I repeated, "It's not about the money."

# Sticks and Stones and Broken Bones

The exact reason why Judge Michael Stacey instructed the eight alternate jurors to participate in the award verdict decision, I don't recall. However, in a few short hours, the jury made a decision. A moment of silence. Holding my breath as I stood there with my attorney. It was surreal, but I heard it. Loud and clear "in favor of the plaintiff."

My knees were knocking, my stomach was queasy, a hand gently rested on my shoulder, and I heard my father's voice, "Breathe, Linda."

Tommy was all I hoped for in a man. A .357 Magnum took him away. One gunshot and our future disappeared. The man I loved and trusted with all my secrets from the past now carried my heart with him to the grave. Without the comfort of time to set my broken heart, it had shattered into particles of dust when the trigger was pulled. I have lived with this flashback everyday, coping with emotional scars one episode at a time.

The impact from witnessing Tommy's death was a magnitude level near extinction. This event triggered many emotional episodes. Dark days from the fallout were ahead—there would be no light to search for the remnants of my broken heart. Eventually, I would have to crawl out of hell to find these pieces of history that are part of my human condition.

The jury had found Tommy was "unnecessarily shot" by a Grosse Pointe Park police officer using excessive force. After the verdict was read, I thanked the jurors. Daddy hugged me as we walked out the courtroom. Joe said the defendants may file an appeal, but he had his doubts.'

Since the day the wrongful death suit was filed in the mid-seventies, it never crossed my mind I would lose. It wasn't arrogance—I just *knew*.

On that particular day when Joe called to inform me the papers were filed, a childhood memory came to mind. I was *begging* God to make me rich so I could give the money away to the poor. That's what a good Catholic is supposed to do—care for others.

"Linda girl... you hit the mother lode," Daddy said. "What a shame it happened this way."

It was a shame. It was also a burden impacting the entire family. It was in Daddy's red, swollen eyes. He felt my pain. He loved his son-in-law. What was waiting for us all in the future weighed heavy on my father's heart. The irreversible consequences of an early Tuesday morning regurgitated in my mouth from the taste of bittersweet tears.

Something invisible was warning me all along. This day had been coming since childhood, long before I met Tommy, but I never pieced it together, the strange daydream or the vision I had experienced in the back of the police car when I was eight years old.

It was a cold, snowy day in February of 1959 when I ran away from St. Timothy's Catholic School in Trenton, Michigan. I was tired of the abuse and false accusations by the nuns. I crawled out a window and took off.

I had walked three miles before someone picked me up and drove me to the Riverview Police Department. The ride back to the school was memorable because of the strange pictures in my head.

If that strange dream, nightmare or whatever it was that played in my head wasn't enough to get my attention to listen to the voice within, I saw the actual date Tommy died—7/16—in another dream approximately fifteen years later in early January of 1972.

What troubled me more than this? *Tommy knew, too:* Our time together was short. "I won't live past thirty, Linda." He was twenty-four years old. A man is gunned down... and I get paid?

*Anticlimactic* best describes what it was like when the jury awarded me and Tommy's two children, Michael and Sheila, 1.2 million dollars, plus interest.

I *earned* nothing, yet gained a world of wealth. An angry cop had changed my life with his .357 Magnum packed with hollow-point bullets, giving me a mission: Speak for the dead.

As we left the courtroom, a few of the jurors approached me near the elevators. An older black man looked particularly sad as he wished our family "the best."

"I knew the cop was lying," he said. Wishing us well, the man headed out.

## Sticks and Stones and Broken Bones

It didn't feel right walking away from the Wayne County Courthouse while my attorney, Joseph Crehan, was singing out loud, "Another One Bites the Dust."

"Why aren't you jumping up and down?" he said. "You should be shouting."

Joe did a good job—in fact, a great job. He left his firm to take on the case. He believed in himself and worked hard; his belief in the case was from a legal perspective. Still? Celebrate blood money? Join him in a happy dance? Inconceivable, "celebrating" a hollow victory for *our* personal loss. The money meant nothing except that bills would be paid on time and the kids could explore extracurricular activities previously unaffordable.

Hell, I had the distinct impression Joe wanted to settle the day the trial began. Watching Joe do his happy dance, it crossed my mind that he didn't get it. He didn't get *me*. The jury was very interested in the testimony from the eyewitness, me. This determined the outcome of the case because, win or lose, I was willing to stand by my convictions.

"As I said before, Joe, it was never about the money."

Meanwhile, neglecting my mental health, the grief I harbored kept the anger alive with seven years of tears and depression. I got the money, but the cop was never charged for the shooting.

The same night Tommy was killed, a Lincoln Park police officer from the other side of the tracks—the poor side of town—was involved in a gangland slaying. I soon learned about political justice—and how the people pulling the strings make the decisions.

A few weeks after Tommy was killed, Wayne County Assistant District Attorney William Cahalan visited me at my Detroit home on 360 Alter Road, to inform me that charges would not be filed against the Grosse Pointe officer, stating it was "not the officer's fault." I knew it was politics. I was too young and grief-stricken to understand why the Lincoln Park officer was being charged for shooting five unarmed men in the head, and not the Grosse Pointe officer.

Cahalan said one of the victims lived to testify that the Lincoln Park officer pulled the trigger. It was my word against two Grosse Pointe officers and in my case, Tommy was dead and could not testify against the cop. "What!?!"

I wanted this man charged, but that wasn't going to happen. In the Lincoln Park case, the district attorney's office filed criminal charges. Why? An easy case to win. After Cahalan left, I called my parents with the news and my father, disgusted, grumbled before making an arbitrary remark.

"I bet you it has everything to do with money and politics."

A random statement but something in it pried at me to make a connection Later on, during Cahalan's run for office, it became apparent that he had ties to Grosse Pointe Farms. I'm sure he had many wealthy friends who contributed to his campaign.

The community of Grosse Pointe, Michigan, where I met my last two husbands, consists of five communities that reek of money.—old money, dating back to Henry Ford. The quaint suburb is a picturesque scene of waterfront mansions gracing Lakeshore Drive, where many residents are afforded special privileges, and the rest of us go directly to jail.

Grosse Pointers pay very high taxes for schools and special services. Cops are known for driving drunken old ladies home and turning a blind eye to entitled kids caught joyriding, drinking, and other delinquent pranks.

Tolerating pranks and giving a kid a break is one thing, but when a police officer gives the privileged adult offenders a free pass over and over, it simply reinforces entitlement, and constitutes a slap in the face to the majority of people who can't afford to pay the price of justice. Our basic civil right is to be treated equally and fairly. Wealthy people have the power to change things, but they keep racism alive by doing nothing when it comes to their home turf.

The wealthy whites of Grosse Pointe have separated themselves from Detroit's poor, black population by turning a blind eye whenever law enforcement engaged with a black person just walking down the street. People of color had better be on their way to or another specific destination, or they'd likely to be placed in a patrol car and escorted back into Detroit. Usually, the poor person would be dropped off at Chalmers and Jefferson Avenue, a very dangerous section in Detroit similar to Harlem.

Yes, I have witnessed this myself one summer afternoon in the 80s when I drove in front of Grosse Pointe South High School. I intentionally followed a Grosse Pointe Farms patrol car after I saw an officer placing an elderly black man in his car. I was curious—I'd heard about this, and I wanted to know if he was taking the old man to the police station or doing the usual drop-off. The cop was heading out of the Pointes into Detroit. At the corner of Jefferson and Chalmers Avenue, the officer let the man out and made a right turn down Chalmers. The black man went about his business.

Witnessing this, it felt very shameful to be white. The next time it occurred, it made me angry because some people truly believe their money entitles them to treat others any way they please and to protect the wrong people.

The "mother lode" indeed—it was Blood Money. I had no respect for it because I didn't earn it. Another vow, but this one to my father, that I would not allow money to change me or pretend to be better than anyone else. I honored that promise, I think, because according to my father, money didn't change me a bit. "You're still nuts!" he maintains.

The following dream came to me almost a year after Tommy died, when I was dating Leonard, my next husband. Over the course of many nights over four decades, it has evolved into a complex futuristic world.

*Again I appeared, standing on a steel staircase leading to another level, where racks of colorful garments were being set up. While I was being dressed by staffers in black camouflage, someone put a gun in my hand, and I heard, "You need to protect yourself. They will be gunning for you. You'll need another disguise."*

When I met Tommy, my life was unresolved, struggling with serious issues. Every wrong I faced in my past was buried in silence until we found each other. Then everything fell into place. My emotional pain eased by the comfort of love as he held my guilty shame close to his heart. I found a renewed purpose. And, though we were penniless, once upon a time I was on top of the world planning a future, a family: We wanted something more than just dreaming about a future—we wanted to live our dreams. Tommy had given me unconditional love, ending the nightmares that startled my mind as a child, proving that love can heal our flawed psyche.

What did I do with all the money? Anything I damn well pleased. I spent it. I lent it. Fulfilled fantasies until I grew quite demented. What happened next blew me away.

What are the twisted odds that fate should unleash its cosmic eye on my family? During the trial, I had a horrible, but a precognitive dream of my third husband, Leonard, talking to a dead man, who was Tommy.

Precognitive dreaming is a representation of our thoughts in pictures of future events. During the trial I had concerns for Leonard's well-being. He had lost weight and was under a lot of stress while I dealt with the trial over Tommy's death.

*Leonard and I exited the vehicle, a red Plymouth Fury, and walked toward the auto store. We were talking, laughing, but on the way out, something changed. Leonard ignored me and began walking ahead faster toward the car. I called his name and demanded that he "look at me!"*

*Leonard didn't flinch. He walked up to the trunk of the car and opened it. Tommy was lying there and sat up. They started talking to each other, laughing and ignoring me as if I did not exist.*

"Leonard can't hear me because he's dead, like Tommy." I woke up believing that Leonard would soon die.

Clammy enough for the air to give me the chills when I tossed the covers off, I knew this was not a normal dream. Our car transformed from a red Plymouth Fury with the 360 engine to the 1979 navy-blue Lincoln Town Car in which I found Leonard's body on March 23, 1982.

A direct hit to my paranormal heart, my third husband was dead less than a year after the trial. I was widowed again, a very wealthy widow, and another coffin to pick out. The nightmares and flashbacks were back. Sleeping was nothing more than a state of restless dreams and self-loathing.

Doctors said I was just depressed, that it was a part of the normal grieving process. True, to some degree. Paranormal secrets were taunting me, but I didn't share this with anyone who could take my rights away. People had no idea how fucked-up my world was because a few lousy dreams told me so.

Daddy was right: It was a shame. My children were doomed to suffer a lifetime of emotional pain while living with a tormented woman: me, their mother, shrouded in guilt. And a shit-load of money to say, "I'm sorry, your daddies are dead, and your mother is off her rocker."

I was an emotional ticking bomb under the control of the irrational and impulsive nature of my dysfunctional thinking. Depression, anxiety, abandonment, survivor's guilt, and my undiagnosed condition: post-traumatic stress disorder coupled with raising four kids with another set of issues—what can I say? I was one wacky single parent.

It was never my desire to be a single parent, but that's the hand I was dealt. When Tommy died, I was carrying our second child. Leonard left behind two children as well. No question, my four children have suffered secondary PTSD.

It wasn't fair. I wasn't a full-time mother if I had to be head of household. To maintain order, I was more of a dictator when they were little. Strict about bedtime, what they ate, where they were going and doing their homework at a scheduled time. No bending the rules. Basically, I followed my mother's rules. Until... I realized that some rules should be broken, or they may break the spirit.

I began to change. I started letting them finish watching a television show if it ran past their bedtime. I would let them pick a time to do homework and allow friends to come over and play in their room—which I had never, ever been allowed to do. I let my kids pick their friends, black or white; I didn't care, as long as they were good kids. I gave them freedom to be. I wanted my children to feel like they could hang out at home with their friends; at least I knew where they were.

My oldest son, Michael, has suffered the most. It hurts more than the written word can describe what I feel when I look at his baby pictures with his father, the bond they had developed… my heart and joy, followed by painful tears for the child Tommy never met—our daughter he named Sheila before he died.

Later, when my daughter Nicole was born, I was reminded how important the parental bond is for the young child's emotional development. Nicole and Michael have both bonded with their fathers; it did make a difference in their lives.

When my youngest son Ryan came along, I noticed that the bond between him and his father was cut short, just like his older brother, Michael. Of all my children, Nicole knew her father longer than her siblings ever had a chance to, and she is the most stable of us all.

Geographically speaking, stability is my issue: I never sit still or stay in one place too long. Always on the move for one reason or another since 1968. After Leonard and I bought our home in Boca Raton, Florida, I thought the restless gypsy in me would settle down in one spot. Leonard died, and I felt out of place again. I was a restless spirit with money in the bank and kids in tow.

Susceptible to outbursts of angry tears, I tried to make life easier on the kids, keeping them away from me and busy with activities. At one point I sent them to boarding school. My goal was to keep the kids distracted from the bad memories of their past. Helping them create new positive memories for their future, I could avoid the painful questions that I had no answer for.

Each of us acted out our emotions. Leonard died just before Michael's ninth birthday. He took it hard. One day he locked himself in a closet at the Boca Raton Christian school and began beating the door, crying in anger. Apparently, my youngest brother told his nephew that Leonard wasn't his biological father. True. However, Leonard and I planned to explain our past to the children when the younger ones were older, to avoid complications. Now that the information was out there, it created problems.

My youngest son, Ryan, was 18 months old, and couldn't understand why daddy wasn't coming home. Later on, when Ryan was around seven years old, he wanted to die for "just a little while" so he could see his dad. Sheila was almost eight, and it concerned me - she only cried, just a little bit. Nicole, barely six years old, wore her heart on her sleeve; she cried and cried. One day when she was a young teen, she cried out, "I wish you died instead of Daddy."

I was trying to understand why so much chaos in my life. My displaced emotions were out of control, just as my mother had taught me by example. I was trying to read between the lines, but the message was lost in translation.

Through writing, therapy, and time, I learned that my emotional rants came from the unresolved issues from past experiences buried beneath one drama after the next. There's no time to heal the past wounds when the present is still vulnerable and it threatens the future—no room to thrive, just to survive.

Our family's tradition and customs were accompanied in a litany of phrases, clichés, home remedies, and visions. Family secrets were well guarded, and sins were mortal wounds inflicted on our soul.

In the 1950s, children were seen and not heard. Told to speak when spoken to. Women were moody. Soldiers were shell-shocked.

The American Dream was a fairytale where we all live happily ever after. All you have to do is grow up, get a job, get married, have kids, own your home and be king of your castle. How I handled trauma as a child was based on these beliefs: If something bad happens, get over it because everything works out for the best in the end., consequently creating the "happy ending" to the story that began a long time ago.

Without intervention, a child's emotional disorders frequently continue into adulthood. I'm an example of that, with. every stick and stone dragging me down to the bottom of despair. The key component to understanding my debilitating mental condition?

Childhood. Facts show depression among young mothers can influence the mental health of young children.

My mother was more than influential, she was a gypsy who believed in curses and fortune telling, she believed we were guided by the stars and that some dreams were messages from the departed. This is the world I grew up in. I never had a chance. I was the round peg trying to fit in the square box.

# WARNING

### The road to recovery is in constant need of maintenance.

There is no escape from the hand of fate. Eventually, it taps us on the shoulder. A simple reminder that life is vulnerable. Nature proves this everyday. People we love eventually die. Most times, it's a manageable experience. The natural order of dying leaves no profound emotional scars of regret or nightmares. Yet, one untimely death or traumatic incident will distort a person's thinking.

In the wake of trauma, one question comes to us: What good can come of such tragedies? Surprisingly, many positive changes can emerge from grief. Emotional and physical trauma can permanently scar the heart. From these experiences will grow the inner-strength to heal or fall victim to self-destructive thoughts. It's a conscious choice.

The repercussions from trauma are toxic waste. Doctors had it wrong for decades, treating me for everything but PTSD. Moving forward, letting go of the guilt is the obvious recourse, or those we love become infected. It was too late for my children, especially the two oldest, trapped in a cesspool of guilty tears since the day Tommy died. If only I had done more to prevent the shooting. All those stupid dreams preparing me for this? I did nothing to stop it. I replayed the scene over and over in my head: I could have push the gun towards the wall, away from Tommy's direction or worse, step in and take the bullet. Take a chance I might survive knowing the baby wouldn't. I couldn't do that either.

My oldest son was recently released from prison, where he served time for his self-medicating habits. My oldest daughter not only made the local newspapers a few times in Pennsylvania for her emotional indiscretions, but her actions in one incident may have caused in the Scranton Community Medical Center to rethink its security when she escaped from the emergency room to avoid being held over for a mental health evaluation due to her life-threatening actions.

Leonard died before the two younger ones realized he had a drinking problem, and, for the most part, they have a better quality of life than their older siblings.

My youngest son has PTSD from Iraq, and is still in better shape than his older brother, who refuses help and would rather sit in jail to avoid the stigma attached to mental health. "I'm not crazy!" No one said you were.

The stigma of mental illness hinders those who need the most help. This must change for a healthy society to prevail. Besides my own children, I am witnessing Sheila's daughter, my oldest grandchild, Maria in a downward spiral, heading toward the core of her demons.

My granddaughter's current lifestyle is detrimental to her health. She is using hard core drugs to self-medicate, and I'm helpless. She has to make the changes, not me. My plan would be to swoop her up and institutionalize her for six months, minimum.

Her past has left her wanting and needy. She didn't ask for much, only what everyone else had: a mother's attention. Praying to whatever God comes to my mind, I say it out loud, "Keep her alive and watch her."

If she continues on this path, she will die. I have seen it before. The hardest part? I can't fix everything. It's not my job. What I can do is share my insight from the dark side of my life, battling government, religion and blind ignorance while suffering mental disorders from terrible events.

The violent and tragic history of our broken family dates back a few generations that I know of. A more recent chaotic event occurred in December 2009. Held hostage by a doped-up person for over ten hours with my sixteen-year-old granddaughter was another setback. PTSD, violence, and all its ugly triggers.

My oldest granddaughter already had abandonment issues. Her parents, young and emotionally unequipped, gave me custody until her mother decided to take her back when she was four. A short time later, it was obviously the wrong decision. My loving granddaughter was treated like a prop, a status symbol, to reflect the image of my oldest daughter's position.

Somewhere in her mind, my child believed being a *good* mother meant she cooked, cleaned, and kept her child dressed in the best clothes—no Wal-Mart. No material wants whatsoever in the Pocono Mountains. The heartbreak of the matter is my granddaughter would have been happier wearing clothes from Wal-Mart, if only her mother had not neglected her emotional needs.

Then again, my daughter's life began under extreme duress, including complications with her birth. While in the womb, she felt every thought and pain in my heart the night her father died. My baby was traumatized before she was even born. It would be a few decades before I discovered what I *felt* was true: That I had passed trauma onto the next generation in *transgenerational trauma.*

Transgenerational trauma is passed on from the first survivors of trauma, who inadvertently pass it along to future generations of offspring of the survivors due to the complex mechanisms of post-traumatic stress disorder.

New findings in the medical profession have determined that a mother's state of mind during pregnancy does affect the unborn child. Most mothers have known this, and didn't need a study to prove it.

Circumstances were out of my control the night Tommy was shot. No one knew what to do for me except, prescribe pills for my "nerves." Just like they did for my mother.

Now, I was staring at our family history through the eyes of my grandchild at sixteen, when her mother sent her back to me again. A lost childhood. Circumstances got out of control for us. Two weeks later, there was a raving lunatic waving a knife in my face.

The property I was living on had a some single residences on it. My granddaughter wasn't completely unpacked when an issue got out of hand. One of the tenants who lived on the property came banging on my door one morning and pushed his way in. My grand daughter saw the stern look in my eyes when I turned around, giving her the hush sign. For once, she kept her mouth shut. The intruder was too high to reason with.

At one point, I was trapped against a wall as the rambling continued over a piece of firewood. The man claimed it was stolen by another tenant living on the property. It wasn't.

It was pointless, but I tried to explain that the firewood was mine. One of the tenants was chopping it up in pieces as a favor to me and my aching body. At one point I tried to leave, thinking the man would follow, but he didn't. He started preaching about religion to my granddaughter.

What in God's name is happening to my family? Is a family's future doomed to repeat mistakes from the past? Does the essence of our ancestors' dreams leave an imprint in our genes? Our subconscious? Questions I was not qualified to answer: but I could theorize and philosophize all I want, but I was looking for facts.

As a family, we tried to make sense of it. Why did so much sorrow and drama follow us. Is it really true that history repeats itself? Does it also apply to family? Yes, it does. Too many complicated questions when I had one complicated problem to solve. How to get this nut job out of the house? First, I attempted to lure this man away from Maria by leaving the house. It almost worked.

He started to follow but then turned around and walked back in the house and continued talking to my granddaughter about God. I went to the end of the driveway and made a call to my son. Why not the cops? I couldn't trust them with my granddaughter's life.

People who suffer with mental illness or who are impaired often have problems with excessive force from law enforcement encounters because police officers admittedly lack the training to deal with the mental issues that affect thousands of individuals who are arrested each year.

I then went back in the house, hoping to diffuse the situation. No such luck; the ranting went on for hours. I listened while Maria remained quiet on the sofa. The man then went into the kitchen and picked up a knife, waving it in the air, using it like a pointer, as the conversation exploded into a tale of thieves, the Bible, and the evil deeds of others. *Where was this insanity coming from?*

It was getting late. I needed food and attempted to cook dinner, trying to ignore this ranting lunatic who picked up the kitchen knife I laid on the counter. What is the problem? I thought this can't be about the firewood.

The ugliness behind the spoken words made me vomit in the kitchen sink. So much for dinner. Fully animated, this person ranted about a pot thief who'd been stealing "weed" every year while making jerky moves toward me for two hours. I was getting dizzy.

My body's reaction to the stress finally made an impact. No one likes to watch another person vomit. My tangible state was obvious. The angry druggie calmed down long enough to realize my physical condition was in a critical state.

He insisted I walk over to their house for something to eat. I followed, a guarantee to get this person out of the house and away from my granddaughter. I took the plate of food offered, then started back to my place. The doper was on my heels.

"God, no." I thought, "Stay home."

The telephone rang. *I am lucky.* The druggie turned around to answer the phone. Making a getaway. I walked in the front door, locking it behind me. I hugged my granddaughter quickly made a call to my youngest son, Ryan.

"You have to get us the hell out of here!"

This is not what I wanted for my granddaughter. Her life was rough enough. I had known the family would send her back to me. The very day I picked her up at the Redding Airport, I recalled a visionary dream I had a few years earlier while living in Hawley, Pennsylvania:

*The room looked like a hotel room, decorated in golden tones, and I noticed the drawers filled with new clothes. We were living there. Like most dreams, it was the future. It was just a dream... Or was it?*

Before Ryan arrived in his pickup to move us out, he had called the Shasta County Sheriff's Department to inform them of the situation. A sheriff's car was placed on standby. They had dealt with the individual before.

Forced out of my home, moving into my youngest son's house wasn't easy, and it took months to find a place in California. I needed a good school district for my granddaughter. Three adults with issues, and an angry, emotionally disabled teenager: it wasn't pretty.

A few violent, knock-down, dragging-her-out—the-door incidents, it was obvious the girl needed professional help, too.

It was not right for her to be forced to sever family ties and moving two thousand miles away to live with me because no one could handle her. No wonder she had abandonment issues. Like a hot potato, tossed to the next of kin. I love and care for her but I'm not her mother. The girl made that loud and clear.

We argued and fought nearly every day until she graduated. The key component in all this? Emotional neglect and abandonment affecting her mental health.

For a break, I opted to stay at the Gaia Hotel in Anderson. Site unseen, I turned the key. I walked into a dream. The room was exactly as I saw it a few years earlier.

"I should have known the dream was a warning," I told a friend, "I *knew* they were going to send her back to me."

My emotionally neglected granddaughter didn't deserve this. Our family's history of emotional neglect must cease. Someone has to open that door, so it might as well be me and my big mouth. As my mother always said, "Not everybody is going to like you." Oh, well.

The human condition of any family speaks volumes of our beating hearts' quest to share unconditional love and be accepted for who we are, quirks and all.

This is a convoluted story, not easy to tell. Let alone having any expectations, people will believe what they read. That's my problem. My goal is to entertain the many avenues and possibilities to raise the consciousness of humanity, even if I embarrass myself in the process.

# "VISION IS THE ART OF SEEING THINGS WHAT IS INVISIBLE TO OTHERS"

Jonathan Swift

**B**efore going further, one equation that needs to be addressed is the complicated matter of the supernatural traumatizing my spirit. Barely two years old, something bizarre happened. A ghost in the room. Followed by an out-of-body experience.

These unforgettable experiences have been daunting throughout my life. A wedge between me and the tangible world I seek to fit in. It was an unresolved problem interfering with most aspects of my life, including this piece of work.

My problem? I needed clarification, a witness, validation, some documentation to collaborate that the strange things I experienced, no doubt in my mind, did happen. Convincing others to open their minds created tensions. No one wanted to admit that the paranormal could be real.

People who haven't had these types of experiences will dismiss what they don't understand as untrue or impossible. No amount of scientific evidence will change a person's view on the paranormal experience, if their beliefs are based solely on science or religion.

Supernatural experiences are also viewed by many therapists as a mental health disorder. This stigma is more damaging than the actual supernatural events themselves. Unless I was too drunk or stoned to keep my opinions to myself, I usually kept my mouth shut.

Mumma was right about liquor: "When yous drink, the truth comes pouring out."

Rambling on about ghosts, the boogeyman, or my wacko dreams was a sure way to lose friends. Oh, well. Wacky thoughts and theories with nowhere to go but in circles. It wasn't until the 1980s that I embarked on this dubious journey to find other people who had experienced paranormal events, and realized that for many people, it takes a personal experience to become interested in the paranormal.

In the recent decade, enough people have come forward about their experiences to rekindle scientific interest in the paranormal world. Science is catching up with the rest of us moonbeams. Researchers are trying to determine if there is a spiritual link connecting us, body and soul. No more dabbling; scientists are now testing their theories on patients and test subjects.

Out-of-body experiences, ghosts, precognitive dreams and other mind-bending experiences are still in the infancy stage of research and discovery, but at least the door is opened.

Everyone dreams. Based on personal observations and experiences, we humans are probably all capable of having ESP (extra sensory perception) and premonitions from dreams. Knowing when to pay attention to a dream is important. Perhaps a dream won't let you go, sticking with you all day long, popping in and out of your head. Trying to wake your inner senses, something is happening, but you don't know what to expect... you feel it.

Dreaming or awake, the brain is wired to watch out for danger. What about the spirit? Does it sense danger? Science is suggesting there may be some truth to the sixth-sense theory. An uneducated guess, I'm inclined to agree. Chalk it up to anecdotal evidence.

Understanding a message from the subconscious is key to the spirit's path. Considering the number of people who believe in God, in signs, miracles, ghosts or their local psychic, I have to wonder?

"Is it possible, some dreams are portals of information from the future? While some dreams trigger past events with flashbacks?"

Some psychologists are suggesting that prophetic dreams reveal an individual's anxiety toward the uncertainty of the immediate future. True, but if a child's dream describes a future event that in vivid detail and it occurs later on, the dreamer recognizes an urgency to change their conventional belief of dreams and their meaning.

Some scientists claim there is convincing evidence that a number of people possess psychic powers. I agree, not based on science, but the lifestyle and beliefs I grew up with. I am the product of my mother and father.

My father did not believe in religion, God, or Jesus. The facts didn't add up in his mind. Mom believed all of it, including dreams, tea leaves, and the third eye. There lies the rub. Raised to be a Catholic by a Hungarian gypsy and an agnostic. Conformity? Out of the question.

Premonitions in a dream have been analyzed and discussed throughout history, including by President Abraham Lincoln. Two weeks before his assassination, Lincoln dreamt of his own body lying in a coffin. He told his wife, a few friends, and his bodyguard, Ward Hill Lamon, about this "wake." Lincoln did believe some dreams could reveal the future.

Do you think Lincoln could afford to spend his political capital sharing this with the general public? Probably not. This was parlor talk for old women to amuse themselves, not to be taken seriously or risk being labeled unstable. Yet, Lincoln felt *compelled* to tell someone.

Deciphering dreams, talking about ghosts added fuel to the ongoing controversy I had with the nuns in religion class. It was heresy and superstitious to believe in anything other than the Catholic Church's teachings. I felt compelled to disagree.

Psychologists say there is an evolutionary theory behind our dreams: to protect ourselves for upcoming events. As time moved forward into the future, I found it to be true. My mother *knew* things before an event. It was as natural to her as sleeping and eating.

In the dream world, we face life-threatening situations such as drowning or being chased by predators; man or beast. The theory is we learn to shield ourselves from harm by practicing "how to" survive immediate danger when presented in this dream state.

While dreaming, the mind pieces together bits of information a lot faster than the conscious mind can realize. President Lincoln is a great example.

Lincoln kept the Union together during the civil war, then freed the slaves, it is possible that in his dream of assassination, his sixth sense was tuning in. Lincoln's unconscious mind was working on the information he already knew. There was much talk and discontent after the war. Many people wanted him dead. Just like my second husband, Lincoln *knew* his lifetime was nearing the end.

Another event brings me back to a dream I had since I was seven years old, and as untimely it seems, Tommy's death arrived on time, just like the dream.

One evening after Tommy's death, I was playing the Neil Young album I gave him for his 24th. Birthday when a spooky feeling came over me with a shiver. *Someone watching me?* I smelled Old Spice. "You're here!"

Tommy's spirit lingered around me, filling the room and the empty space in my heart with his familiar scent. I took a deep breath, hoping to breathe into the partials of the argon atoms he once breathed and capture the essence that was him. Tommy's favorite song began to play when I felt a small stinging pinch on my right butt cheek at the exact moment "Old man look at my life - Twenty-four and there's so much more..."

"I felt that! I knew it! I knew you were here!" I cried until I nearly lost my breath. "Don't go."

In the spring of 1975, my personal mission was find people like me. "Birds of a feather," Mom would call them. Searching for people in need of help when I needed it was probably the last thing I needed. Ironically, I was looking for dysfunctional people—and that's when I got Leonard. Another childhood dream unfolding, my third husband.

## Sticks and Stones and Broken Bones

Looking for another point of view on the dead, I discovered a book *Life After Life* by Dr. Raymond Moody, an authority in the field of near death Experience (NDE). The number of non-gypsies and Catholics who believe that dreams as personal, spiritual messages are many. Many people today are admitting their paranormal secrets.

As a Catholic child, I was taught these experiences were not real, or the work of the devil. Even worse, anyone who talked about ghosts or heard voices were called crazy. Yet, with all my faith, an army of nuns didn't stop these strange dreams or the dead souls that came around. To me, it was personal. The paranormal was the normal, at least in our household.

"Yes Sister, I do believe in ghosts!" I repeated, again and again. A verbal affirmation that usually preceded with accusations of being disagreeable to disrupt the class.

But the ghosts weren't some figment of my imagination—they were real.

Listening to other people's opinions outside the homogenized world I grew up in was an education. Open-minded discussions on philosophy, politics, and religion. Debating countless perspectives to the endless questions of life and death, I discovered I was not alone. Yet, no one would admit in a public setting what it is they saw go bump in the night.

It seemed I was always grasping for a lifeline to breathe new life into my heart and soul with each strange encounter. Also, there in digging into everything related to death, dreams, and the supernatural can pique an insatiable curiosity. This obsession had nothing to do with my anxiety, OCD, depression or PTSD issues. It had everything to do with the soul of humanity, the depraved indifference of many so-called Christians to human suffering, and the narcissistic attitude "Who cares..? It doesn't involve me."

To witness the last breath a person or any living creature exhales is raw pain. Under violent conditions, a bloody death may occur, giving mankind cause to bleed tears of reasons to care about humanity, and to share the wealth the planet has to offer because there is no reason for anyone to die of hunger. This is a grave evil that need not exist.

There is too much money wasted on weapons. Why build more devices to kill? Oh, I get it—it's cheaper to kill the poor than to feed them. Every living creature born deserves a chance to experience living, and most will fight tooth and nail to live another day. Or, in some instances, they may come back to haunt you.

Push a person to their limits - a primitive being will be unleashed. Hunger is a driving force behind many indiscretions. Perhaps, if we remove hunger from list of things that kill people, it might make a difference how the world treats one another? Most of the negative experiences I endured, I have had to work out in my head. No one wanted to listen. So, I would write down every crappy thought, experience and dream, just to have a timeline of evidence for myself as proof, it wasn't all in my head when an event took place.

Writing enables me to cope with my distorted thoughts before sharing them with others. Talking to anyone who would listen when I felt out of place with my surroundings, I discovered the world became my therapist.

Often, I drank myself into bed, but not to dream. Regardless of hard-core efforts to slumber, the alarm clock nagged in the back of my mind at 1:16 a.m. on any given night. It was the hour a childhood dream became a living nightmare, it was the hour of Tommy's death. Every night the alarm would go off in my mind, waking me to my harsh reality. I was on my own to figure things out.

Researching the science of dreaming, I found articles and books above my pay-grade. I would read and reread chapters with a dictionary next to me. *The Interpretation of Dreams* by Sigmund Freud was perhaps the best explanation for dreaming.

The founder of psychoanalysis, talk therapy, Freud realized the significance of dreams, referring to them as a "window to the soul.' This dream state is a place where hidden thoughts are kept. Freud introduced the theory of the unconscious, which opened up a window for controversial discussion among the scholars as well as figures from the nonacademic world, such as Edgar Cayce.

Cayce, a well-known psychic with a ninth-grade education, was called The "Sleeping Prophet." Cayce would go into a sleep-like trance and was able to give life-readings to individuals seeking answers about their mental, physical and spiritual health. His "gift" was to dream, to see into the unconscious mind the information that the conscious mind is unaware of.

Cayce was in a class of his own—allegedly he could do it all: heal the sick, see the future, dream of the past, and talk to the dead. Cayce was unusually gifted. I shared this information with my mother, but she already knew about him.

Despite her Catholic upbringing, mom had a gypsy heart, so *strange* was normal. The lack of scientific evidence never stopped Mom from having complete faith in her gut. Mom's standard for evidence was based on gut feelings.

And everyone who knew Mom respected her gut. Mostly for the odd premonitions. Some of us knew to stay away if she was in "a mood." Deep in trance as she vacuumed the floor. Sometimes mom was a little scary. I have the pictures to prove it.

Mom *was* the paranormal. Her eye contact energized you to your feet. "Get the hell out of my way!" Mom could be one pissed-off lady. As far as I knew, she was an unwilling messenger, and not the cause of any events.

As time passed, unreasonable conclusions developed. Did mom curse the cop? On the night my husband was killed, I called my parents. On the way to the house where Tommy was shot, Daddy asked Mom if she had anything to do with it.

"No, I didn't curse my own daughter," she snapped. "Someone already did it."

"Well, you're always putting a curse on somebody," he yelled. "Put a curse on that cop for what he did to Tommy and your daughter."

"It's done," she said. "but I didn't do it."

Now what kind of questions are these to ask? Do other families go around talking about curses and asking each other these kind of questions? Years later, daddy asked me if *I* did it! Did I put a curse on him? *I don't know?* Sure, I cursed *at* him, but it was only words from the anger and pain I was experiencing.

We curse people out of anger, but no one thinks it means anything. I didn't believe it was a *real* curse, but sometimes... knowing what I know, I wondered? Did the universe hear my tears and angry words that fateful night?

For whatever reason, it would take years before I learned why my mom had so much unresolved anger. She was OCD, depressed, and of course, her visions kept her on edge. Mom claimed that so-called *gifts* were a *curse*. The poor woman suffered undue guilt for sins based on the double standards of philosophy taught by the Catholic Church. Can I get an amen?

Dreams and visions were bestowed only to the prophets of God, the Church told us: Anyone else having such experiences were simply subject to a demonic ruse to steal the soul. Give me a break. Is God promoting favoritism?

"Why would God give you a gift and then say you can't use it?" It wasn't logical.

A person's perception of the truth is based on acquired information, as they know it. The same scenario applies if comparing, "wetlands to swamp land," what an individual perceives is true, is in fact, all that matters to them.

In time mom would talk about some of the things she kept hidden from us, but I had to press her. The past controlled her fears but not her heart. That belonged to us.

One afternoon in the 70s, mom was reading her favorite rag, the *National Enquirer.* I walked into the kitchen and the first thing out of her mouth was,

"I know I'm going to read about yous one day. I know it."

This was getting old. By the time I was nineteen, I had already made the newspapers in three instances I was aware of. Mom was right: There may have been a dark cloud toying with me but it never stopped me from trying to find the silver lining that would pull me out of it.

Mom and I both believed in paranormal energy. Dreams shed its secrets in the light of day, revealing what matters most to the dreamer. When I left home in the '60s, my sister was next in line to pick up where I left off, she was mom's new workhorse and was paying for my rebellious lifestyle. One night, I had a dream of my sister, she looked sad, very hurt and crying; there was a rabbit lying dead on the ground. The next day I received a letter from my sister. She wanted me to come home, she missed me. And my mother accused her of killing the family's pet rabbit. My father said it was an accident, that the dog tripped over the rabbit-breaking its neck. Mom never believed him.

Sometimes, you become the dream that you desire, but only if you go after it because destiny is a choice that requires action by the individual. Fate is an unavoidable event caused by the actions of an unseen force, like a tree struck by lightening, and falling on a parked car.

"Speaking of gut feelings and predictions, ma, I have one of my own." It was something I never told anyone, but I had to tell her.

"I'm going to be rich one day. I don't know how, but it will happen. I know it. I saw myself." Careful what you wish for... the universe has ears.

# PART II

# The Human Condition

## Dedicated to my children: Recognize destiny is a choice.

Inevitable life events such as birth, childhood, adulthood, love, and death make up the human condition. Understanding of the emotional and moral issues people face is based on these human experiences.

Growing up the first eighteen years as a shy, extremely sheltered, and very naive child, it was inevitable I would be who I am, today not by choice, but of necessity. I could remain a prisoner to the shy little girl inside me or change. And change I did. Opinionated, fearless, spiritual, loyal, *a god-damn gypsy*.

During my human conditioning was the Catholic Church. At that time, the world in general was in the dark about the Church and all its ugly secrets. Besides the pedophile shuffle, child abuse was also hidden during the 1950s and '60s. This is an account of the mental and physical abuse by the hands of a few cruel nuns that left many classmates feeling undeserving, dirty, and sinful.

How life events impact us during childhood is critical, determining our behavior and our opinion of the world. No matter what happens to us, we have a choice to make. To allow the event to overcome our life or use the event to empower your future. Sometimes I wondered, if the choices I made were really my own or inspired by an invisible world where our ancestors roam as guides?

As I was growing up, my parents sheltered me from the world, but one thing you can't hide from is DNA, the bloodline. Many of our quirks and phobias may very well be inherited through our genes.

# A PRODUCT OF THE 1950S

## Baby Boomers & Gypsies

After World War II, America got busy. The Baby Boomers arrived in force. Not only did the population grow, but the economy was improving. Opportunity was knocking on every front door in suburbia.

The 1950s was an era when modern technology wooed consumers into buying the latest gadgets. Many homes were bought with the GI bill, some on just a handshake, and ours with a small down payment. From televisions to washing machines, homes were filled with these necessities for the nuclear family of tomorrow.

Commuters were born when the roadways improved and interstate travel expanded, providing easy access to these bedroom communities of the future that would one day breed the social revolution of the century.

You could say that the 1950s was the calm before the storm. Fast cars, fast food was breaking ground, life was moving in the fast lane. Unaware these changes of modern times would stir the consciousness of these Baby Boomers "to dream the impossible dream."

Born a Libra to a Virgo mother and a Scorpio father, I was already in the middle between the two of them. Mom was stern, critical, demanding that the house stay in order. Daddy was adaptable, and with his independent nature and quick wit, he swept mom off her feet.

According to my schedule, I arrived on this planet just in time. But to hear mom tell it, it was an act of rebellion—I was three weeks late. "Better late than never," Daddy said.

Daddy gave mom a sense of balance. Weighing in at 8lbs. 5 oz, I was the first of the next generation to carry on the perpetual state of love, keeping the world populated, our bloodline—and possibly a family curse of broken hearts and trauma.

Compelled to balance the scales of justice, I learned how unfair the universe could be in matters of the heart. How recklessly cruel fate is to anyone in its path. So, when the opportunity arises I have made it my mission "to right the unbearable wrong." Feed the beggar, the broken man on the corner, or give a dying man his last drink. People are more than their issues and addictions. Someone loves them.

Some believe there is a space where souls are born between the world of the dead and living. I call it stardust. Mumma was aware of this invisible world that would never fade away from memory, always on watch for omens and signs.

Often, Daddy said, *"She's strange that way."*

Perhaps the fact I was born with bronchitis may be one of many reasons Mumma told Daddy, the day I was born, "This one is going to have a hard life." The universe must have been listening.

Mumma saw my illness as a foreboding sign. But maybe, it wasn't that scientific: It could have been the red birthmark on my right arm that was shaped like an upside-down heart but with a piece missing from the tip. Was this a curse or an omen of great sorrow and wealth? Some believe it's a sign of reincarnation and sometimes, I wonder if it could be true.

A hard life indicated by a broken piece missing from the otherwise perfect, upside-down heart? Love was never far from sorrow. Violence, too, found its way to my heart, as it did for my mother and grandmothers. Tears would fall, hard. There was turmoil in the mist.

"She was right," Daddy said I always had to learn the hard way.

Daddy was right, too. Blindsided by youth; many things could have been avoided by making better choices. Hindsight can be *so* pretentious. Don't ya think?

Still, despite many personal triumphs and mistakes; no one can escape the hand of fate, the world of dreams, the dead, and unfortunately, some of the living.

What I saw in my mother's eyes growing up was the same look I saw in my grandmother and great-grandmother's eyes: The face of the human condition, the look of shared hardships, the heartaches of past mistakes, lost dreams, and absent lovers. None of it mattered when the future is sitting in your lap ready to carry the family torch of the perpetual sadness following our bloodline. Depression became a way of life.

Unprecedented events can change a person's perception of reality and spirituality. Such events from my childhood are imprinted in my memory as if it were yesterday. These phenomenal experiences leave room for discussion, if not a straitjacket—but they *did* happen.

You never forget the first time you see a dead body, someone gunned downed, a ghost, or an out-of-body experience. The core impression lingers in the back of your brain, a core reminder to see what *isn't* there.

Before trauma toyed with my brain, I lived as a child in a world of dreams, where paranormal entities haunted me long before I learned the words to call them *ghosts*. Here, in my dreams, thoughts were planting seeds of mystery and grief. And, like a disturbing Grimm's fairy tale, she grew up to be me. In spite of it all my attempts to forget these dreams; some dreams were meant to be... an open door to set our mind free from the confinement of the physical world.

*Countless trains passed the tiny wooden frame house that sat next to the railroad tracks on Thaddeus Street. Night after night, clackity clack, I slept through a lullaby of air horns blasting as trains approached the railroad crossing. But one night, all it took was a click to awaken me from slumber.*

*The first memory rooted in the back of my mind is clear, the baby was me. Except for the light coming through the crack under the door, the bedroom was dark. I couldn't see, but something was with me in the room. I felt it. I was screaming and holding on to the rails of the crib when Mumma came in.*

*Mumma settled me down, hoping I would go back to sleep because I was sick with a high fever. She left the room, closing the door behind her as she did before. 'Click.' A moment later, the door quietly opened of its own accord, but no one was there. Mumma entered the room to a screaming baby. Reluctantly, she closed the door. Click.*

*The damn door opened up again! Something was in my room! This time Mumma decided to let me "cry it out."*

*At what point, I don't remember what triggered me, but a different feeling came over me. My little body was stuck in bed but I could see myself below. I remember seeing the back of my head with its wet, wispy curls. A voice said, "Go back—not yet—it's not time."*

I never forgot that voice. I couldn't explain it or what happened to me. I was still learning to talk. Astral projection wouldn't be in my vocabulary for at least twenty years. And that *something* in my room was a spirit.

For a long time, Mom never wanted to talk about or admit she had visions. It was *crazy* talk—yet parts of the future *were* hers to see. If I asked her anything about growing up, often she responded by singing, "Que sera, sera, whatever will be, will be."

Years later, mom told me about the man who lived in the house before she and Daddy rented it—he died in the kitchen. *BOO!*

As mom walked out of my bedroom that night, her long, wavy, dark auburn hair was hanging down her back against her white blouse. The same blouse she wore the day I saw her standing to the right of the dining room window, looking out into the distance.

"You looked worried," I said to her. Mom was remembering something, but she wouldn't tell what it was. I wasn't going to pry. This was for another day.

Something about these maternal women from my mother's side of the family, *you knew* what they were thinking without speaking. Their eyes spoke in code. Their elusive conversations too were in some genetic code designed to be read between the lines."

Growing up, Mumma continued predicting my fated future before it began. All I ever heard out of her mouth was: "*I know. I just know.* One day, I am going to read about yous in the newspapers."

What can I say? The woman was right. Most of my horrific events are documented, public information. According to Daddy, with or without my help, trouble could find me anywhere.

"You have a great instinct for being in the wrong place at the wrong time," he said.

Every decade of this most interesting life, my name has found its way into the news. Some chapters made front page news. It seemed that I was dealt a losing hand, but it didn't mean I had to lose. "It's how you play your hand that counts," a lover once said.

While I was growing up, many mental health disorder symptoms surfaced as a result of too many traumas. Fair to say, I'm jumpy as hell.

My childhood was pretty good considering my emotional problems. My parents didn't drink. I wasn't beaten, burned, or mistreated - though sometimes mom went overboard. My parents were solid as a rock. Raising us on a foundation embedded with morals, rules, and hard work. Above all, they loved us.

Everybody loved Daddy. No one had a bad word to say about the man. This held true on the day of his funeral: People from all walks of life came from everywhere to honor his memory, filling the main room to capacity and requiring an additional room, though there were so many mourners, some people still had to stand. The personal statements were so glowing that you would have thought a state dignitary had passed.

Welling up in tears, the service moved me consciously to another level, inspiring me to live more like my father; to be there when people need you, not only when it's convenient. To find a reason to laugh away the pain, since it's better than crying.

Most people, including those of us who loved her, didn't understand my mother. She was a hard woman to love, but when she hugged you, her grip was so tight, you were almost breathless, and you knew she loved you.

Whatever happened in my mother's past had frightened her so much that only my father could carry her heart. When he died, it was the saddest day my mother ever faced. "I'm nobody's baby anymore."

"That's not true, Mumma. You're my baby now." Our roles were changing, and our relationship grew stronger. It became clear: She needed me. I needed her to know that I loved her.

"You're the only one who calls me Mumma," she cried. "I really like that."

As a child, I didn't understand my mother's "moments of mean." She was a stubborn woman to a point, a flaw that formed the great divide between us. "My way or the highway." Say this long enough to an impressionable kid, you get your wish.

Like most parents, Dolores (Rusty) Marie Bodzsar and James Leroy Bogard did their best protecting us from the world's wicked ways. They wanted the best for their five children. To have happy and healthy lives. To know we were loved and wanted. To work for what we wanted. It is this love I cling to in times of doubt and sorrow. The nurturing strength gained from a family rich in history and whose culture reminds me *who I am. What I wished for.*

# THE MAGYAR LIFE

Delray, Michigan, a.k.a. Hunkeytown - 1950

A suburb of the city of Detroit, Delray was a little village of prosperous Hungarians that flourished for decades. Sadly, progress and greed encroached on this community and its rich cultural and traditions, to be replaced by steel and stench.

It was inevitable: Delray was dying. I was lucky enough to be born to a Hungarian mother just in time to experience the life of the Magyars as a community before they were scattered to the suburbs, leaving this part of my cultural background to the history books.

In early childhood, I was raised by three generations of Magyars on my mother's side. Delray was once a colorful reminder of the Old World. Statues of saints and the Virgin Mary sat among a menagerie of floral and vegetable gardens outlining the manicured lawns, showcasing the pride of homeownership and independent living.

Carved around the doorways of many homes and shops were strange symbols and designs from the Old Country, an inspiration for the living to remember where they came from. Thaddeus Street was a homage to that powerful combination of American pride and the Hungarian way of life.

Mumma was among the first generation of children who were natural-born Americans from Hungarian immigrants who were as proud to be U.S. citizens as they were of their Magyar roots. This group of immigrants were living their American Dream. They worked hard for it. They showed their appreciation for a good life by caring for what they had.

Summer nights were a social gathering for family and neighbors. Forever implanted in my tiny brain, I can still hear Grandpa (Steve) Beno chatting with friends about current events and other nonsense "not of my concern" while performing the nightly ritual of burning leaves and lawn clippings.

Soon as Grandpa was finished washing away the burnt ash off the sidewalks and driveway, it was time to go in and get ready for bed. Life was following both a routine and the orders that accompanied it. No child ever talked back because we didn't have the right to an opinion.

"You're not old enough to put your two cents in," Mumma said. The metaphor went over my little head: I didn't have a penny to my name and somehow, I'm supposed to pay to talk? This was family life, and adults ruled.

Though the odorous haze from the factories smelled like one big fart, Delray was the cleanest community in Detroit. Despite the smokestacks spewing amber haze that billowed over the Fisher Body plant; the streets and alleys were washed down and kept cleared of debris, making way for the "sheeny" man and his horse-drawn cart.

The sheeny man a "rag and bone man," an aged gypsy who bought and sold junk on the streets. Daddy said he collected other people's junk to resell. "One man's junk is another man's treasure," he said.

Clip-clop, clip-clop, I could hear the horses hooves hitting the pavement. The sheeny man was coming, calling out his trade as he made his way toward grandma's house.

"The Sheeny-man is here. Get your knives and scissors sharpened!"

Running out to see the horses, I pretended to spy on him as he rummaged through trash looking for anything salvageable. He tossed a broken chair in the back of the wagon on top of a heap of scrap metal, mumbling, "I can fix that."

The sheeny man inspired me. I wanted to find "treasure," too. And I did.

## Sticks and Stones and Broken Bones

My first discovery unfolded a secret that led to another. Eventually, it led to my mother's childhood. I would learn that secret while harboring a few of my own. After all, I had the best teacher on the planet, my mother.

Istvan Bodzsar was born in Dregelypalank, Hungary. He was my grandfather; not the man I knew as Grandpa. I never met Istvan Bodzsar, and was unaware of him until it was time to get my driver's license. Even then, not much information was given "Because I said so!"

Great-Aunt (Nagyneni) Margaret and Great-Uncle (Nagybacsi) John Toth lived with my mom's cousin in the house across the street from Grandma Stella Beno's house. Mom's sister and her husband lived on the second floor of grandma's house with my three cousins.

Old customs still applied to us, the second-generation born. We were spanked, not beaten. We were told it was our "job" to listen and learn. We had grandparents, aunts, uncles and neighbors enforcing most of the same rules.

Daddy's side of the family lived on the other side of Delray, which allowed Grandma Alma Bogard and Grandma Stella Beno to take turns babysitting me. There was a big difference staying with the Bogard side of the family. They laughed more. The rules had "exceptions," and as the first grandchild of the Bogards, I ruled the first five years.

The Bogards were not Magyars, but they were strict Catholics. They never took life for granted or as seriously as mom's family despite the sorrows they endured. They learned to accept Mom's strange ways and grew to love her quirky ways. Aunts, uncles and cousins often laughed out loud, "Your mother's nuts!"

Mom would just *know* something was about to go down in our little family's universe—and she acted on it. One night she told my brother Jimmy not to go home, "just wait a few minutes." He did. It probably saved his life. There was a car accident on I-75 that happened moments before my brother would have driven by the exact location. It was mom's *thing*.

My relationship with my mother was always cool to the touch. She rarely held me, and kept her emotional distance. She didn't mean for this to happen, but something happened to my mother that eventually had an impact on everyone who loved her. Trauma can be buried for years before it resurfaces.

Something had prevented my mom from sharing her experiences. In the times she grew up, no one called the cops over family business. No one would ever see a shrink, because the stigma was like a plague. "Don't air family laundry in public."

Mom worried all the time about one thing or another. One day it would come out. In the meantime, growing up was like waiting for the other shoe to drop. It was simple: Mom's quiet ways and out-in-the-distance stares was "her thing." She couldn't help it, gut feelings were her tools. This is how it was in our household. This was normal.

As families go, we were close. Maybe too close. Because there is no escaping the wrath of God when most of your family lives in the same town, some on the same street, and in the same house. *Close?* More like kept on a tight leash for our own safety.

It was Delray, but it was still in Detroit, a dangerous city—and I was made aware of this early on. Staying alert was part of training a kid. Having an uncle for a cop, I learned that it was mandatory to pay attention and lookout for danger.

Childhood is filled with discovering a world within our reach of perception: picking flowers, watching birds fly high, embracing our imagination with surprise. Like most young children I didn't worry about anything except "when do we eat" and "can I go play?"

Food brings people together. Many of my memories are centered around food for a very good reason. Smells trigger our memories and open our hearts to the past. A favorite memory that comforted my heart was the aroma of baked goods coming from the bakery around the corner on Westend.

For a while, the sweet aroma helped to diffuse the city's ongoing industrial pollution lingering in the skies above us. Soon enough,

## Sticks and Stones and Broken Bones

nothing would disguise the smell of death, but for now it was all about the fresh bread and Grandma (Bodzsar) Beno's Sunday soup.

Grandma's special soup was homemade chicken noodle, Hungarian style. It took a day to make the noodles and hours to simmer the fresh hen for broth; a very exciting time in my young life. to be on the cusp of old-world customs with new-world dreams.

Grandma and I would take a walk on a Friday or Saturday to the poultry shop where she hand-picked a live hen for "Sunday soup." The butcher killed it, cleaned it, wrapped it in brown paper, and handed it to her, chicken feet included. I couldn't wait to get home.

Waiting for chicken feet doesn't sound appetizing, but I loved this ritual with my grandmother and great-grandmother. Grandma would clean and cook the chicken feet while I sat in great-grandma's lap eating another one of my favorite Hungarian dishes, *szalonna*, bacon made from pork backfat.

Great-Grandma Barbara Berecz was a big woman who always smelled like onions and insulin. She spoke to me in Hungarian while we ate the crispy chunks of pork backfat with raw onions and tomatoes on bread that was drizzled in grease from the *szalonna*.

"You need a little fat. In case you get sick," she said.

That was my last memory of great-grandma alive, telling me I needed "a little fat" to stay healthy. It stuck with me and served a purpose later on, as did all the lessons I was taught by my elders.

Grandma (Bodzsar) Beno took care of me quite a bit while my mother and father worked to put money away for a house in Trenton, Michigan. I walked everywhere with Grandma. This routine taught me true independence. You don't need wheels to get out of town, just the will to do it.

Almost every Saturday, I would sit on the basement steps watching Grandma below, rolling out the dough on the table she used just for flour. She would then pick up a knife, wipe it off on her apron and then slice the rolled dough into perfect egg noodles. Loosely separating the cut noodles, Grandma would spread them out to dry. Every few hours, she went to the basement to turn them over.

Sometimes, Grandma let me turn the noodles because she knew I wanted a few for myself.

Sunday morning arrived, and Grandma would wake me up around four a.m. to get ready for five o'clock mass. It was always dark out when grandma went to church. She went to early mass so she could start her Sunday soup on time. Grandma held my hand tightly while we walked quickly and quietly in the middle of Thaddeus Street.

"Leen-da, always walk in the middle of the street when it's dark," she said. We avoided the sidewalks for one reason: "So no one jumps out of the bushes and grabs yous."

Grandma explained that the street lights let "yous" see if someone is coming from behind. This lesson in street smarts also proved to be valuable later when I was attacked while walking home one night in Detroit in 1969. It was the shadows from streetlights that alerted me to three men approaching from behind. It was enough of a warning not to panic. Thank you, Grandma.

As Grandma and I continued walking in the dark toward Sloan Street, we turned right and walked to Yale Street. A few blocks ahead on South Street stood the impressive Gothic structure of the Holy Cross Hungarian Catholic Church, beckoning its parishioners with its tolling bells.

The Catholic Church was just as mysterious and complicated as my family. The miracles, life after death for the soul, stories of angels, saints and martyrs, prophets with visions: This was our religion, and the root of conflicts to come.

People often joked to me, "Your mother's a gypsy." Mom wasn't a godless woman or a thief living in a caravan, and she didn't go around casting the evil- eye (so I thought) but she did get "these feelings." With an open heart and a desire to share what most people try hide: the worst events of their life; I present mistakes and ignorant choices made based on superstitious lies and traditions endorsed by the Catholic Church.

Before the Catholic Church or any Christian faith would allow gypsies into the fold, these religious organizations persecuted gypsies

## Sticks and Stones and Broken Bones

for their fortune-telling and palm reading. Mom was reading horoscopes before it was popular.

Some cultures still believe in the gypsy curse. My mother did. She also read tea leaves. How else was I suppose to grow up but believing as she did when I saw with my own eyes what happened when she put her mind to it?

The Magyar way of life is about music, too. I have heard violins that could make you cry or jump to your feet, dancing with tambourines in your hand. Every song a celebration of life or death. And timing is everything.

Grandma was always humming a tune around the house, but never before noon. One morning while I was singing, "How much is that doggy in the window?" Mumma cut me off.

"Don't sing in the morning, Linda—your tears will fall by night."

No wondering why, I wanted to wander like a nomad, sing and dance my way through life. It's in the blood. The rituals, the music, life and death, strange, superstitious sayings: This most suspicious mystery was my birthright to live like a damn gypsy. I was Catholic, too, but there was no room in heaven for a gypsy.

It was a good thing that the houses on Thaddeus St. were crammed close together— you could smell supper on the table. Good thing too, because it helped cover up the increasing farty factory and sewage smells. One day, the sheeny man disappeared into history never to be seen, only remembered. Soon the vegetable truck man would also disappear.

The City of Detroit's master plan of 1955 supported industrial development. Then the Feds backed it up with a study of their own in 1963: end game. The expansion of I-75 began, and more than a hundred years of immigrant families would slowly die out and fade away into the history books.

Generations of immigrants, my parents included, began moving downriver to the suburbs to escape the encroaching death of Delray. Grandma and her sister stayed behind on Thaddeus Street.

South of Detroit, along the Detroit River, the expanding eighteen communities collectively called the Downriver area, and its residents the Downriver Rats, mainly because the area was populated with blue-collar, middle-class workers employed by the dozens of auto factories, steel mills, and shipbuilders in the area.

Like all things, the Downriver area would change, with more upper middle-class workers moving in communities focusing on boating and fishing. Trenton was a mixture of upper- and middle class.

In the Fall of 1955, I would start kindergarten. It was a culture shock for me when my parents bought the house in Trenton. Little matchbox houses made of concrete and red brick, all looking the same. No trees shading the newly paved streets, no alleys for the sheeny man, and no friends.

A day would come when all the homes on Lynn Court would be transformed with trees taller than the houses. The streets would crack, and houses would appear not so ordinary after time. Until then, I would do my part, being a kid: Go to school. Do what I was told. Help around the house and pull weeds.

This transition from old-world charm to this new world of cookie-cutter homes was my fate. Adjusting to the changes would take time.

The problem was, my life was now heading in a different direction, this was my fate. I had no choice. Every friend I had was family, and they were forty miles away. Then a scale of events ranging from tragic to exciting evolved during the summer of 1955, proving that everything changes.

Daddy owned a two-seater prop plane and taught himself how to fly with the help of his buddy, Al Kovacks. There were few FAA regulations back then regarding pilot licenses. In fact, nothing kept my father from doing anything he wanted to do. He even convinced my mother to do something she was afraid of: fly.

"If I was meant to fly," she Said, "I'd have wings."

Somehow, Daddy did it. We were off, with me stashed in the luggage compartment, where I could look over mom's shoulder and out the window as Daddy propelled the little two-seater prop plane up into the wild blue yonder and headed over the lake.

## Sticks and Stones and Broken Bones

I had all but nearly forgotten the out of body experience and the spooky ghost, but looking out the window for angels in the sky, that memory was creeping into the back of my mind as I watched the white clouds swirl above. It reminded me how I saw my body in the crib. I finally knew a word to explain what it felt like: *flying*.

> Staring down at the water, how little the houses appeared along the shoreline. I wasn't afraid of flying like the birds we saw below. Daddy and I were very comfortable in the sky, but not Mom: She was angry and scared to death. She tried to be a good sport, but had enough.

"Get me down, Jimmy! Take this goddamn thing down right now!" She didn't have wings. Daddy loved flying, but he loved Mom even more. Eventually, he sold that little plane and devoted more time to his other passions, drawing and building things.

My father's life was about the *doing*. He was a freethinker with no restrictions on philosophy or possibilities. Mom needed his carefree spirit, a blessing compared to her self-imposed restrictions on fun. If you're having too much fun, something must be wrong with you and something will go wrong. Mom was a nervous, jumpy woman, and her anger level would rise from zero to sixty in a heartbeat.

Mom coped with her demons by cleaning excessively. As Mom instructed, I headed to the basement to clean our second living room that daddy had remodeled with a little help from me. Mom was dusting the hallway when I had to ask her about the constant cleaning. "I mean, ma? How dusty does a thermostat get in twenty-four hours?"

She laughed a little, "I know. It's a habit, it's hard to break." It turns out she used cleaning as a way to block the outside world from disrupting her thoughts. Mom was always deep in thought.

The summer of 1955 changed me forever when I witnessed an event children should never see. Mom was visiting Grandma Beno, and I was outside playing in front of the house. I was told not to cross the sidewalk or get anywhere near the curb. Naturally, I stayed within my boundaries or faced a spanking.

While amusing myself with the local insects and butterflies, I noticed a little girl coming out of the house across the street. She looked at me as her mother yelled for her to stop.

For some reason, she didn't listen and ran into the street, falling under the wheel of a car traveling at fifteen miles per hour. The crushing impact distorted her skull. All the screaming, the blood, compelled me to get closer to the scene of the horrific accident. I crossed the sidewalk and stood at the edge of the curb, watching her body move slowly, then stillness. Death came quickly.

The family was in the kitchen when they heard the commotion out front, more screams and tears. I was too close to the curb. Someone spanked me because I disobeyed, but there was not one word about the tragedy. I was then whisked away by Grandma, but it was too late.

Who could forget a little girl's short life in a pool of blood being washed away into a sewer drain? It was forever an emotional scar. Buried deep in my psyche, a destructive seed was planted. Decades later it bloomed into a thorny wild rose, invading my garden of happiness with its diseased thoughts. In some way, I miss her.

That little girl's sad ending was only the beginning of the bittersweet journey into the mental madness of PTSD throughout childhood into adulthood. No one suspected this tragedy would have such an impact on my life.

There are right and wrong ways to deal with a family member who's been violently assaulted or witnessed something horrific. Depending on how a family deals with trauma has an impact on the victim's recovery. It can also determine how long a victim will actively struggle with PTSD.

No one said a comforting word to me about what I had witnessed. Was I suppose to forget this? How was it possible? They punished me for being there. In some ways, the child assumes the guilt.

Maybe, if she didn't look at me before running out, she would not have died. No one said anything different. It wasn't too long after this horrible accident that my Great-grandma Berecz died: August 17, 1955. A sad day.

"It was her time to go." Mumma said. "One day we will see her again. Until then, don't cry too long, Linda. Her spirit won't rest."

My parents made plans to move away from the city once it was time for me to start school. I had thought I would go to Holy Cross like my cousins, and didn't want to move away, but I had no say in the matter. Like every other generation before me, until I had my own wheels, I was along for the ride. Trenton, Michigan, was my new hometown. Adjust, be happy, or be miserable that was the choice I had, Mom said.

Shortly after great-grandma's funeral, I went to spend the night with my grandparents. It was strange sleeping in great-grandma's bed without her. I missed her warm hugs… the way she squeezed my cheeks before giving me a kiss. Always shoving Hungarian food in my face as if I would never have it again.

Lying in her bed, I was thinking about the fading yellow chalk outline that was still faintly visible on the street where the little girl died. At four years old, I didn't understand why it happened but I knew that, just like my great-grandma, she was never coming home. Was it *her time* to go, too? Did she know she was dead? Finally, I fell asleep.

Something touched my cheek like a butterfly kiss. I was awake, eyes wide open. Across the room near the dresser was a misty glow. *Someone* was in the room and, it wasn't Grandma checking in on me. It was a see-through lady!

It appeared that candles were being lit at the feet of the Virgin Mary statue on the dresser. There was a distinct moment when I thought, "Who' that?" As an answer, strong scents filled the room with a blend of burning wax and onions. The air prevailed with great-grandma's perfume. My heart pounded. I remembered sitting on her lap with my face burrowed in her apron that smelled of onions while she squeezed me with her hefty arms, kissing me on the top of my head.

Out of the mist, the lady moved, not so much walking, but flowing toward me. This apparition was young, not old as I had known my great-grandma, but somehow I knew it was her.

Scared and excited, I ran right into my grandparents' bedroom, jumping into bed, not saying a word. I still did not know the words to describe what happened, but it made me remember my first ghost. It was the same spooky feeling: *Someone* was there.

I believe that great-grandma was communicating, transferring a message to my mind through the sense of smell. How thoughtful. She was watching over me. She knew I was upset about the little girl and the spanking, too.

Oddly enough, the meaning of "soul" is defined, in an earlier edition of Webster's dictionary as:

1. Immaterial essence of an individual life
2. Relevant

The very essence of her life was lingering, definitely relevant and my point, *she was there.*

I do believe that generally, a child of four has not yet been corrupted by deceit, nor has the knowledge to recognize trickery.

My birthday was in October. I was a little younger than most kids in my kindergarten class, who were bigger than I was. Adjusting to my new life at school and making new friends was a lonely journey. I pretty much avoided the other kids. I didn't know how to make friends.

My mother's family's influence had repercussions. I had a slight accent because of my background. I spoke a few Hungarian words mixed in with English. Of course, the kids made fun of me because I was different. "You talk funny."

Mumma would chuckle, "You *are* a little different. Who cares? Ignore them."

"Not everyone is going to like you." Another one of her favorite mantras: "Sticks and stones may break my bones, but names will never hurt me." *Toughen up* was her advice.

You could call Mom a "hunkey" or a "gypsy"—proud to be insulted, she just laughed, telling us to do the same. "So what if yous talk funny," she said. "Everybody talks funny." Mom had a slight accent, mixed with grammatical errors.

In due time Mom self-corrected herself, dropping the *s* in "yous." Occasionally, they slipped out in anger. Something else was noticeably odd: My father's speech patterns changed anytime he was pissed off. The words that mostly stood out were "not at all," which sounded almost Old English: "notta tall."

Daddy agreed I was a *strange* child even at the age of two. He began calling me *eccentric* one day and it stuck. Really? How does a seven-year-old come to be eccentric? One incident at a time.

In the mid 1950s, the exodus began. Residents of Hunkeytown were leaving the community that had been home for nearly a century to this small group of Magyars. They headed to the suburbs, along with generations of other cultures that formed their communities within the larger town.

Grandma and Grandpa Bogard, too, along with my Uncle Red and Aunt Dorothy. The Bogards relocated to Dearborn, on the other side of the suburbs. With miles between us, weekly visits were routine. For certain, the family was growing.

Being the only Bogard child for a few years understandably gave me reason to believe the world revolved around me. Then, like a parade of ants, one by one my dad's siblings got married, and soon cousins arrived. And they kept coming! Our family was doing its part to keep up with the Catholic tradition of raising a minimum of three Catholics per family.

The age differences among myself, my siblings and cousins positioned me as a role model and babysitter by default. My job to "set a good example for the younger ones." I did not want to be an example to follow because restrictions were in place: Don't do anything that could get the blobs hurt.

It wasn't much fun at first. These little blobs didn't talk and couldn't walk, but they could crawl and waddle, following me everywhere. At six years old, I wanted playmates. Though disconnected by age as we grew older together, we learned about our parents, our collective history as a family, and about each other. We had fun.

Mom was dealing with the move to Trenton in her own way, which was usually explosive. It was hard on my mother to be so far away from Delray and her mother. She started blaming my father for feeling "cooped up." It was about this time I noticed a violent streak in my mother. In early spring of 1956, my parents were shouting something about "the rabbit died."

Rarely, my parents would argue with me around. It shocked me. Mom screaming at Daddy as I lay in bed, praying for silence. The screaming would stop until the next time.

If Mom felt trapped or wronged in any way, she hid it long enough for things to build up before expressing her true feelings. This went on for years until a doctor advised that she speak her mind or suffer a nervous breakdown and get an ulcer.

As a couple, my parents were usually loving towards each other, no bitter words to resent when the storm blew over. Together they talked, laughed, and sang around the house. They exchanged looks that said, "I love you."

But not tonight!

My bedroom door flew open, with Daddy diving to the floor for cover. On his heels was a dining room chair that crashed into the closet door at the end of the hallway, next to my bedroom. Seeing Mom act like King Kong and Daddy taking cover, I knew something was wrong.

Daddy, laughing like nothing was wrong, crawled up on his knees to lean on the bed and whispered. "Your mother's pretty mad at me. I think she needs to cool off."

All I heard was the rabbit died—code for you're going to have a baby. Mom blamed Daddy for getting her drunk on New Year's Eve.

Mom had a few triggers that would set her off. Booze was one. Her father, Grandpa Bodzsar was a bad alcoholic. She was probably feeling guilty, but it went deeper. Mom had displaced anger and abandonment issues that surfaced in a fit of rage when least expected.

Over the years she threw a number of shoes, hair brushes, and a sewing machine at me. Poor Daddy was unsuccessful at dodging the glass ashtray that nicked his knee. And then there was that pot of spaghetti sauce I had to clean up after she pitched that at him, too.

"Dinner is served!"

One incident that could have been deadly was the time mom was throwing knives at Daddy. Later, I found out that she witnessed her father hold a knife to her mother's throat as a child. A few decades ago, I was in a similar scenario when my gay husband held a knife to my throat. There seems to be a pattern here, but that's another chapter.

Mumma couldn't forgive her father's drinking and abuse. She was very close to her mother and would do anything for her—something we were lacking as mother and daughter, not that we didn't try. We were too much alike in ways yet to be determined. The last thing most young girls want to hear: "You're just like your mother."

What did that mean? I did what any girl does when compared to her mother. I rebelled by doing what I could *not* to be her. In the long run, it didn't work. I am every bit like my mother with a few exceptions: I hated secrets. Mom was full of them.

The Baby Boomer population hit its peak in 1957, when roughly every seven seconds in the U.S., a baby was born. In one of those seconds along came Valerie, the cutest and goofiest baby I knew. As an only child, I was spoiled for six years by default. I never needed anything that I was aware of. But it was immediately pointed out when Valerie arrived that September that I was the "big sister," and things had to change.

Since I graduated from the only child in rank to the oldest, Mumma said. It was time to grow up. A year and a day later, my brother Jimmy was born. That's when the Bogards realized Mom didn't like girls and was exceptionally harder on us. It was years before Valerie and I knew this to be true.

"You two were dropped like hot potatoes." Grandma Bogard, along with other family members agreed that Mom thought the boys could do no wrong. This observation seem to explain Mom's endless comparisons between men and women, which I didn't understand as a child.

"A man can shit in his hat and still be called a man… but," Mom added, "a woman has to act like a lady at all times, or her reputation is ruined."

The Bogards tried to compensate for her favoritism by giving us special attention that our mother didn't know how to give. These changes may not have been as significant as I make them out; but they do timeline other events responsible for my *odd* behavior, my mother's temper.

Trenton's population grew, with a need for more schools. My parents first sent me to West Road Elementary for kindergarten. Meanwhile, the new high school was being built. For first grade, I was moved to Anderson Elementary until St. Timothy's opened its doors in September of 1957.

Switching from public to parochial school was similar to culture shock. We were all Catholics. In public school we were taught patriotism: "I pledge allegiance to the flag…" In parochial school there is no greater law than God's, so we learned our prayers: "Our Father, who art in heaven…"

Regardless of what institution was accountable for my education; any and every incident of indiscretion would become part of my permanent record to follow me everywhere I went in life.

In a few short years, my emotional well-being was severely compromised by the acts of violence I was experiencing. The culmination of these acts, changing schools three years in a row, impacted my social life and self-esteem. The family dynamics were changing, too. Mom was suffering from postpartum depression. Or, what they use to call the "baby blues."

My sister was a year old when my brother was born with colic that lasted over six months. The constant crying was more than any of us could handle. Mom concocted a tea remedy from caraway seed, which was good for the digestive system, according to Grandma Beno.

Grandma and her home remedies always seem to worked, but not this time—it was only a temporary fix. The pain resumed, as did the crying, heart wrenching and nerve wracking. Mom was at a point she was afraid she would "choke him," I heard her say.

## Sticks and Stones and Broken Bones

Daddy was working all sorts of odd jobs at all hours to put food on the table. Mom was losing it, crying she went to the neighbor's for help. She didn't trust herself, and handed the baby to her friend for the night.

"I can't take it," she cried. "I don't know if I'm coming or going."

Women in general were having issues in the fifties. They were all sold a bill of goods after the war to stay at home; make babies, raise families so the men could have the jobs. Mumma was no different in her thinking, and she was training me to be the same way.

"Get a job, get married and have kids."

Daddy was working long hours at odd jobs and, like a lot of blue-collar fathers missed most of the day's drama: The men worked; the women stayed home. Home alone with three kids, with nothing but chores to do is a thankless job, Mom would say.

It was normal to find Mom cleaning, cooking, and doing yard work, but she went overboard. No one noticed she was a servant to the weight of her secrets, though her compulsive cleaning was well-noted in our family. Everything, every day, including the thermostat, had to be dusted.

At first, she was just being "Rusty." No one noticed mom's obsession with cleanliness was a sign of mental distress until it got out of hand. No one, even the Pope, was allowed to enter the front door.

It was "bad luck," and "your shoes are dirty."

One occasion, the insurance man stopped by, unaware of Mom's rules. He knocked on the front door, with mom barking orders to meet her at the back gate, as she told him to do in the first place. She escorted him past the watchful eyes of our German Shepherd to the back door. "Take your shoes off."

As the salesman took his shoes off, he commented that the Japanese did the same thing. *Oh, boy.* Another can of worms! Don't compare mom to the Japanese. Her hatred would not be contested. There was no forgiveness for Pearl Harbor, with prejudice running deep in her veins. If you think about it, how could mom forgive Japan if she wouldn't forgive her own father?

Compared to Detroit, living in Trenton was relatively safe. However, the suburbs only reinforced Mom's fear for people of a different race and color. The 'burbs were legally off limits to any non-Caucasians. It was this lifestyle that segregated us as a nation. My sister and I were often told, "You better never come home with a nigger."

Despite the threats of being disowned from both sides of the family, a time would come "to fight the unbeatable foe." Detroit would burn. My family would be at odds with over racism and unrealistic religious rules. In the 1950s, there was a sense of urgency to "be prepared." Stay guarded. After all, this was the nuclear age.

The Cold War was on. Bomb shelters were being built. Even whispers of "little green men" from outer space were circulating, and we practiced "duck and cover" drills in case "they (Russia) drop the big one." Teachers instructed us to get under our desk. "And keep your eyes closed." As if? I didn't believe it. I saw what we did to Japan.

Every week with my father, I watched documentaries and war movies that had real life scenes from WWII, including the bombing of Hiroshima and Nagasaki. "More like kiss your ass goodbye," Daddy laughed. It was not possible to be saved from a nuclear bomb while hiding under a piece of wood. You have to "go way underground." I believed him. We were all "shit out of luck."

According to the National Institute of Mental Health, there are many risk factors involved in whether a person will be affected by post- traumatic stress disorder. I was a prime candidate.

We were one of the first families to move to Lynn Court in Trenton. By 1957, every home was occupied; many of them with kids of all ages, but not one girl or boy my age. It was a neighborhood dominated by boys, and a few were mean and nasty. *Damn!* Mom was right again. Stones hurt!

Six years old, and trouble was just a few doors down. Three brothers lived a few houses away. One of them had the bright idea to grab me. While holding my arms behind my back, they ordered their younger sister to throw rocks at me. I was being *stoned*! How biblical is that?

After dodging a few rocks, one made contact above my left eye, splitting it open. The sight of blood running down my face chased the bullies away, but the scar was permanent in many ways.

With an ice pack on my eye, I heard Daddy on the telephone, half-joking to Grandma Bogard, saying that Mom had "put a curse" on them. Strange enough, that family soon moved away. It wasn't the last time this happened either.

A few neighbors who crossed my mother over the years moved away. I'm not saying Mom had anything to do with it, but it was ironic and often a topic of conversation whenever something weird happened.

"Don't get on her bad side," Daddy teased. "Don't push her buttons. That woman's nuts. She'll put a curse on you."

In hindsight, there was a good reason to be paranoid. But realistically, Russian bombs dropping on my head was the least of my worries. I had bullies at the end of the block to worry about, and a new order of law was about to be imposed by the changing of the guard: the Sisters of the Immaculate Heart of Mary.

# MOTHER SUPERIOR

### A lesson in abuse

Second grade at St. Tim's was indeed a milestone year of events. Rules were enforced by Mother Superior, a.k.a. Sister Mary Bede, who would "beat the devil out of you" if you crossed her. Any student will testify that she was infamous for her paddlings, among other cruel punishments, we soon found out.

Let me say this to all world leaders: Torture is no way to get the truth from anyone. A person will lie to avoid the pain or worse, act in defiance.

Some of the nuns at St. Timothy's added fuel to my developing PTSD eccentricities. Vivid dreams and nightmares began when I started school, dreams that took my breath away. *Why* do we dream? Their meanings pose a question that most people address at some point in their lives. I was no different, wondering if my intense dreams and visions had any meaning at all.

After a few violent incidents with the nuns, I learned to pay attention to repeating images from my dreams, including tornados and black crosses. Dreams warning me to be prepared, be on the lookout for myself, and to watch out for the nuns:

*I was looking up at the bright sunny sky, but the weather drastically changed—a storm was coming. There were dozens of tiny tornadoes whirling in the sky, coming at me, turning into little black crosses burrowing into my forehead. They were evil crosses.*

No matter how hard I tried to stay out of the nuns' way, something would happen that managed to put me under their radar. For the next seven years, the students of St. Tim's endured humiliation, verbal, and physical abuse by God's representatives in blue.

In 1957, St. Timothy's school opened its doors to students from grades one to three. As the first students to enter the building, we saw that it was clearly, brand spanking new—which drew even more attention to my scrawled name, which stood out on the freshly painted bathroom door a few months later; which I didn't do.

All I remembered was pleading with Sister to believe me. I wouldn't write my own name on the bathroom door because, despite my grades, I wasn't stupid. I pointed out to her that somebody misspelled *did* **Linda Bogard** *dad* **this?**

"I didn't do it. I know how to spell *did*."

Sister Margaret Cecile and Sister Mary Bede kept calling me a liar. Then she called me *stubborn* and said that I was afraid of the truth. But I would not be badgered into admitting something I didn't do. "I didn't do it," I repeated. But that didn't matter to the nun. For decades, it preyed on my mind. Five decades later, a classmate explained what she knew.

Carol Stepanski remembered an incident when a nun slammed someone up against the wall in the bathroom. "Was that you?" In that moment, I remembered falling down next to the sinks after the nun slapped me hard enough to knock me back against the wall. A memory blocked out for too many years that taught me to accept abuse at an early age.

Like a good Catholic, I accepted the bullying as a badge for God, believing the more I was abused, the more favor I held with him. The nuns explained that those who loved God will face great pain and hardships. Well, he must really love me!

The nuns at St. Tim's were nothing like the kind, selfless ones in the old Bing Crosby movies. A few pious nuns were too strict with the rules, never bending an inch because they were never wrong, and "nuns don't lie."

Most of my classmates who survived St. Timothy's have spoken about how they were abused—Too many of us, as far as I'm concerned.

I know most have been through hell since those days. Sad too, the bonding we experienced as classmates was a violent one. Another nightmare, but it had nothing to do with the nuns. There were other evils to guard against and I wasn't alone:

*Tornados, black crosses, and murky waters, I was drowning. Again, the black crosses were in reverse, turning into little tornados that attacked me. This time I found myself crying in a sea of gray waves that were crashing over me. I fought to keep my head up, looking at the dark sky I could see a light breaking through the stormy clouds. I would be saved.*

Sometime in the fall of that same year, I was sexually assaulted when a neighbor boy pinned me in a corner of the chimney wall outside his house, trying to poke me with a stick where it did not belong. I pushed him away and ran home with shame on my bright red face.

Crying, explaining to Mumma that the boy was hurting me with a stick. Afraid and embarrassed to show her where, I suppressed my anger for being violated. A day would come when I would lash out and hurt those least deserving. The signs were there, but not recognized because of the era.

When I was a child, it was easy to mislabel PTSD as a behavior problem. According to the nuns, I was "disruptive in class." I had a sense of fairness and justice. I didn't appreciate condescending answers or speculation.

Our weekly trip to visit Grandma in Delray included riding through some of the Downriver communities, where subtle changes were becoming obvious each year. Crime and violence encroached on communities closest to the city limits of Detroit, with Trenton one of the farthest away.

My cousin and I were always told to watch out for strangers and stick together. We were like most little girls growing up with childhood dreams. Crime wasn't the first thing on our mind. We talked about becoming mothers. What we wanted to be and we were more excited about was making our First Communion. We pretended to take communion with our little saucer-shaped candy wafers we bought at the candy store across the street from Holy Cross.

## Sticks and Stones and Broken Bones

We also talked about boys. Who was cute? Who did we have a crush on? Like good girls we planned to remain virgins until we were married: The purest state of grace in the eyes of God, but *"What's a virgin?"*

The nuns, just like my mother, avoided talking about body parts to explain any mysterious terminology. Instead, we're told, "A virgin is a woman who doesn't have relations with a man before marriage."

All Catholics pledge allegiance in the Apostle's Creed, but the most important ceremony is the First Holy Communion. It is a rite of passage for the young to receive "the body and blood of Christ:" A little white wafer transformed into our Lord and Savior for consumption. Hard to swallow, literally and figuratively. But a small child wants to believe someone is watching over them.

While many young girls imagine their wedding day, a Catholic girl will also be wondering if she has "the calling" to be a "Bride of Christ." Especially on First Communion Day. Staring at myself in the mirror with my wedding-like dress gave me a feeling of personal pride.

It was time to testify our faith in God, along with promising to fulfill certain obligations to the Supreme Being. I was ready if God "called" on me.

Or if God made me rich, my plan was to help "poor people" Buy them food give them money. It was a kid's wish made from a heart of innocence. What could possibly go wrong? Each step I made towards the altar felt like a floating cloud.

As I knelt on the prayer bench to accept the body and blood of Christ, I started weaving side to side. Father Eppenbrock attempted to place the wafer on my tongue, but everything went bright-white, and I passed out. Was that my sign?

Vaguely, I remembered falling backward. I didn't make my communion. I was picked up and sat down in the front row with my head between my knees, regaining my composure I waited for a redo.

Meanwhile thinking, what was the bright white light? Was I hungry, like Mom said? Maybe I can't be a nun. I was a bad person rejected by the body of Christ. Religious instructors ought to be more careful how they present spirituality to a child.

Every day we were trained or brainwashed in the merits of being a good Catholic. We were taught to accept our fate as a challenge to prove our faith to the Holy Trinity; to be willing to die for our beliefs "in the name of Jesus Christ, our Savior." I did what I was told, but bad things still happened.

Paying attention in class was easier said than done. Inattention was another PTSD indicator something is wrong. Wandering thoughts, daydreams of islands, lurked in the corners of my imagination. I would live on an island with my family when I grew up. A self-sufficient island away from all bad, scary things like the boogeyman.

Stephen King wrote about his own "boogeyman," but I was living with one. Many parents used the boogeyman to keep young kids in line. "Behave, or the boogeyman's gonna get ya." "Go to bed, or the boogeyman's gonna get ya." It works.

Like most kids, I didn't like going to bed because I was afraid I might miss out on something. But some nights, I worried. Was he under my bed or in the closet? Who was the spooky *someone* I couldn't see? I do remember a sound. "Click."

Hiding with the covers over my head, holding my breath and praying to God to keep me safe from the devil, suffocating in fear. I believed evil was in me because I was subjected to it daily by the nuns. We are all born in sin. Penance was the only way out of hell. Between the church and my mother, what was I supposed to think?

Mumma wouldn't go to Sunday Mass when I was a child. She never talked about premonitions, just told you what to do when it "hit her." Pretty regular for her.

"Answer the phone." But it's not ringing? Seconds later, it would.

Over time I began to understand why Mumma kept quiet. It was a spiritual conflict. The Church delivered mixed messages. On one hand, God guided his earthly servants through dreams and angels. On the other hand, anyone else was influenced by the devil.

My emotional problems were escalating. The trauma over the past few years was surfacing, not only affecting my schoolwork, but my overall concentration. I was obsessed with other things. It was

## Sticks and Stones and Broken Bones

evidently clear that demons were lurking in my bedroom, waiting for me to fall asleep to invade my dreams with their nightmares. But were they all bad spirits?

What about guardian angels? *Aren't they supposed to be watching over us?* Is my great-grandma a guardian angel? I began obsessing prior to falling asleep, reciting the times table, but only sixes and nines, which I repeated three times.

In my head and in the classroom, I argued with the nuns about these questions. Why wouldn't God talk to us in our dreams, or send a warning message when trouble was coming? The nuns were wrong. The spirit being within me didn't agree and I always paid for it, with a slap across the face or some other punishment.

Sometimes our dreams are more than they seem. They open up a vivid future, sending a message for the dreamer to understand. My "sixth sense" philosophy I base on my need for self-preservation. Hindered by my lack of understanding as a child, I didn't know *how* to defend myself against the church's unwavering stance on the paranormal and dreamers. So I keep these thoughts isolated from rebuttal.

Many dreams were just that, dreams. Nightmares too, nothing more than "something you ate." A comforting hug, and Mom would say, "It's only a bad dream, honey. It can't hurt you." Most times I believed her, but sometimes, there was more to it than a bad dream. Something was waiting to infect my mind.

A few days later, the same boy who assaulted me the first time tried to pull my panties down right in front of our house. I was yelling at him to stop it when mom came running out. Mom screamed at the kid to go home, while giving me that 'look.'

She was disgusted. "Why would you let him do that to you?"

"I did try to stop him." Traumatized and angry. I had nowhere to go. No way to defend myself. This was handled all wrong, too. Instead of comforting me, I was punished, again. I resented mom for blaming me. She had it in her head if bad things happen to you, there had to be a reason that meant it was my fault. How could she think that?

One consolation, I never saw that family again. One day, they were just gone. Moved out without notice. Daddy seriously, teased mom, "You gave them the third eye? Didn't you?" She laughed at the idea. "That kind of power, I would be the president."

Sexual trauma is a helpless feeling, bearing down on guilt. It is hard enough to deal with this as a grown woman, but when a child who hasn't even discovered their own body is sexually assaulted, her issues will compound daily into a mess of displaced anger and shame.

The emphasis on being "pure" is a lot of stress for a Catholic child who has no control over the action of others. My father could see his little girl was afraid and embarrassed, too. Mom told him what happened. And Daddy handled it his way.

"That boy was wrong to do that to you, Linda," Daddy said. "Next time a boy tries to hurt you and won't leave you alone, kick him in the nuts!" Pointing to his genital area, he added, "Right here at the family jewels."

Shy, quiet people are easy targets for bullies. The newness of another school and all it entailed was becoming repetitive. When you 'talk funny," you learn to keep your mouth shut. The less I communicated, the more I learned to be alone in my daydreams.

Leo King was cute as a button. The first time I saw him, he was singing, "I Dream of Jeannie" on stage. I was infatuated and began having dreams of Leo. *Something* connected, but what was it?

Next to my dad, Leo was a childhood hero. Because he was a grade ahead of me and an altar boy, I barely knew him. We had near to no interaction with each other except a few years later, when some bullies pushed me down on the way home from school. Leo stood up to them. "Pick on someone your own size!"

He then asked me if I was okay. It made all the difference in the world to me. Someone showed me kindness in a time of need. That's all it takes: one person to make a difference in another's person's life to change things for the better.

A month after First Communion, summer vacation began. Pulling weeds and being the general "go-for" was my summer routine,

## Sticks and Stones and Broken Bones

along with a new list of chores to do because I was the oldest. It also meant more freedom. Work hard, do the job right the first time so you're not stuck doing it over again "the right way."

When my chores were finished, I rode to the park on my bike. On a typical summer day, my Schwinn and I covered a lot of ground. One morning the sun was high up against a brilliant blue sky, perfect for swinging and daydreaming.

I was making promises to God that no matter what the devil would do to hurt me, I would never give up believing. The next thing I remember waking up with my mother standing over me. I had fallen off the swing, flying over the bars, and had been knocked out. No one told Mom what happened. "I just knew something was wrong," she said.

A big bruise formed on my lower back. It was tender and sore, but that wasn't causing the excruciating pain. I actually, broke my butt. The tip of my tailbone was gone. It wasn't discovered until 25 years later on an x-ray revealing this old injury.

My broken butt hurt too much to sleep comfortably or think about any times tables. Instead, I stared at the moonlight peeking through the slits of the curtains. Eventually, I did fall asleep, forgetting the pain, and dreamed this vision:

*I heard babies crying. I went to go see what was wrong when I saw the back of man's head, dark and wavy hair. Haven't we met? "Leo? Is that you?"*

*He turned and looked at me with grin. But it wasn't the boy I knew as Leo King. He was a different person—a man. A reasonably tall and handsome man with a thick moustache. Who was he?*

*"Don't call me Leo." He preferred* Leonard.

*It took me another moment staring at the other person in the room before I realized that it was a grown-up me, with four small children. Two children crying were mine and someone else's. The smaller two were ours. Leonard then disappeared, leaving me was alone with the crying babies, wondering why they were crying?"*

A feeling of overwhelming sadness, I was crying hysterically when my mother woke me up. "Linda, it's only a dream."

"But Mumma, *it was real.*"

# NUNS DON'T LIE

## White lies only

Fourth grade was relatively smooth until the winter of 1959. It was around February when I was again accused of doing something I didn't do: Talking in church during Mass. Completely unexpectedly, Sister Margaret Cecile motioned for me to exit the pew with a sour look on her face. "Linda, no talking in church!"

Too shy to speak, let alone open my mouth while in church other than to sing, I couldn't help but to defend myself. Who would if I didn't?

"I wasn't talking, Sister. I was singing."

It didn't matter. Sister didn't believe me and made damn sure I was humiliated. As I knelt in the pew on the other side of the aisle, all the students walked by me as they left for lunch. A few kids made snide comments, but the kids next to me in church knew I was falsely accused.

"Wait here until I come get you," said Sister. Sick with worry about what she would tell my mother, I waited on my knees as I was told to do. I heard the lunch bell; it was time for recess. I panicked.

The bell rang again. It was time to go back to class, but I was still on my knees, hungry and waiting for Sister. She never came. On impulse, I left. I crawled right out the church window. Eight years old, and I was on a mission. I was going to grandma's house, back to Delray.

It was frigid outside, with every inch of ground covered in snow from the night before. It did not hindered my escape; it was sheer will: I was not going back to class. Not today, anyway. I waded through the hip-deep snow along the building and ducked down below the classroom windows to avoid being spotted.

When I reached the sidewalk, I ran as if the devil were after me. Certain that no one was coming after me, I started walking down West Rd. towards Fort Street. I knew that this road would take me to Delray—all I had to do was follow it until I reached the (Woodmere) cemetery.

It seemed like forever, but I finally made it to King Road. My first landmark, the Sibley Quarry, was coming up on the right. I had walked over three miles with thirty-seven more to go when it started snowing again. I needed a ride. I put my thumb out.

An eight-year-old nomad on the road in the cold. What was I thinking? Obviously, God has a soft spot for fools and idiots, because I'm sure it was more than luck when a kind woman pulled over to see if I was lost. After explaining that I wasn't lost, the lady offered me a ride to Grandma's house.

The woman lied. Worried for my safety, she drove me straight to the Riverview Police Department. This was the first, but certainly not my last encounter with the law.

Did I make it any easier for the police to take me back to school? Hell, no! I wouldn't say anything, not even how old I was. They came to their own conclusions after looking inside my prayer book, which traced me back to St. Timothy's.

Visibly upset, I begged the officers to take me to Grandma's. Instead, the officer sitting on the right side of the car turned and smiled, hoping to distract me with the car radio.

"You want to listen to the radio?"

Maybe it was the lack of food or that I had been crying so much that I was dehydrated. But whatever the reason, *something* was wrong with my head. The amplifying static and muffled voices over the police radio agitated me. My head was hurting, and I felt dizzy.

Behaving like a caged animal, I began kicking and screaming in the back seat of the patrol car. I covered my ears to block out the radio sounds, begging for "it" to stop. There was an image in my head: I could see blood on the ground, more police, and a man bleeding. I was eight years old.

On July 16, 1974, Everyone knew, Tommy was the man I saw in my head while riding in back of the patrol car that winter's day, but I couldn't explain. Meanwhile, the "Holy Office" was waiting my arrival.,

Mother Superior, the head nun in charge, Sister Mary Bede: unforgiving and strict, her customary mood complementing her customary harsh tone of her voice. "Why did you run away?"

"Sister didn't come back to get me, like she said. She forgot me."

Sister Margaret Cecile not only abandoned me, but lied to cover it up. "I said no such thing." The nun continued her fabricated report. "She was supposed to be the last one in line—a reminder not to talk during mass."

"I wasn't talking!" I blurted out in my defense. "Why would I talk in church? I love God. I love going to church."

"Are you calling me a liar?" Sister demanded. "Are you calling Sister Cecile a liar?"

"No, Sister, I di..." But I was cut off.

"Yes, you are." Sister insisting. "You're arguing with me; you're calling me a liar."

How do you answer a question when any answer is wrong, because "they said so" by putting the words in your mouth. A child confronted by an angry adult will shrink into silent terror. I didn't know what to say. I said enough by not answering. Sister's hand struck me across the face before I knew it.

Pleading with Sister Mary Bede to believe me was a waste. She called my mother and explained their version of what happened. According to them, I started the "commotion" when I was caught talking in church. Sister hung up the phone. I wanted to scream, "I hate you!"

Boy, could these two nuns inflict pain. Quick to slap your face, Sister Cecile also loved to pinch and pull hair. What the hell was wrong with these people? The imprint left a burning red mark across my cheek, warming a desire to leave these horrible people behind. They were not godlike, they acted like evil bitches from hell bent to break our spirits. As an adult, I believe they lied to my parents to avoid a lawsuit.

All the way home I cried with worry. I was a wreck. The world was a serious place if a nun could get away with her own kangaroo court. After all, "Nuns don't lie." What was Mom going to say? THIS was a woman you didn't mess with when her emotions were jarred. Boy, I sure wished I had been in a sealed jar and buried when I walked in the door.

It was a MOM attack brought on by fear-induced anger—one of the worst emotions a mother experiences after realizing the life-and-death situation her child may have encountered; a conflicting perspective she can do without.

On one hand, the mother is overjoyed her child isn't dead. But it's the other hand the child needs to be worried about. "Ouch." Twice in one day? How could I ever forget this day?

"STAND THERE!" she commanded. Yep, that's right, two feet within striking distance. Another slap in the face before I could get my coat off. She had my attention. "Why did you run away?"

"I wasn't running away. I was going to Grandma's house because Sister left me. She said I was talking in church but I wasn't."

I don't know if it was my pleas, my tears, or my refusal to take blame for the situation, but my mother, decidedly, rectified the immediate damage between us. Mom sat down at the kitchen table with her hand cupping her right cheek.

"What am I going to do with you? I know I am going to just read about you in the papers. Tell me, why would the nuns lie? It's a sin to tell lies."

"I don't know, Mumma, but I was singing, not talking."

Mom motioned for me to sit on her lap. For the first time I could recall, my mother showed remorse for hitting me. She couldn't say it, but it was the way she hugged me. I knew she believed me. But it was no excuse to leave school.

"Don't ever do that again," she said, squeezing me tightly. "I was scared to death something bad had happened to you." I promised not to do that again. Sitting in mom's lap was rare moment, but I was safe. I soaked it up. I wanted to tell her about the strange headache I had experienced, but decided it was best not to.

Daddy wasn't keen on nuns in general. As a child, he had had his share of their methods of discipline. He came home that night and found me hiding in the bathroom doing a series of times tables as punishment. Daddy sat me down at the kitchen table while he listened to the details. He didn't believe a word of it.

"She wouldn't run away if they were doing their job," he said. "I've had enough of their pious bullshit! They have no business putting their hands on her." My father was pissed off. "I've half a mind to go over to that nunnery and read them (nuns) the riot act!"

Daddy, always to the point and to the rescue, paused a moment to catch his breath, bright red in the face. "What time do those penguins go to bed, Rusty?"

Penguins? Who said anything about penguins? It was a rhetorical question. Mom started laughing. I got the joke.

"Yeah, daddy... they do look like birds in tuxedos. Don't they?"

Shaking his head, Daddy noticed I was paying too close attention to his rant. I never heard my father express such disrespect for their authority.

"It's time for bed, Linda, girl," daddy said. "Forget the extra homework. Your Ma will send you to school with a note. Now gimme a kiss goodnight."

It wasn't the answer I expected, but enough information to know my ordeal was finally over. And for a little while, my scary ride in the patrol car was forgotten. When I lay in bed, I worried if something was wrong with my brain. Luckily, I fell asleep with a major change to my nightly routine. After two years, no more times tables repeating in my head.

Near the end of that school year, another minor but memorable incident occurred when that phantom *someone* struck again. To this

## Sticks and Stones and Broken Bones

day, I'm not sure if the sound I heard was a pencil breaking or if someone just threw it, but I was the one in trouble.

Festering inside, an angry and frightened little girl was tired of being a scapegoat. I wanted to lash out, but again didn't know how to. I panicked. My heart was racing, and I tried to catch my breath as I walked to the front of the class as directed. With each pounding beat, it hurt to breathe. Clutching my chest in anguish, I was freaking out.

"My heart, my heart, my heart hurts!"

It lasted a few moments, and the pain was gone. After being escorted to the office, my mother was called to pick me up. Mom accused me of "acting dramatic, faking a heart attack."

Whatever ails the soul, laughter is the best remedy to keep things in perspective. With her hand over her heart, mom reenacted my *performance*, "My heart, my heart." It wasn't fair. Mom was making me laugh at my expense. You can't whine when you're laughing. This didn't exactly help the case for my "hurting heart," but I knew the truth. I could care less if anyone believed me or not.

The pain was real, as were the intrusive thoughts that wouldn't go away. It wasn't a heart attack: It was a panic attack. Another symptom of post-traumatic stress disorder, but who knew? It was the '50s.

The 1960s: a new decade was around the corner. Delray was fighting for its last breath. By now, most of the Bodzsars and Bogards were peppered throughout neighboring suburbs. Only a few stayed behind, living out their days in Delray.

As time went by, the less I went to Delray, but Mom still went at least once a week. One Friday, I had to go with Mom so my grandmother could heal the boil on my knee with a dry fried onion. Mom watched with great concern while Grandma lanced the boil.

"Everything will be alright, Mariska," Grandma said. "Yous see."

*Mariska* was my mother's Hungarian nickname. I thought it meant *Dolores* until Aunt Nena corrected me. "She's (mom) a *little bitter.*"

The contrast between my parents was obvious over time. Mom was a full-blood Hungarian, Daddy a self-proclaimed "mutt."

Sometimes, "us kids" were in the middle of it, not knowing exactly what it was.

When issues not meant for young ears would come up, I would be excused from the room. It perpetuated my curiosity. I listened at the top of the stairs while Mom and Dad were in the basement. I was doing more and more of this, spying on my family to find out what the hell was going on.

My parents and their siblings were small children growing up in the days of the Great Depression. This generation survived the '30s and a World War, but not without repercussions that affected them throughout their lifetime, instilling the importance to save for a rainy day. These adult children stocked shelves with goods to last months in the event the economy took a dump. Mom saved for deluge.

"Just in case daddy gets laid off," she explained. While Mom was doing laundry, I heard my parents discussed remodeling the basement into a combination family room with a second kitchen. Mom needed more space to "stock up" on supplies.

"Jesus Christ, Rusty... You got enough soup in here to open up a goddamn soup kitchen! How many cans of tuna fish do you have in here, anyway?" Daddy named a few other items, his voice got quiet, and then I heard a giggle.

"It was on sale," Mom said. I don't think they were talking about groceries, but it does explain the tune Daddy was singing coming up the stairs.

"Hey, good lookin', Whatcha got cookin'? How's about cookin' up something special with me?" He caught me spying. Smiling, he gave me a wink, then went to read the paper on his "throne." I heard Mom coming up, and tried to get out of the house, but it was too late.

"Linda. I need you to go to the store," she said. Thank God, I didn't have to pull weeds. The note read, "Please sell my daughter, Linda, one pack of Pall Malls and a loaf of bread." Mom gave me the money and went back downstairs to her cubbyhole..

Daddy made the shush sign and placed a dime in my hand. "This is for you."

The somber, survivalist lifestyle of my mother's Hungarian past was drilled into me. Work hard from sunup to sundown, learn to adapt, and eat what you're served because it could be your last (meal).

"Appreciate what you have, Linda, and don't make waves, don't cause a scene, keep your mouth shut."

Mom wouldn't give me an allowance. So, now and then Dad would slip me a few coins. "Don't say anything to your Mom. I wanna keep the peace around here." I did learn to keep my mouth shut.

The 1950s were a precursor to the birth of the Great American Subculture of the 1960s. It was time to rock 'n' roll to the sound of a new beat generation. Uncle Johnny was younger than my parents, closer in age to the beats and hipsters, like Marlon Brando in *The Wild One*, he was a greaser with a cool hair-do. One tough son of a bitch.

My uncle didn't like the nuns, either. He had been mistreated: smacked around a few times. Other issues stemmed from childhood, but I never pried. One evening in 1959, Uncle Johnny invited me to tag along and ride up to the store with him and his date.

Uncle Johnny turned the radio up as the DJ announced, "Next, Elvis Presley and *Jailhouse Rock*." Tapping his fingers to the beat on the steering column, he looked over at me smiling. "You like that, Linda?"

It was fast-paced, like my mind. Uncle Johnny's music was *cool. Rock n' roll was cool.* Nodding my head and tapping my knees to the beat with my uncle was the moment I knew I wanted to dance and sing. It made me feel better, like I wasn't so strange after all.

The early days of rock n' roll when Elvis hit the scene put a bounce in my mother's step, too. She would dance around the basement with me, attempting to teach me how to jitterbug, do the two-step, and we twisted. Family parties would find us all dancing and rocking out. Those were good days with Mom. The music and dancing made her feel young, alive with hope. It helped balance the bad days that impacted our family life.

Violence and severe trauma happen in war. Not to a little girl. So I lived with it. Untreated disorders continued to interfere with my life. Giving it a home to secrets and strange dreams. I began to keep a journal of my daily events and issues, documenting dreams and opinions no one cared to hear, but the universe was paying attention.

Over the next few years, my issues were typical of a child with emotional problems, and my grades were proof of that. The academic world ate me alive. Maybe if I could concentrate, but I didn't care. School was a place I was the least comfortable.

My "permanent record" already tarnished with comments. "Linda is not applying herself." Unless it was a subject I cared about an A or B wasn't important to me. Not being noticed by the nuns was. Hey, I wasn't planning on being a rocket scientist, but I did reach for the stars.

Secretly, I planned my escape into adulthood. Leaning toward the convent at first. Regardless, I was seen as being "too serious" for my age. Mom said, "Don't worry about the rest of the world. Just worry about yous."

All dreams, to her, had one outcome. "You'll get married someday and have kids." Mom was sure of it.

Hungarian girls are raised to be wives and mothers. Preparing for my wedding day was my mother's goal. It was her job to see me go down the altar, unscathed, untouched, a virgin.

Eight more years of relying on my parents for financial support before I could get a job, buy a car and go where I wanted to go. Or, join the convent and be a better nun. That was a plan. After all, what do you when you're a kid, but make all sorts of elaborate plans and toy with the question adults never seem to tire of asking:

"What are you going to do with the rest of your life?"

I stood there, trying to avoid my mother's eyes. Mom shouted, "Look at this report card!" God, I hated report card day. It was never a good day. I was a bad apple, and we know what people do with bad apples–Toss them out. "It only takes one bad apple to spoil the bunch."

"Look at me." She demanded. "Look me in the eye and explain why yous got a U?"

U, was unsatisfactory, the mark of failure. Sheepishly, I replied. "I don't know."

## Sticks and Stones and Broken Bones

It was bad enough my grades were failing, but it was the teacher comments that would set my mother off year after year. "Linda does not pay attention in class. She still needs to concentrate." I didn't know *why* it was so difficult to pay attention and focus in class. I tried, but I always found another place I wanted to be in my head. Why would I trust what they tell me is the truth? If anything, I learned fear and doubt.

Children who have been sexually molested, bullied or otherwise victimized cannot think about anything but when the next attack will take place. I didn't participate in group discussions or activities. I lacked self-control and had a problem with authority.

Every report card indicated underlying issues. This should have been a sign that something was seriously wrong, but that's the way it was in the '50s. No one made the connection between school performance and a child in need of help. It was all my fault.

A person hears something long enough, they may be fooled into thinking it's true, or find a way to prove it wrong. Most of the time I avoided mischief to prove I was being a "good girl." From time to time, that sleeping giant awoke, to stomp around making noise and then head back to slumberland.

It was time for the annual Csardas Gypsy Dance in Delray. The Csardas, the dance that defines the soul of the Hungarian people, was introduced about two hundred years ago. It was rejected by nobility and pastors alike because it was a dance of revolution against foreign oppression.

Created from a thousand years of tradition, the national song was used to recruit soldiers for the Hungarian army. The Csardas was an annual reminder the war against oppression is never over. Mom said it was very important to be there and support the tradition.

My cousin looked like a gypsy princess from a fairy tale in her colorful gypsy skirt and headpiece. Her full skirt bounced as she tapped and stepped, twirling with her partner the dance tempo speeded up. The revolution was on. Kind of like a rock 'n' roll sound, except different.

Feeling the momentum of the dance under my feet, I really wanted to be a part of this, but I couldn't. Holy Cross was no longer my church. Saint Tim's was homogenized. No ethnic celebrations other than Saint Patrick's Day.

This is what I craved, my roots, but what I grew to love was disappearing out of my grasp. I was a gypsy at heart. Watching my cousin do her part to keep tradition alive, it became clearer... I had to go the bathroom.

No one noticed that I slipped out of the dance to go explore the hallways of the school. Standing next to the stairs by the second floor was a group of older girls, whispering and giggling. They were up to something, and I was going to find out.

"You pull it," one said to the other while the other two girls listened on.

"No," she said. "You. It was your idea."

Pull what? I wondered? More squabbling, then one of them slightly moved over. They were planning to pull the fire alarm in the middle of the Csardas, but they were arguing who would pull the alarm. I was frustrated. No one made a decision. I wanted to see what happened.

While they quibbled, I pulled the red lever. What chaos! It was a *rush*. Watching nuns fly down the stairs like hell was at their heels with their habits hiked up to their asses, showing their white petticoats. People were running everywhere. I would have gotten away with it, but the girls ratted me out.

In trouble again, but I didn't care. It was worth it. I did it! "I pulled the fire alarm, Sister." I don't recall what my punishment was. Probably, because I deserved it.

Nevertheless, this defiant, bold action gave me a sense of security in the person I was becoming: Someone of action, a risk taker, someone who couldn't conform to the standards of the day, just because "that's the way it is." But instead of being admired as a risk taker, I was a troublemaker, an outcast, and for the longest time held the title of the family's Black Sheep.

## Sticks and Stones and Broken Bones

Considering the Magyars' political history of oppression; understandably, Hungarians are skeptics at heart, and a Hungarian gypsy most certainly didn't trust anyone outside her group. Gypsies were persecuted, hunted down like animals, and treated like the scum of the earth.

The Catholic Church displayed a certain arrogance, making claims that it was only true religion. Everyone else was going to hell. Pretty harsh concept. Difficult to accept. I was skeptical.

"It's best to be skeptical," Mom said. "Don't believe everything yous hear, or read in the newspapers. Yous make up your own mind."

It was part of the Magyar disposition not to trust the clergy or government—my mother and grandparents were proof of that. Though mom and my grandmother both had pierced ears, they refused to wear pierced earrings. Mom wouldn't allow me or my sister to pierce ours because of its "gypsy" stigma.

"You'll look like a goddamn gypsy," was all she said. So, I pressed her. "But what's wrong with that? I thought it was okay if people called us names?"

"I can't explain it to yous," she said. "Yous too young to understand." The conversation was over. I was sent out to play, or she'd find something for me to do... I boogied out before she changed her mind. I had other things to do besides be the workhorse.

The Trenton Library was my refuge. I could be left alone to learn what interested me. For hours I would sit in the aisle on the floor, reading about nature, heaven, death, whatever questions arose from unsatisfied answers the nuns fed us.

Behind the library ran a creek alongside a trail where I rode my bike, pretending I was somewhere else. Often, I went into the woods by Westfield and King Roads, looking for wounded animals to rescue, and of course, adventure.

Most of the time I spent alone, riding my bike along the creek or hanging at the park. Freedom to be alone, think, and discover my heart's desire, without the undue influence of others quick to criticize what I thought or hoped for.

Like my mother, I preferred animals. Mom had a way with them— she said they could sense a person's true heart. It was obvious that animals trusted her. Squirrels would run up to her, waiting until she knelt down. Then these little buggers would steal the nuts right out of her coat pocket, putting a smile on Mom's face.

Birds too, outside the kitchen window, pecked at crumbs she placed on the windowsill. These neighborly creatures counted on her daily routine to supplement the harsh consequences of urban sprawl that replaced their nested homes in blocks of concrete.

I was beginning to understand why my mother spent so much time with critters—they didn't talk or ask questions. Squirrels, birds, chipmunks, and baby rabbits made better company than most of the humans. No need to be guarded or worry about what critters thought of me while I narrated random thoughts and dreams.

My first rescue was a baby squirrel that fell from its nest. It was lying next to its dead mother, and I took it home to Mumma. Concerned about the "infested" wildlife I was carrying, she instructed me to wash my hands. Mom prepared me for the inescapable truth.

"Honey, he's hurt pretty bad," she said. "He isn't breathing right. He's going to die."

Sadly, it barely lived an hour. Stroking its little head, I kept praying God would change his mind and let him live. Instead, with a sudden jerking motion, the baby squirrel "went to sleep." It wasn't fair.

My obsession with death couldn't be helped. The little dead squirrel triggered memories of the horrific death I witnessed at age four. A fascination for cemeteries developed, along with a need to learn more about how life began and what happens after death. I cried for days. Why did it hurt so much?

It was getting harder to believe Genesis: "In the beginning God created the heavens and the earth..." Why no mention of dinosaurs? Were they a mistake? Maybe people don't know everything about God they claimed? Maybe animal souls do go to heaven? Why do we dream?

My time at the library was well spent. Picking up one book led to another. Some books were off limits to kids under twelve, but at

## Sticks and Stones and Broken Bones

the age-appropriate time, I made a point to follow through. Without intending to learn, this little habit of collecting facts taught me how to do research and find answers, a useful skill that has served me well throughout life and has aided with the career choices I've made.

As the years passed, newer kids moved in the neighborhood and became my friends. Though still younger than I was, it was OK. It gave me purpose. I took it upon myself to be in charge of the younger kids because I was older. Keeping an eye on them and keeping them out of the street. No one was going to get hit by a car if I could help it.

Bullies were still a problem. We had a few mean ones who lived on Lynn Court, and looking back, anyone could make an uneducated guess some of these bullies had sociopathic tendencies. A hard lesson learned.

One afternoon, while walking home from the park, I heard a popping noise and noticed the neighbor boys that lived down the street on the corner, lighting firecrackers. Like all kids. I loved fireworks and just wanted to watch them go off.

What I found was upsetting beyond belief. These boys were killing frogs and garter snakes by placing firecrackers in their mouths and tossing them. Instant rage. I screamed at but they laughed at me. I wasn't big enough to stop them but that didn't stop me from trying.

Running over to the frog they tossed next to a 2X4 laying on top a rock, I saw it was dead. There was a small garter snake in a can I grabbed the snake and when I stood up, one of the boys jumped on the end of the board. The other end of the board flew up, coming down on the right side of my head, smacking my ear.

The hit was so hard it knocked my glasses off, the injury left me with permanent tone damage, which I found out later when I was in a recording studio.

It was not easy dealing with bullies if you were a girl raised to turn the other cheek. I wanted to fight back, but the church and Mom had two different views. The church says, "Turn the other cheek." Mom says, "Stand up for yourself."

When I came home with my ear bleeding and broken glasses, Mom yelled at me, "You need a strong constitution to make it in this world." Obviously, confused. Girls don't fight. Mom said it wasn't ladylike. The sight of blood, a screaming child, she was singing a different tune. She wanted me to fight back. She was giving me permission: "HIT 'EM BACK!"

"I don't care about turning the other cheek crap," she said. "A person can take so much..."

My glasses were broken, too, and I was in trouble. It didn't matter *how* it happened. "It's your responsibility to take care of them," she yelled. I should have walked away and headed straight home like I was supposed to.

"It never would have happened," she said.

So, what do I do the next time my glasses are broken? I overreact. I caused pain and undeserving tears by doing the meanest thing I could think of to the next kid who broke them. I grabbed Frankie's arm and twisted it behind his back until I heard a "pop." I thought I broke his arm, but luckily I hadn't.

The emotional and physical abuse turned into aggression after a distant cousin sexually molested me. Three sexual assaults in a four-year period compounded by bullying, made things worse. I did what any kid would do—I lashed out at the wrong person.

I felt like a monster when I grabbed Frankie's arm and whipped it behind his back, pulling it up until I heard him scream. There was a sick satisfaction knowing that if I had to, I could hurt someone, but I didn't want to be that kind of person.

The aggression was an act of defense. I was terrified if I didn't do something about my broken glasses, Mom would. Damned if you do and damned if you don't.

Mom threatened to punish me the next time I didn't stand up for myself or if my glasses were broken again. Over the years I discovered when I lose my glasses or if they break... I still panic. A stupid trigger, too. I thought this was behind me, but a few years ago...

Driving on I-5 in Shasta County with the windows down, singing my heart out, *whoosh* came a wind, and out the window my glasses flew. I panicked—a blind woman was driving. Mom was the first person I thought of. How would I have explained this if she were alive? Would she believe it?

Hurting someone out of anger doesn't feel as good as I thought it would—at least I know I'm not a sociopath. I was covered in a blanket of guilt and shame for my cruel acts.

Hurting Frankie was wrong, and not how I wanted to remember our childhood. He wasn't a bad kid. In fact, I had a little crush on him. Mental note to self, "Don't be mean." Yet sometimes, wishing I was strong as a man, I wanted to beat up mean people.

PTSD, woven into my character, was changing my life in more ways than one. According to Mom, I was a bad apple, a *"bad seed."* No, a product of my mother's predictions. You hear something long enough as a child, you will begin to believe it.

Today, anyone with a psych degree would review my report cards and recognize consistencies between teacher comments, my grades, and the emotional maltreatment I had experienced, and I would have been properly diagnosed long before things got worse.

The Bogards and Bodzsars; day and night. Around the circle of life we spin. Holidays, weddings, baby showers galore; we had more things to do and places to be as our clan grew in numbers. The first sibling to arrive was Valerie; then Jimmy, David, and Johnny followed.

My sister Valerie was a funny baby. She made the goofiest face when she was excited and happy. Her giddiness threw us in a fit of laughter. Daddy would just look at her, sitting in the high chair as she waited for him to scrunch his nose at her.

Valerie giggled, responding in her own way, making a bug-eyed face and showing her teeth while twitching. Daddy did this repeatedly, my side was hurting from laughing so hard. We might have been having too much fun. Mom picked up the bubbly baby and went into the bedroom to change her diaper.

Daddy went to a neighbor's house. I was still washing the dishes when mom called. My job was to put a clean shirt on Valerie and keep an eye on her so she wouldn't fall off the bed. "Don't let her fall," Mom warned.

Simple enough, I put her shirt on. Mom was distracted doing something in the kitchen. Valerie kept making distorted faces when I had a brilliant idea; let's see if her diapers were as padded as Mom kept saying they were.

Let's face it, two-year-olds can be boring but Valerie wasn't. Let's bounce the baby! I thought Valerie would bounce just a little, so I picked her up and dropped her in the middle of the bed. Much to my chagrin, she bounced off the bed onto the floor, right on her butt. The wailing began. Hers and mine. A lesson in chain reaction as a result of my careless action.

Mom shouting, "Think, before yous do something."

Mumma supported the theory, "if you want the job done right in the first place," do it yourself. Translation? "Do it right the first time." Mom stared at me. "I know, I am going to read about yous in the paper."

Looking back it almost was impossible not to get noticed. Yet I wondered? Was there an *I told you so* in there waiting to come out? There was. Down the road, it would come out. "You made your bed, now lie in it."

# A BOGEY IN THE HOUSE
## Everybody needs an ally

The Bogards love for music appealed to my emotional needs. Uncle Frank never passed a piano without running a tune over the ivory keys. Daddy, softly whistling while he worked, often crescendoing into lyrics. Uncle Red's talents weren't musical but they were creative. Looking back I can this as combat –fatigue-inspired art.

Grandpa Bogard wrote songs, played the violin, and the piano. Aunt Joann too, played the piano. My father had a nice voice, he also played a soulful harmonica and was one helluva artist.

No one ever considered my mental health as the issue complicating my life as a child but my behavior singled me out as, being "odd." Lucky for me, the Bogards had a soft spot for me. In their eyes, there was a reason for my odd behavior.

While watching TV in the basement, I could hear the adults arguing over something that was *none of my business*. Maybe not, but someone said my name? Wasn't it my business? I came upstairs, thinking I was in trouble? Mom said curiosity killed the cat. W*hat cat?*

"Don't be so nosey," Mom said, "yous don't put your nose where it does not belong!" But what about the *cat?*

"It's an expression!" I *was* that naive. How was I suppose to know that? As for the cat? What cryptic message was this? Or was there one? Telling Mom that I learned from Grandma that the cat had eight more lives because "satisfaction brought him back." Well, that was me; being a "smartass." I paid for that one, too. *SMACK!*

Linda Lee King

It would have been a lonely existence, if it wasn't for my allies in the Bogard family. Rules, were meant to be broken if there was an exceptional cause at stake, like homemade cherry pie.

"Linda, go pick me some cherries from the tree at the corner." Apprehensive from previous experiences, I questioned Grandma about going on people's property. "Go on—you have *my* permission." Grandma Bogard said. That's all I needed, right?

Ha! Grandma just wanted them cherries. She knew the owners but thought they were out and sent me in to do her work I found out later.

"No one is going to wonder why a kid's up in a tree grabbing some cherries," Daddy laughed. "But your Grandma would sure look out of place trying to explain why she was stealing cherries."

It's kinda funny. Both of my grandmothers and my mother, too, inadvertently were teaching me stealing, food is the exception to society's rules. Grandma Beno would wheel me around the fruit section of A&P popping grapes, cherries and anything else she wanted fresh into my mouth. "Is it good?" Then pop a grape in her mouth.

Mom did the same thing. They all insisted, it wasn't stealing!?! My thoughts? Going hungry during the Depression may have adjusted their moral compass.

Growing up around the hearty Bogard laughter and love of music, invoked many capricious ideas to spun around in my head. What to do? What to do? Watching Grandpa Bogard string horsehair to the violin bow, I knew I wanted to play an instrument.

Aunt Joann played beautifully, her passion for music illuminated when she played. When she had time she taught me the scales and how to read the notes. "Every Good Boy Does Fine." And if, Uncle Red didn't have one of his "migraines" I practiced whenever I came over.

If I wasn't practicing the scales, I would teach myself to play a song. It was fine for awhile, but if I was going to fully understand "how" to play, I needed lessons. My parents barely afforded the heating bill in the winter, let alone the money to pay for lessons or a piano. I made do with what I had. Like I always do.

## Sticks and Stones and Broken Bones

One afternoon mom walked in the living room where I was teaching myself, "The Marines Hymn (Don't ask)." Without warning, she yanked me off the piano bench. No clue what was wrong and I never found out *why* mom started spanking me. Grandpa Bogard pulled me out of her lap and onto his. Hugging me tightly, covering my head, and hollering for her to "quit it!"

"What's wrong with you?" Grandpa shouted. "She isn't doing anything wrong!"

The atmosphere in the room suddenly changed. Something between the adults was going on that I didn't understand, except Grandpa told mom, "You're wrong."

Mom loved her father-in-law and refrained from saying anything else. The chain of command, and Mom wasn't in charge. I learned respect for your elders still carried weight within the family structure and Mom practiced what she preached. You have to respect that.

Funerals, the final milestone in life. It was a cruel joke, Grandpa Bogard died on October 18, 1960. Happy Birthday, Linda. The legacy begins with Grandpa. Tommy, Leonard, my father; all the men I loved in my life died on a Tuesday. Not strange at all, if you were me. Adding to this, I recently discovered my first husband, Thomas Rousku, died on March 19, 2013; a Tuesday.

What message lie in this coincidental time frame? Probably none, but then again? Why do I feel there is something, missing? Do the sins of the father come back to haunt us? If so, what else do we inherit from our family besides genetic traits and property?

Life is full of surprises and mystery in general when you're young. Our parents have all the answers. Then one day, we begin to challenge those answers because something has changed: you.

Often I went with my father to visit his family. I never felt worthless, stupid or weak when I was around the Bogards. Their choice of words allowed me the freedom to dream. Mom repeatedly squelched any dream with, "You can't do that because..."

The Bogards lived like an open book. I learned more about my father than I'd ever hoped for. I didn't have to sneak around, hiding behind sofas or under the tables and chairs to find things out. Secrets are destructive tools of separation that divides a family. Pitting one against the other, corroding the core of the family unit.

The insight to my father's childhood revealed that life lessons ought to be shared with family, so the next generation can learn from it, laugh at the ignorance of youth. The good stories, the sad ones, and the bad ones, too. All valuable lessons to pass on to help the new and hopefully improved model of our next generation born.

The best were the stories of the many stupid shenanigans Daddy and his brothers pulled off as kids. Ah, the stupidity of youth. Believe me, I thought about doing this stunt myself as a child until I heard Daddy's story.

"Your father thought he could parachute off the roof using a bed sheet," Grandma said. "Fool. Lucky he didn't break his neck instead of his leg."

Grandma would have broken it for him. He scared the hell out of her. That's what moms do when you scare the crap out of them. They make sure you remember what you did. Grandma Bogard's favorite weapon? A straw broom she wielded like a pro, wailing the hell out of Daddy's brothers for letting him do a stupid thing. Grandma said it didn't hurt the boys if she bopped them when they acted "brain dead."

My father, a man with a wild and crazy past, only Mom could curb. They were yin and yang. Mom was leery of change. Daddy adapted to it, if not, caused it. Mom buried her problems, and Daddy dug them up.

My father also relied on his wits and ability to go after what he wanted. The man sat in a airplane and taught himself to fly while reading the instructions. I repeat: He was reading the instructions while in the frigging air!!! *Who does that?*

"A couple of numbskulls," Daddy laughed. "That's who."

Though his buddy Al Kovacs sat in the co-pilot seat, no surprise—he wasn't a pilot either. It was time to land the two-seater when they ran out of gas. Yes, *Ooh, God, yes,* they did that. Gliding with the wind. They were laughing in the face of possible death all the way down.

## Sticks and Stones and Broken Bones

"Bogey managed to get us down without crashing," said Kovacs.

Without the other crap in my life, childhood was perfectly grand, the best of both worlds. Mumma was a little nuts, but hey? Aren't we all? Daddy was funny and always listening for the call of adventure, a legacy I couldn't let go of. Certainly, I was becoming more like my father when it came to taking chances; this was a "bogey" trait.

Taking a risk was in the blood. I contemplated exploring the world to meet new people and experience new cultures. My big thing was Africa—I wanted to swing from tree to tree like Tarzan. Go to Kenya, save the lions like *Elsa*, just like Joy Anderson wrote about in her book *Born Free*. That was another plan for a while.

Like each summer before, a repeating dream clouded my sleep with memories yet to be. What did it mean? A question I asked myself every year until, I was seventeen:

*Darkness cloaked the cemetery. Through the fog, a young woman walked quickly between the headstones. How did she get there? Overcome by irrational fear, she started to run. A man appeared out of the shadows, dressed to kill, but who? Like some kind of a spy movie, he stood in his cloak, holding a butcher knife in his hand. The woman turned her head toward the sound of his footsteps—she could see the blade's edge reflecting in the moonlight.*

*Blindly she ran through the fog, unaware of the open grave in her path. Her feet gave way for lack of earth, tumbling into the blood-filled pit. The rich red blood ran in rivulets down her bright yellow dress as the man ran closer and closer. The woman was frantic when she fell in the freshly dug grave, half-filled with blood, but not a drop on her dress.*

*"Wake up!" A voice screamed in the dream.. "Wake up or be dead!"*

Ten years, repeating the same dream. As I grew up, I recognized the woman: It was me running, falling into a pit of blood. Not a drop on me. I noticed when I fell, the dream turned into color. An ominous warning. But what? Why the same dream for so long? It was warning me not to marry my first husband, a gay man—the dream was relevant to my future. Its meaning I would understand later instead of sooner.

Repeatedly Mom called me a late bloomer. And she wasn't talking boobs, which were taking their sweet time developing, too. "You're a slow learner; it takes you a while to learn some things. Don't worry, you'll catch up." Oh, I caught up alright. In fact, deep-seated ambitions were coming into full bloom. Soon the gypsy rose would outgrow her garden.

A young teenager entering high school should know the basic anatomical terms of body parts; like hands, feet, breasts or penises—Mom had never talked about sex, let alone say the word *vagina*. That *area* was referred as: *down there*. I know, right? Sounds scary, silly? How crazy is that? Regardless, before high school, mom decided it was time to discuss "down there." Once a month, I was going to bleed.

No explanation *why* my body would do this. Mom then demonstrated how to: attach safety pins to the Kotex pad and to my special underwear. That was it. No discussion except that it was going to happen because I was becoming a woman. Naturally, my curiosity piqued, I went back to the library.

Society had a new breed to contend with, the American teenager, a direct product of suburban living in the 1950s. Teenagers no longer helped to support the family—they worked to play. They spent their money on a good time, buying non-essentials like records and hot rods.

Baby Boomers, we were little rebels growing up, unaware we would change the old-world thinking with music, demonstrations, and with purpose. We did not accept the old, traditional ways of thinking. It was a new generation.

The Vietnam War and the civil rights movement would impact the country. Racism, too, was destroying cities, dividing families and neighbors. Music seemed to be the only positive outlet people enjoyed. Religion and politics just pissed people off.

Underneath the constraints of suburban life, I was growing restless every day. Like other Baby Boomers with too much time on their hands, the wheels started turning. Teens were *ready to rumble*. I wasn't far behind.

## Sticks and Stones and Broken Bones

With post-war prosperity, more teens could afford a car or at the very least have access to the family wheels. These bedroom communities not only segregated races, they encouraged rebellion among the youth to seek their own identity and question authority. A job defined autonomy.

The road was calling me long before I put my thumb out that wintry day in February. Commercials enticing us all to "See the USA in your Chevrolet." One day I would see the USA.

It wasn't a big deal to my parents that they did not have high school diplomas. "Hands on" experience was the most common method of training blue-collar workers. These laborers gained prosperity after the war by the sweat off their backs. But it was a big deal for my parents that their children have an education for a better future.

My parents were among the two million young adults dropping out of high school during WWII to support their families and country. Civilians were needed to take over the jobs left behind after droves of men went off to war. Mom had worked odd jobs and landed a "good job" with Vernors before marrying my father, and expected me to do the same. Get a job. Then get married.

My father had some of the worst jobs in the world before working for Ford Motor Company. One in particular offended my father's loving nature, the slaughterhouses. The cruel experience traumatized him. He never ate veal or lamb again. Who could blame him? He couldn't bring himself to smash the brains of baby animals. It was brutal. Daddy wasn't.

Over the years I must have heard this story a dozen times or more. The pack of dogs, flies buzzing and the bloody trail dripping off the truck from dead animals body parts, not meant for human consumption.

"Jesus Christ! You should've seen it," he laughed. "The bodies were piled high. Flies everywhere! In your eyes, in your ears, and we had a pack of dogs chasing after us down the street! It stank like hell, too."

Daddy would stare off in the distance for a brief moment, reminiscing. He vowed never to eat veal or lamb again. "They cried like babies." He shrugged off the memory by changing the topic. He told this story to make a point. He wanted a better life for his kids.

"Get your education, Linda. The world is changing."

The older I became, the more stories I heard of the personal hardships my family went through as children and young adults growing up during the Great Depression and a World War. These young adults were among the many people who kept the labor force alive.

Patriotism was my mother's other favorite subject of interest. Mom was red, white, and blue. She could put a spark under anyone's ass who listened. God help you if she thought you were a "no-good commie traitor" or Japanese.

Women, especially, were encouraged to hang up their aprons to build war machines; leaving children with grandparents. Many young adults (they weren't called teenagers yet) left high school, like my mother, who was fourteen when she dropped out to work. When the war was over, she was seventeen. Women were sent back to the kitchen after the war or took lower-paying jobs. What society didn't expect was the upcoming change in women's role in society.

Women proved in a time of war and chaos that they could do many jobs once considered men's work. After the war, many women were not satisfied to stay at home. Modern appliances had shortened the time women spent on housework, leaving them with more time and reasons to be involved in the workforce, politics, and improving their education, gaining independence and equality with a paycheck.

On a larger scale, women were opting out of family life in the 60s and 70s to have careers and/or be free of male dominance and the undisclosed domestic violence that would be mainly ignored until the 1980s. They demanded equal rights.

School was out of reach for my mother, but not the desire to learn. Mom was also looking for an outlet when she decided to become a beautician, and it did not require a high school diploma. Mom did very well and loved doing hair. She had a bounce in her step again, and it was actually fun to be around her. She joked more and opened up more how things were when she was a young girl.

## Sticks and Stones and Broken Bones

Mom was twenty-one when she married my father. It was expected of her to marry; she was groomed for it. "You'll get a job one day and get married, too," she said. "But you have to graduate, first."

These expectations were my mother's. I had no idea what would be in store for me. Maybe I would get married. Maybe I'd be a Bride of Christ. Maybe, I'd be just a pain in the ass the next time someone asks. "What do you want to be when you grow up?" I didn't know where I was heading, but I didn't want to be my mother.

Our financial health was all on Daddy, who worked –eighteen to twenty hours a day to put food on the table. We never were hungry. Before securing a permanent employment with Ford, my father was a tugboat captain on the Great Lakes based out of the Port Office in South Chicago. He would be gone weeks at a time, but never left us high and dry.

September 25, 1963 was a bad day. Three men from my father's crew were killed in freak accidents. That same week, my Uncle Johnny was in a car accident, and my father's paycheck was short, but we weren't. He sent $135 of his $138 paycheck, keeping only three bucks for himself to get by until the next paycheck. That's a good man.

Raising the children was all on Mom. In a way, Mom was a single parent. Every penny Dad made went to her because she ran the household, paid the bills, and took on the financial worries. Everyday Mom kept an eye out for the mailman, waiting for his letters. Over and over she would read them until the mailman delivered a new one.

Everybody had a job to do—if you failed to do your part, it made it harder on the rest of us, which meant me. I was put in charge of my siblings. A big job for almost thirteen years old. One evening before supper, Mom was fit to be tied. All hell broke loose. She was angry at Valerie; she didn't do her job "right."

"What is so hard about washing behind your ears? The bottoms of your feet are still dirty. Did you even wash?" My sister was still crying downstairs when my mother came to get me.

"Linda, finish the dishes after you give your sister a bath." Mom instructed me to scrub her body, especially her feet, with the brush in the sink. I gave Valerie a bath and was scrubbing her feet. Mom came downstairs to pull the clean clothes out of the dryer.

"Do it harder—get that dirt out of her heels," she said. "I just changed the sheets and I don't want dirty feet in the bed." Mom then went to check on dinner.

The dirt wasn't coming out so easily. It wasn't dirt—it was motor oil from the driveway. All I knew if I didn't get her squeaky clean, it would be my ass next, so I scrubbed her feet with Ajax. It did the trick, but Valerie was traumatized. I overdid it. I didn't see that the gnarly scrub brush was hurting her feet.

Mom was screaming at my little brother Jimmy in the background to get off his ass and pick up his toys. The baby, David, was just a toddler. Mom was losing it fast. All the demons were on the loose.

Two months later, President John F. Kennedy was assassinated. We were in class when the news came in. Many of us started crying; the nuns too. My enemy, Mother Superior, was humbled by the news and shed tears, as well. I felt sorry for her. We all knelt in class to say a prayer for the President and his family, then sent home. When I walked in the door, I noticed the grocery bags were still on the floor by the back door.

Mom was glued to the TV set, waiting to hear any news on the "traitorous killer." She was at A&P when she heard the news on the speaker. "You should have seen it. Everybody was crying." Tears rolling down her cheeks, my mother was devastated, too.

"This! This is awful!" Alarming, the amount of anger and passion she demonstrated. Cursing and crying, a bad combo. We watched the news play back the moment Kennedy was shot. I gasped. Mom covered her mouth. It was a side of her I never saw. Mom would personally "kill" this man who shot Kennedy, if she could only get her "hands on him." She wasn't the only one who wanted the killer dead.

The next two days we sat and watched the updates. Capturing Lee Harvey Oswald gave Mom some satisfaction. Then on live television, Oswald was murdered by Jack Ruby. It was unnerving, traumatic, to witness a man being murdered. The nation, the world, too, an eyewitness to this new evolution of live social media news, living up to its daily mantra. "If it bleeds... it leads."

The nuns were very quiet, subdued by the killing of their favorite Catholic Irish President, and pretty much left most of us alone for a while.

How I ended up on the girl's basketball team I don't recall, but after the game, one of the girl's wanted to meet my parents when they dropped me off. Word got around that Daddy was very cute. A few of the girls wanted to see how cute for themselves and jumped out of the car, giggling before I did.

Daddy was "handsome" and "very good-looking." These girls were flirting with my father! It stunned me. I never would have noticed, if Mom didn't point out that's what they were doing. Yes, I was that innocent. My father was in the backyard with my brothers. The boys saw us girls and stopped what they were doing —that's when Dad decided to show off for mom and us gals.

"Hey, Rusty, you think I can make it over the top?" Dad didn't wait for an answer. He was already on the move.

Dad was running at top speed toward the crossbar and planted the pole directly in the box. He almost made it. It appeared he had cleared the top bar. Then a brief, almost slow-motion pause in mid-air, he dropped like a sack of potatoes. "*Thunk.*"

The poor bastard cracked a few ribs, and was laughing about it. "*Umpff,*" he moaned, trying not to laugh. "The spirit is willing, but the body isn't."

Watching Mom helping Daddy to his feet, talking sweetly to him, they were a happy couple despite Mom's bouts with depression and anger. Daddy looked sheepishly at her. I realized my parents truly loved each other. Why couldn't Mom be happy like that all the time?

"I'm getting too old for this shit, Rusty." She squeezed his arm, chuckling. 'You're not that old, Jimmy." They weren't. They were in their early thirties.

No matter what they faced, they were a team. This is love. I wanted a happily-ever-after story, too. Whatever that was. I didn't have a plan, except entering the Dominican Order of Missionary Nuns in San Diego. I could be a postulant when I turned sixteen. I had a little more than two years to wait.

In those two years, the world changed drastically. We were on the edge of a new era, baby boomers were taking over the social consciousness of society.

We were reminded on eighth grade graduation day that our duty as Soldiers of Christ was ongoing. Fighting the war between good and evil was a battle I could manage. PTSD had already changed my developing brain, but who knew in 1964 that this was possible? No one. I was ready to kick ass, but it was more like teenage hormones kicking in.

# WELCOME TO THE 60S

## Ready, set, time to rock n' roll

Years of unresolved traumas eventually surfaces. It could take years before all the symptoms of PTSD become clear, providing nothing traumatic happens in between healing old wounds. Most people get a break. I didn't have an option.

My emotional well-being was severely compromised at an early age due to trauma. The facts state over 40 percent of children and teens will endure at the very least one traumatic experience that will result in PTSD. Also noted, up to 100 percent of children who endured sexual assault have a tendency to develop PTSD.

Impulsive, aggressive behavior is a dangerous symptom of PTSD. It usually doesn't occur in children or adults, but shows up in teens because of raging hormones. I was no different. Well, maybe a little bit. The day I enrolled at Trenton High School, a flood of memories hit like a ton of bricks.

An emotional flashback is triggered by the familiar surroundings of an event. Literally walking in the door of Trenton High School was like doing a 360. I was back where I started in 1954, at West Road Elementary School where I attended kindergarten. And now, it was my high school. Ten years later, *I was still mad at Mom.*

Mom showed up at school waiting for the recess bell, waiting for me. As I walked out the classroom, Mom dragged me down the halls. Out the door we go. Mom yelling all the way home, smacking me on the ass because I "wet the bed." Mom didn't care what I had to say.

Mom spanked me, and sent me to my room without realizing I was dealing with traumatic events. The general consensus in the 1950's was: "little children were too young to remember." Not true. You don't forget what makes you conscious of your surroundings, good or bad. I was adjusting to a new neighborhood, new school, my great-grandmother died, then her ghost visited me, and fresh in my mind was one dead little girl.

Public humiliation, if warranted, can be a good lesson learned, but intentionally embarrassing a child for no other reason but to humiliate them will compromise their self-esteem and self-confidence. I wasn't a bed wetter; it was the one and only time it happened after a nightmare. Apparently, it literally scared the piss out of me.

In the morning I stripped the soiled sheets off the bed and placed them in the laundry room. A sensible act for an almost five-year-old. I thought I did the right thing. I knew she would see the sheets but not telling her was a "cover-up." I didn't know I did anything wrong.

A memory of one dead child in the street causes me to react today. Kids running in the street, squealing tires, sirens, all triggers of my PTSD. Anytime a kid goes running in the street without looking, I yell at them. Dead was dead.

The physical and verbal abuse I experienced as a child were never addressed at the time of the incidents; neither were the sexual attacks. I was simply a *strange*, quiet girl until I reached high school, still strange but not so quiet. Soon enough, I would heed the call of teenage rebellion like a slave fighting oppression.

Ma noticed I didn't socialize like most kids when I started high school. No school dances, no boyfriends. Just me and my animals. On my way to school I happened to find a fallen nest with baby birds. I didn't know what I was going to do with them except I had to feed them every 15 minutes and figure out an excuse to leave class so I could feed them.

A few hours went by and I didn't know how I was going to pull it off all day. How many times can I leave class to use the bathroom without drawing attention to myself? Well, I didn't have to figure it out. The janitor did it for me. He kept hearing "tweet, tweet" until he finally located the sound coming my locker and called the office.

The Dean of Girls, Mrs. Bard, wondered why did I bring them to school? How could I leave them there to die? What to do with them now was the problem. The solution was take them to the biology class where they could be watched all day long. Not sure what happened, but they died anyway.

Almost fourteen years old, I was bored with hanging out at home with the neighborhood kids and babysitting. I was looking for fun and adventure. In ninth grade, I joined the Girl Scouts. It seemed like a good idea. I wanted to make new friends and have good times like Mom wanted.

As a troop we were planting flowers at the Trenton Library when I managed to fulfill Mom's prophecy. My name, along with the others in a group photo ran in the local paper with the worst quote ever, from me. "My hair's a mess." I was talking to myself.

Soon after my embarrassing debut our troop went on an overnight camping trip. This was why I joined, to be in nature and explore new places. Some girls wanted to explore each other. It freaked me out on all levels of Catholic reasoning, but the main reason? I didn't like anyone touching me without permission. Waking up with some girl on my back, touching my breasts triggered my survival instinct: this was a predator.

Quickly, I got up and left the tent. Standing at the water's edge wishing I was home, I thought about *why* they did that? I stayed awake most of the night waiting for dawn.

To this day I don't remember who the girls were—don't care, either. At the time, it never crossed my mind girls would be touching other girls. Why would I? Hell, I barely thought about boys. I still had a semi-crush on Leo King, and there was a new beau I was head over heels: Paul McCartney, the cutest of the Beatles, who taught himself to play bass and he played left-handed.

The first light of morning appeared I went back to the tent where the girls were sleeping, and within minutes of lying down, so was I. The next day, I told Mom the Girl Scouts wasn't "my thing." I just didn't tell her about the girl. Homosexuality was not part of my vocabulary.

Seven years of looking over my shoulder wasn't an easy habit to break. Like a prisoner released back into society, it took a while getting used to freedom. No nuns roaming the halls looking for prey. It was a public school. We were treated like people, not slaves of sin. With so many unfamiliar faces, it was intimidating.

Almost everyone intimidated me, especially the girls, with their stylish hair and clothes. Mom rolled curlers in my short hair every night before bed. I looked like an old lady with a poodle cut. Certainly, I was old enough to wash and set my own hair, but Mom objected.

The hairstyle I wore was Mom's vision of what I should look like. I was accusing her of making me look ugly, like a bookworm, a geek with an old woman haircut. She laughed and kept cutting my hair. My father heard us arguing in the basement.

"Rusty, she's fourteen years old, for Christ's sake! Don't you think she's old enough to wash her own damn hair and have it the way she likes it?" he yelled. "No one told you how to wear your hair when you were her age."

"When I was her age I had a job!:" Mom yelled back.

"So? What's the difference? What does that have to do with it?" Dad said. "Sometimes, you make no sense at 'tall, Rusty." (Did I hear an accent in my father's voice?)

If Daddy couldn't get through to Mom, it was hopeless. He said goodbye and left for work. Dad drove eighteen-hour shifts for Ford but at least he was home every day for a few hours as a buffer.

Mom did everything to stunt my emotional independence from cultivating who I was becoming, a free spirit on the run. I grabbed my coat and ran out the door before she could put her scissors away, and I left without permission. The family was right. Mom liked the boys better than her daughters. As soon as I could, I would leave home.

Just like my mother, I talked to myself. "I'll grow my hair out and never, cut it off!" And I swore I would never be like her. "Not in a

## Sticks and Stones and Broken Bones

million years!" Out into the freezing rain I ran. My hair, dripping wet, stiffened into strands of icicles by the time I reached Stephanie's house.

Stephanie Asbury was a new classmate from Chicago who recently transferred to Trenton during freshman year and was assigned to my homeroom class. Stephanie's vivacious spirit encouraged people to come out and play, she was a happy person.

Most girls are ecstatic shedding their parochial school uniforms for the latest fashion trends, but not me. Oh, at first I was, but wearing hand-me downs from an older cousin made me look frumpy, crimping my style of fashion at a time a teenage girl needs it the most, in high school. Stephanie, had style and lots of cool clothes, very mod.

It was fun trying on new looks, sharing girly talk, listening to the Beatles, our favorite band. This was all new to me. A friend. Sharing ideas, making future plans, I found more self-confidence when I was away from home. Attempting to share my new interest for photography with Mom by showing her A's and B's I attained in art and music class was disheartening.

"So?... What good is that? Yous got to eat. Taking pictures don't pay the bills," Mom said. "Get a real job."

My grades never improved much with the exception of Mr. Eugene Bacon's Theater Arts class and Mr. Thomas Deku's English class. Writing was my niche, Mr. Deku said. "You have a gift."

Seeing my thoughts on paper, I could reexamine what was behind some very dark thoughts, I didn't know writing was my therapy. Mr. Deku knew writing was my talent. His voice was in my head, too. But sharing my desire to have a writing career with Mom was a mistake.

"You won't make any money and yous got to eat. No one is going to hire you. Look at your grades. What would you even write about?"

"Mr. Deku said a writer writes what a writer knows," confidently, I replied. "He said is was my 'niche.'"

Mom said I just needed to get a practical job after graduation. "Maybe work in a factory or be a secretary," she said "You want to make enough money to live on."

Working in a factory was the last place I wanted to work. I knew first-hand what an auto factory looked like, and it was no place for someone like me: too jumpy, too many noises to distract me, and standing still was difficult to do, I was "high-strung."

"Wrapped too tight, just like your mother," my father said.

There had to be a job out there fitting to all my quirks and dreams. Again, I attempted to share another desire: to sing, dance, and act. Mom opposed the idea for reasons that made no sense to me. "You can't be an actress. You'll become a whore." That threw me off.

Acting class was fun, an outlet helping to crack the inner shield around my shy and wounded heart that prevented me from believing in myself. Hear something long enough, you will doubt yourself.

What the hell was she talking about? Reading about the personal and mental history of many well-known actors, I recognized a common connection: most come from a dysfunctional family. Many entertainers and writers select this line of work of expression as a method to purge or heal personal struggles.

What was I going to do with the rest of my life? Mom didn't support any dream or talents that I naturally was good at. She wanted me to be realistic, while I needed to cultivate my garden of dreams into a banquet of choices to feed me with inspiration and the determination to succeed. I would keep these secret desires close to my heart, quietly planning my get-away.

The following spring, a letter arrived from the Dominican Order of Missionary Nuns in San Diego. My application was approved. Joining the convent or the priesthood was a good alternative for young Catholic adults with no road to follow. I could enter the convent in my senior year.

Again, another dream squelched. Mom needed me. I took it as a sign. Pregnant with her fifth child, she was embarrassed and depressed, giving me strict orders to tell anyone on her side of the family. I said, "W*haat*?" How the hell was she going to keep this a secret? I mean, this wasn't a hickey, like the one she tried to cover up a few months ago. A baby just doesn't 'go away.'

## Sticks and Stones and Broken Bones

Crying while she peeled potatoes, mom expelled her guilt. "It's a sin, women shouldn't have babies after forty."

Technically, mom was thirty-eight, but it was her habit to add a year or two when making a point. I could be sixteen years old and a day, she would say, "You're going to be seventeen."

A Hungarian woman, bred for marriage since she was born. That was her future. "What was I supposed, to do?" Mom said. "I shouldn't had kids right away. I was too young to be strapped down."

Why did she think that way? Mom wasn't an unwed teen, she was twenty-two years old. when I was born. Again, she made no sense, but I listened. Apparently, Mom missed out on her youth, recapping stories about her old stomping grounds and hanging out with friends or heading over to the Roller Rink where she danced on wheels to the music.

Mumma longed for the people she grew up with: the Kovacs, the Nagys, the Horvaths, the Papps, and other Delray families. Some of these people I met as a child in Delray. Obvious by the warm smiles and hugs, these people loved my mother in a way I could not understand. They knew her history and understood her childhood issues: This is what she missed and needed to feel grounded in her life, but Trenton was forty miles away from her past.

Mumma seem to have a far-away stare when things bothered her. Something from childhood troubled her. She had a secret. The kind not meant for children to learn about, but I was no longer a small child.

Perhaps mom was too young. Her teenage years were cut short by war. When my mother died, I took all the letters I could find, searching for meaning and answers to my mother's secrets when I found a letter to an old friend, Bob.

Mom wrote about the family, what we did together. My father was making over $50,000 a year driving a truck for Ford's in the 60s. The extra money he treated us with discretionary toys. Go-karts, a new color TV, a bright yellow surrey with the red fringe on top, and a trip to Niagara Falls. We thought we were rich. It was his overtime.

My father would drive eighteen-hour stretches to give us more than he had.

What my mother wrote next struck me as very odd: *"I was an Elvis fan since I was a teenager."*

Not physically possible. Mom was born seven years before Elvis Presley. She was twenty-five years-old when his first singing debut album was released in 1954, but in mom's mind she was just a teenager. Standing in front of me was a woman lost in religion and stuck in a time warp.

Mom admitted she didn't want another baby; she was just getting her freedom back. Then confessed she didn't want to be pregnant with me either, and pleaded with me to wait before I settle down and have kids.

"Go out and have some fun, Linda," she said. "You'll have plenty of time to cook and clean." All I heard was that she didn't want kids right away. This is why she was always mad. I represented her lost youth.

Not only did Mom dictate what hairstyle and clothes to wear but she also tried to prevent me from using the family car to take my driver's test. That pissed the old man off big time. Not sure what day it was but Dad took me down to take my driving test, which I passed with flying colors. Waiting for the paperwork to be finished, I took another look at my birth certificate.

Mom's maiden name was Bodzsar, not Beno, as I thought. She never spoke of her biological father, Istvan Bodzsar, my grandfather. Mom was pretty much tight-lipped about the past, but after years of being annoyingly persistent, she figured I was old enough to hear her parents were divorced when she was a little girl.

"He was a mean drunk." End of conversation. "Because I said so," Mom resumed cleaning. Dismissing me, but never my curiosity. One day, I would find out because Mom said, "The squeaky wheel gets the grease."

Stephanie was a big part of my life during high school. She wasn't shy like me, but a girl who spoke her mind and willing to test the waters of youth. We both had a little tomboy in us and pulled a few

## Sticks and Stones and Broken Bones

crazy car stunts, one of us on the hood hanging on for dear life, while the other zigzagged down the dirt road. I was challenging my fears. A dangerous stunt, but we were young and dumb. I was becoming a wild child.

Questioning authority, rejecting traditional values, taking risks and taking drugs. Teenagers across the nation were giving birth to a new sub-culture, the hippies. Most parents viewed this as a "phase" of teenage rebellion that would fade away in time. They were wrong.

This was the generation to rock and roll, live out loud without fear, to prove we had the right to be part of the living constitution and voice our opinion how to run our country. "No more war. No more bombs." Make love, not war: our generation's slogan. A virgin in high school when the sexual revolution began, I was nowhere near ready for sex. It was "bad" for girls who were not married.

Mom was tripping out. According to her, the new generation would ruin America. Her red, white, and blue came out. Draft dodgers were traitors. Any guy with long hair was "a lazy bum" even if they made millions singing *She Loves You*.

Mom couldn't stand the Beatles—they were responsible for the hippie generation. The mere idea that rock and roll began before the Beatles with Elvis, Chubby Checker and others like them set her off. "It's not the same thing."

The first time listening to the Beatles on the radio, I became an instant fan, obsessed. Then, a taste of success. I was the "lucky caller" to win two tickets to their first concert in Detroit, at Olympia Stadium. Naturally, I had to take my buddy, Stephanie along. She was a *crazed* fan, like me. We screamed the moment they walked on stage.

My obsession was obvious to other classmates. Overwhelmed by the Beatles' positive, poetic, and mystical lyrics of love, hope, and faith, I was hooked and found a new voice in me. I would crusade their message of love. To thrive and succeed in a world submerged in conflict and violence. *"All you need is love."*

Writing down hopes and dreams in a journal soothed my troubled mind. At one point in high school I imagined myself as Lois Lane, writing stories about the "little guy" who couldn't defend himself. Writing helped to build my inner confidence. Music kept the beat alive in my heart. Secretly, I was envisioning what I wanted.

My new plan was to get on the Robin Seymour Show that aired on CKLW. Somehow, I managed to call in to the station and once again, I won tickets to the show. Mom didn't know about the tickets until they arrived in the mail. Dad said, "Let her go—she earned it."

As I waited with the other kids in the lobby, someone walked up to me and asked if I wanted to dance on stage. I had no clue what to do but I was "Bobbin with the Robin." Joe Tex was introduced and was singing, *Skinny Legs and All*. For a short time I was noticed for having courage to step up to the platform and dance my heart out on live TV even if I did look like a spaz.

My eight-year-old brother Jimmy watched the show, thinking I was rich. "Anyone on TV gets paid about a million bucks," he said. Even I knew that wasn't true.

"You have to be famous first," I answered. *How does one get famous?*

Most of my summers growing up were spent working around the house and yard for my mother. Each age I attained, the more responsibilities I had. My brothers were too young to help Dad with home improvements. which allowed me to work with him when he was home. Together, we put up the basement ceiling tiles.

Dad taught me to hammer a nail correctly into a 2X4, how to frame a wall, put up plaster, and cut bathroom tile. I was part of my father's "gopher" crew when he built his garage, and I learned how to lay shingles on the roof. Learning these skills from my father kept me away from Mom's meltdowns.

This allowed me to developed more independently and realize the satisfaction of learning something most girls didn't know how to do. These skills were used to renovate my own homes later on.

A couple of months before my "spaz dance" on television, on November 22, 1966 my youngest brother, John Fitzgerald was born. And my awkward moment of fame by embarrassment, was temporary. Johnny, the poor bastard, named after a fallen president, took a lot of

## Sticks and Stones and Broken Bones

ribbing growing up. Meanwhile, motherhood was having a toll on Mom. After the first week home, it was me, getting up in the middle of the night to feed my brother a bottle.

Mom was suffering from the "baby blues." Another name for postpartum depression. To the outside world, everything's fine. Mom would never tell the truth about anything going on in the family, and she did so by not sharing what problems she was having or anyone else. denial was fortification.

*"Everything's fine, everybody is doing fine."* No, it isn't fine, but sooner or later it will be when you figure out where you need to be. It was not my job to be my baby brother's mother, but I did it anyway. For the first year and half, I had a major role in my brother's care while Mom slowly recovered from her depression.

Mumma wouldn't share her problems. Not until a doctor prescribed valium to calm her "nerves" with instructions to either speak her mind or get an ulcer. After a few months popping happy pills, expressing her true feelings, it revealed an unhappy woman.

Addiction to prescribed drugs wasn't well-known in the 60s but my mother had a feeling she was suffering from the side effects of Valium. It was physically addicting.

One afternoon when Mom ran out of pills, she had one of her headaches until the prescription was refilled. In her words, "I put two and two together." That was the end of it. Mom did not like to depend on anything. She walked the talk. A woman to respect and admire for standing by her convictions. The come-down was a rough ride. Mom was anxious and suffered with migraines for a few weeks until the narcotic was out of her system.

Teenage angst and hormones out of whack intensified during Mom's interim with happy pills. We were at each other's throats. We did not communicate without a shouting match, reverting to something I'd done as a kid. Bringing up these past mistakes was teaching me to hang on to guilt as a form of penance.

Except for my "hands off" attitude from previous sexual assaults, I was like any other teenager. But the furthest thing on my mind was sex. I still didn't know what it was when I was in tenth grade and Michael Ballard gave me my first kiss. That was it. I could not handle it. The conflicting emotions, my mother's traditions, and the Church's expectations held me hostage to rules I could not completely accept.

Emotional outbreaks usually are triggered by something similar to a past experience. The turmoil of teenage years compiled onto my emotional plate and was spilling over. I started lashing out again.

A girl I was becoming friends with lived down the street. She was outside waiting for me when my mother started yelling, embarrassing me as she always did in front of others. The girl said something, but it was the way she looked at me that gave me cause to push her off the porch, landing her in the snow with me on top of her, trying to smack her face.

My aggression was building up. The following summer Chris Woodward, a long-time neighbor kid, had pushed the wrong button. Chris was relentless, always teasing me, but he started poking my arm with a stick, which triggered a flashback. I went commando on his ass, grabbing a switch, slashing him violently across the face till he cried out.

This was pent up anger contained over the last ten years. Anyone who betrayed or touched me without permission had exploded into a dangerous rage. My body was shaking uncontrollably, I couldn't calm down. I got on my bike and rode away into the woods.

Years later at a wedding, I apologized to Chris. He barely recalled the incident that left me feeling miserable and guilty for years.

"I probably deserved it," he said. "Linda, you were always looking out for us kids. You were like *our* guardian angel." That stumped me. I felt anything but angelic. Too much Catholic guilt.

God only knows why people do what they do to one another, but the lasting effects of their actions affect their victims and families forever. Forgiveness brings peace. Chris Woodward left me with a better memory of our childhood and a subtle message that a stranger repeated when he saw me give a donation to a homeless man in 1997.

## Sticks and Stones and Broken Bones

"You looked like a guardian angel walking down the street... an angel from God." Not really. It was the dress. Wearing a full-length, white cotton dress flowing behind me created more of an illusion of a nun's habit as I walked down the street. I loved the idea that nuns were suppose to be gentle and kind, loving to all.

By the time I was seventeen, I was the "eccentric young lady with strange ideas," my father would say. Mom frowned at my new style of clothing, a cross between the mod look and a hippie-gypsy, hair hanging in my face shielding my eyes from the world's all-knowing glare, I wasn't one of them.

Exactly what path I was taking after high school was unclear to many, but not to me. I knew I would be a good person, but what I wanted to do was many things. I couldn't seem to stick with one idea. In the back of my mind, I figured I'd go with the flow. Let fate take me down the road for a while and see what happens, because according to everyone else, my options were dwindling.

My grades were still poor, college wasn't a goal, the convent was now a memory, and a desire to "do something" that had meaning persisted—but what?

The issues young people faced were about to reveal itself. On July 23, 1967, Detroit was burning in prejudice and hate. The 1967 Detroit riots nearly exceeded the New York draft riots during the Civil War. My father was in the middle of it.

Rioters were attacking the firefighters, volunteers, and other emergency service vehicles attempting to help. Ford Motor Company asked for company employees to volunteer and deliver supplies to the National Guard. Daddy was one of the lucky ones.

By Monday night, almost two days into the riots, it was getting worse. My father was gone, my mother sat, staring at the news. I knew how serious the situation was. My father could get killed because of his kindness and sense of responsibility. Mom had "a bad feeling."

I hopped on my bike and rode almost six miles to the I-75 overpass, staring north toward Detroit. The glow of the burning city had the same effect as it did in the film *Gone With the Wind*, except it wasn't Atlanta blazing down years of oppression, this was Detroit, a city of hardship. A sense of pride and worry came over me, knowing my father was among the many heroes helping people in need.

The night before the Army was deployed, the National Guard was taking gunshot fire as they attempted to bring the wounded to Henry Ford Hospital. My father was riding in that vicinity when he heard a *ping* under his ass. He kept going until he got back to the River Rouge Plant. There was a bullet hole right under his seat.

"I almost got shot in the ass, Rusty." he laughed. The Polaroid photo of my Dad pointing at the bullet hole said it all. He was happy to be alive and not number 44 on a list of the dead.

After the curfew was lifted, I took a ride with my father. More than 1,100 people were injured, a few thousand buildings destroyed and reduced to rubble. It looked like a war zone, but it felt like home. I could relate to this destruction of oppression.

Black or white, in the 1960s, Detroit cops were brutal, crooked, and out of control. Racism spewed hatred among the older generations, attempting to soil the new generation with their prejudice. It didn't work. Another mantra chanted by the disenchanted youth of the '60s: "Don't trust anyone over thirty."

The Civil Rights movement was a significant cause I could agree with, ensuring that the rights of all people are equally protected by the law, including the rights of minorities. Hell, yes. I believed in equality of all mankind; furthermore, I was taught God loved all his children. Mom called me a "bleeding heart." I was offended at first because she didn't respect my opinion. Eventually, I wore it like a badge of honor, voicing my opinion against any and all injustice.

One afternoon, the king of the hippies, John Sinclair, walked into our classroom to enlighten us about the war. Sinclair, a political activist, was on the Detroit Committee to End the War in Vietnam. Sinclair explained that if we wanted change in the world, it was important to be active in politics and to vote.

All my childhood training pointed in one direction: a life of hardship, as Mumma predicted. Still, I believed in dreams that only

## Sticks and Stones and Broken Bones

I could see. What I lacked was direction. I didn't have a plan or a road map to take me where I needed to go on my journey. I followed my gut at every beck and call.

One afternoon while in my counselor's office, it became perfectly clear to me I was wasting time with high school. My counselor said college wasn't for me, but insisted that I should focus on graduating high school because it was important.

"Then you can find a job as a secretary or clerk until one day, when you'll probably get married," she said.

Even without a diploma, securing employment as a clerk or any other office job was easy back then if you could type, spell, and use an adding machine. I was qualified for plenty of jobs without having to wait for a piece of paper.

"What am I doing wasting my time here if I'm just going to get married? I quit." And, like an idiot, I walked out the door three months shy of graduating and never went back.

Secretly, I wanted to join a rock 'n' roll band, write songs, books, and poetry, something entertaining and artistic, but I was lacking the means to find the path I desired. Tired of being discouraged whenever I shared my hopes and dreams with my mother while I was growing up, I kept the ones that mattered most to myself until I figured it out.

Growing up in Delray inspired me to seek the road less traveled. When somebody in the neighbourhood died, I remember people dancing in the street, sitting on stoops playing violins with spirited passion, keeping time to the heartbeat with a tambourine. I was out of time. Dancing to the beat of my own drum. Was this fate or destiny pushing me to go? A little bit of both. Fate is unchangeable, but destiny... I could choose any path my heart desired. It is, my life.

# THE 5:15

## Be home in time for dinner

**M**y mother's lifelong emotional self-protection was the underlying problem between us; she was critical of my opinions and ideas, and always accusing me of things I never did. With nothing to look forward to but hang around Trenton, feeling hopeless, needy, anxious but mostly desperate. it was time to go. Pave my own way if necessary.

Money saved from babysitting bought me a train ticket to Chicago. The day I left home was indicative of our ongoing mother-daughter problems. Informing Mom of my plans, I didn't want to live in Trenton until I was married off. I was not going to be my mother, but I didn't tell her that. "I need to get away," I said.

"You can't run from your problems, Linda." Mom said. "You take them with you."

I beg to differ. Some problematic people you *should* leave behind. People who stomp on every hope and dream should be kept at a safe distance. Mom *was* the problem. She never listened without judging, rarely complimenting me for anything I was good at. My attitude? "I'll show her."

A couple of times before leaving, I had mentioned "the 5:15" to Chicago. Mom ignored me, pretending not to hear. Deny it long enough and it won't happen? Mom was washing the kitchen floor when I came up from the basement with my one packed bag.

"Mom, it's time for me to go. I'm leaving for Chicago." She didn't look up. I wanted to hug her, kiss her. I knew she loved me. *Make me stay* because you like me. Instead?

"Be home in time for dinner."

It never dawned on me that maybe, this was her way of asking me to stay, but the damage was done a long time ago. Mom loved her children, but she was emotionally distant. It was a long road ahead but tell that to a seventeen-year-old. Emotionally unfit, I was well on my way to be a perfect victim when I walked out the door in mid-February, 1968.

Adventure, the road to discovery—that's what I was looking for, a future suited to my lifestyle, whatever that was. Determined to represent my generation, I was going to find myself believing the future would unfold with each new day. Mom could not understand why I left her. It broke her heart.

But I didn't leave *her*—leaving *home* was the only option I had. A revolution was going on inside of me. I had to break out from my comfort zone, using the wild zeitgeist of the '60s, I spirited up enough nerve to live up to my own truth.

Complex PTSD never goes away. We are never 100% cured because it is part of us. It may be controlled, but it remains beneath the surface, waiting to emerge the first chance it gets. Who knew in 1968? No one. It festered and interfered with most of my life.

Unaware and untreated when I left home in 1968, my emotional baggage tagged along. I isolated myself from the family when I had bad days, trying to forget childhood bullies, pretending nothing had happened.

Only those personally involved in my trauma knew what they did and they weren't talking. Desperate to hear my own voice above the clouded insecurities that were my mother's, I left home before any more of her doubts rubbed off on me. If I didn't go as planned, I was afraid I would lose my nerve for future endeavors. The 5:15 was my ticket to the world.

Clackity-clack, the familiar sound of the train wheels riding the rails lulled me to sleep with parting memories of Delray. Quietly, remembering Mumma standing in the dining room, staring out the window of our house on Thaddeus St. She turned to look at me, looking very sad and pretty, her long-auburn hair curled softly around her face. A short time later, she cut it all off.

It was around eleven p.m. when the train pulled into the Chicago station. I had enough money for a hotel room, but no clue where to find one. I wandered out into a cold Chicago night to learn they don't call it the *Windy City* to be cute. I had to battle the breeze just to keep a hat on while trying to carry my luggage through the snow that kept coming down.

Waiting at an intersection next to a bus stop, I was blown over by a gust of wind so forceful I had to use the street-sign post to pull myself up. Then my glove stuck to the metal post, pulling it off my sweaty hand. I finally made my way to Lakeshore Drive, but not before falling a half a dozen times.

Ahead of me, a bright marquee shining its red and green lights that spelled something Italian. Hungry and cold, I made my way up the street. A few feet from the doorway, two young sailors were watching me make my way through the snow. One of them opened the restaurant door while the other helped me with my bag.

The draft was active in the 1960s. Many young men took their fate into their own hands by signing up with a military service of their choice instead of waiting to be drafted into the Army. Such was the case of the two sailors who invited me to join them for dinner. No one had offered to buy me dinner before. It was like watching a movie, except *I* was the damsel in need of assistance. The guys were being deployed in a few days, and were curious as to what I was doing out on such a blustery night alone, advising me to go back home.

During dinner, our conversation covered a potpourri of topics, starting off with the Vietnam War. They both disagreed with the politics behind the war, but they could do nothing about it. "You have to follow orders."

## Sticks and Stones and Broken Bones

My two military escorts said, there was a hotel not far from the restaurant. They made certain I was secure for the night and walked me to my room. My room was located next to the tracks that ran above the street. After sharing farewell courtesies, I wished them "peace" and safety. As I locked the door behind them, I heard a train overhead. The familiar old-world charm of Delray would keep me company my first night alone.

The hotel had seen its heyday, but it was clean. The furniture reminded me of my grandmother's furniture back in Delray: old, but nice. The air smelled of mothballs and bleached sheets. I sat on the bed and lit a cigarette. Unaccustomed to smoking, I played with it, looking at myself in the mirror. Strategically, held it in my hand like Bette Davis. I took a drag.

Coughing from the smoke, I realized I'd held it in too long. When I got up to retrieve an ashtray on the dresser, the mood of the room seem to change. It was odd. My reflection in the mirror captivated the attention of my senses. Who was the woman looking back at me? I knew it was me, but it felt like an *old* me. The 1920s came to mind. "You have been here before."

I blew it off as a crazy thought. I was going to get a job and get on with life. There is a lot to do when you're seventeen, going on the rest of your life.

Though my stay in Chicago was short-lived, the lessons remain forever. A job in a furniture factory lasted a mere 15 minutes before I punched my timecard and walked out the door. I was not factory material. Back in Michigan, I stayed a few weeks with my parents until I found a job downtown at Crowley's Department Store.

It was an hour-and-a-half bus ride one way, which I hated. I felt trapped, a situation I could not deal with. My flight-or-fight reflexes were on edge. Similar to an animal caught in a trap, that leg would be gone. I simply didn't feel safe riding on a bus.

Working as a sales clerk wasn't a problem for me, but telling a white lie to a heavy-set woman just to make a commission was a problem. A tent dress with wide stripes? No way could I say, "It looks good on you" to the customer. But I did say to the manager, "I quit."

White lies don't bother me if I'm protecting someone's feelings, but making money off them seemed wrong to me. It didn't bother me too much to tell a white lie to avoid my mother's sharp tongue and critical eye for the next three days. The rule? "Never quit a job unless you have another one lined up."

One night, I decided: No more. No more wasting time placating my mother's wishes. No more wasting time with white lies to satisfy unattainable goals she had planned for me. I rented a room across the street from Johanna's Boutique, my next place of employment.

In July 1968, Johanna's Boutique was more than a job. It was the end of a childhood, but not the future. The woman who owned the boutique was about six years older than me, married, with kids, very much into the art scene and the hippie culture. Johanna became my unintended spiritual guide, role model, and friend for the next five years. She believed in the paranormal, dreams, and other things.

# WAITING FOR THE SUN

## Wild child on the run

**B**aby Boomers were carving out their future. A cultural revolution was on. Bohemians, misfits, outsiders, and dropouts, all mingling with jocks and geeks down on Plum Street. It was Detroit's mecca of hope to improve its image after the 1967 riots tore the city apart. Motor City needed a boost.

Chicago had created Old Town, San Francisco had Haight-Ashbury, but in Detroit we had Plum Street, though it barely survived its three-year run. I was lucky to survive three years after leaving home. Plum Street was my first detour on a life's journey seeking a purpose, a mission.

The first time I made my way to "hippie-town," as dad would call it, the widespread use of recreational drugs was lingering in the streets. I didn't use drugs or smoke when I lived at home. I didn't understand what the buzz was all about, but enlightenment was just around the corner. People get high when distressed because it relieves the misery and pain of reality.

Working part-time for Johanna wasn't enough money. Around the corner was the Plush Puppy, a cute hot dog café, where I got a job for a few more days a week. I had a serious crush on a guy I met at Johanna's but Thomas Gordon Rousku, kept ignoring my flirtations. Everyone told me he wasn't interested but didn't say why.

I told this little pity story to Gary, a college student from Wayne State University who came in for a hot dog. "Instead of waiting for the other guy, go out with me," he said. So I did.

Most of the evening we talked about politics, religion, and bands we liked. While listening to music by the Doors, Gary said, "You want to get high?"

I thought about it for a few seconds. "Sure, why not?"

Here's where I made a leap of crazy. *"Not to touch the earth, not to see the sun / Nothing left to do but run, run, run…"* Crystal meth, my crystal spider: my brain was on fire.. a needle in my arm. The endorphins released a new high, numbing my emotional pain. I felt exceptionally normal. We had no sex; just a couple of motor-mouths.

At one point Gary was going for another hit, but a little whisper in my head was loud enough to hear, "No more."

"Did I say that out loud?" I asked.

"Say what?" Gary asked, still mixing his spoonful.

"No more for me. I gotta go." I fumbled around for my purse. Looking around the place, I realized it was a hole in the wall but kinda cozy in a hippie way. High as a kite, I wandered down Cass Ave. heading to Plum Street.

As for marijuana being a gateway drug? You got to be kidding! I liked the speedy high of crystal too much. Luckily, when I got back to Plum St. I found a co-worker, Tony, who turned me on to marijuana. That was my saving grace.

Tony, too was working for Johanna while attending Wayne State—and he was a stoner, the calmest dude I ever met. We had nothing in common but working at Johanna's and listening to music while we worked. I was "too hyper," He said.

Keeping the shelves organized, stocked, and clean was part of my job. One afternoon, Tony turned up the radio, and again, it was the Doors: the *"Unknown Soldier"* was playing, and I began doing a dance around the store.

*"Ready. Aim. Fire."* I clutched my abdomen as if I were hit, curling up into a ball on the floor. *"It's all over for the unknown soldier…."* Tony looked at me. "You're wound too tight! Go outside and smoke this," handing me a joint. "Mellow out, already."

## Sticks and Stones and Broken Bones

I took a couple of puffs. In a few minutes, my brain felt better. I had a case of the giggles when I walked back in the shop. Listening to my thoughts while I stocked the shelves, I was quieter, too. Focusing on what I wanted from this life, I knew I had to live the dream for it to come true. So many dreams in my head; where do I start?

There he was, Thomas Rousku, the man I had met a few months earlier at Johanna's, watching me. He was cute, bright, outgoing, very artistic and gay as they come. Silly me, when Johanna and my father both said Rousku was gay, I said I didn't have a problem with "happy" people. "So what?"

We spent a lot of time together: not because Tom was falling for me, but because of his desire to transform me into the likeness of actresses he admired. One day he dressed me like Marilyn Monroe, wig and all. It was fun dressing up in antique clothing, pretending to be back in time.

Sex had nothing to do with my attraction to Tom; it was his flamboyant and artistic lifestyle. Tom and his friends were so colorful, lively, and fun, outspoken about everything, and boy, did they know how to dress for an occasion.

"Make an entrance, dahling!" said Rick Cook, the owner of Tres Camp, a favorite hangout of the hippie queens, like Joe and Robin. Robin was in love with Jim Morrison. He was so devastated at the news of Morrison's death, he went into a state of depression. A year later, he overdosed. I suppose making an entrance equally requires making a proper exit.

The relationship I imagined with Rousku wasn't going anywhere. Restless to make something happen, despite I had no clue what I wanted, I was too busy distracting my life from the essence of self-doubt that seemed to linger.

Since childhood, I dreamed of going to California, feeling something *pulling* me. It felt as if my destiny was out west. I was a wild child on the run. An opportunity arose when a group of hippies were heading for Haight-Ashbury, a destination for many flower children on the road.

The sixties subculture was a perfect background to camouflage any dysfunctional disorder one might have. We were all dreamers, believers and stargazers. We didn't trust anyone over thirty.

In August 1968, a group of strangers, headed west and I was among them. As were entering Salt Lake City, I was blinded by the sight before my eyes, truly humbled by nature's greatness. The salty desert shone like a sea of diamonds in the moon's light. This was a true mystery to enjoy, the life and creation of earth, the universe ... something wonderful was out there. I drifted away into a dream that night:

*The night sky started to glow as I walked down a street and across a lawn. I was back on Lynn Court. I had to cover my face with my forearm, leaving enough space to peek at what was happening.*

*The quarter moon was hooked on Saturn's ring, with millions of little shooting stars across the sky. Red fireballs darting towards Earth at me. A revelation of magnitude, and I was not in control.*

When we reached California, our group split up in San Francisco. I spent two days hanging out at Berkeley, getting stoned and informed about current issues we faced. The war in Vietnam needed to end. The draft needed to go. Women wanted equal pay. And the gays were coming out of the closet. And, I had thought it meant *happy*.

The guy I traveled with to San Diego stole all my Beatle albums while I was napping. Luckily, my wallet was on my person. I found my way to the Mission District and jumped in the ocean. Floating around, relaxed, I felt that this is what life was about—experiencing what it has to offer.

Dripping wet and cold, I reached for a towel. There was a young man watching me. Tall and dark, wearing a leather jacket, sitting on a Harley Davidson. Angel was curious. "What's a girl like you doing down here? You don't belong here; it's dangerous."

The Mission District was a haven for the homeless and druggies who would see me as prey. My fearless attitude was slightly miffed by Angel's personal concern that I be gone before dark. My plan was take a bus to Hollywood from San Diego. Since Angel was going to Los Angeles anyway, he said. "Keep your money. You'll need it."

## Sticks and Stones and Broken Bones

Riding along the coastline with the wind in my hair and a few bugs in my teeth, I was living in the moment. Exploring the country on a motorcycle wasn't a bad plan. Angel was going in the direction he wanted to go. I wanted to see Tinsel Town. The land of dreams and fairy tales. I belonged in this land of "fruits and nuts."

Traveling like a gypsy, exploring, moving around from place to place, was inspirational. It was a lifestyle that helped build self-confidence and strengthened my emotional development. I learned to rely on myself. How could I ever go home? I was the same person my mother once knew, but stronger and more opinionated.

Among the cast of characters parading down Sunset Strip when Angel dropped me off was Julius Caesar, greeting me. "Hail, Caesar!" The young man, dressed in an ankle-length toga, begged, "Spare change?"

"You got to be kidding," I replied. "Do I look rich to you?"

Angel laughed, "You'll do just fine."

Standing in front of the Whiskey a Go Go, watching Angel disappear down the Strip, a little voice said, "You are on your own." Looking around me at the collage of young people, I fit right in. A gypsy-hippie with a wild heart and strange ideas. Where was I going to sleep?

A few fellow travelers were looking for somewhere to crash—my new word. Someone suggested the all-night market on Vine Street, known to never close. The Hollywood Ranch Market's snack bar was a hangout for celebrities who working at nearby studios as well as the hippie mob. Plenty of people around to feel safe, sleeping in a coin-operated photo booth just outside the market. Who's going to take pictures at this time in the night?

Cramped, hungry, and feeling downright grubby, I woke up to a new day and walked over to the snack bar for something to eat. As I searched the want ads for a job, a few people were staring, judging me by my appearance. I stared back.

Sure, I looked a little rough—who wouldn't after traveling nearly two weeks on the road? Using the market's bathroom, I went in to clean up and change clothes for job hunting. A few customers at the snack bar had to do a double-take as I passed by.

While waiting for a bus, I was once again hailed by Caesar, still in costume, on Hollywood and Vine Street. I waved back. He was harmless, wandering up and down Sunset Strip with the other characters looking for fame and fortune in Tinsel Town. I had no clue where to begin except to get a job or wander the streets like Caesar, a lost soul trapped in his own mind.

With nowhere to go or anything better to do than find a job, I had plenty of time to fill out applications. By mid-afternoon, I was getting hungry. Already discouraged from the numerous rejections because I didn't have a local residence, a telephone number or any local experience. No one was willing to call *Michigan*, for references.

"How can you get experience if no one hires you?" I asked the waitress who didn't look much older than me when she brought me my fries. She had a soft spot, I guess, because she replied, "We just got an opening here. Why don't you talk to Mike? He's the manager."

Mike was a young man unlike the other, older managers, and he decided that my lack of experience wasn't a barrier. He hired me and put me to work immediately. I put my bags behind the bar and followed my trainer for about an hour before getting a table. I was on track. All I needed was a place to live.

The Eating Affair restaurant was perfect for me. Business was good, and it was a fun place to work. I had food to eat and learned to get better at shooting pool. I was blossoming. People liked me, and I started making decent tips. It was a party hangout at night. Wall-to-wall people eating, listening to music and playing pool. I was never bored.

By September 1968, I was sharing a studio apartment with two other girls at the Sunset West Motel, across the street from the Continental Hyatt. One of my roommates was visiting someone at the Hyatt and left a message at the front desk asking me to bring her camera to her. She wanted to take a picture of Donovan while he painted a billboard promoting his concert at the Hollywood Bowl.

## Sticks and Stones and Broken Bones

By time I got the message, Donovan was finished and back in his room. I walked over to the Hyatt with the Nikon in its case hanging on my shoulder. Dressed up, I looked like a professional photographer. A group of businessmen from Japan were dispersing as I walked across the lobby, and one of them approached me with a weird look on his face.

"You want to make a hundred dollars?" he asked. "To talk."

"You want to *pay* me a hundred bucks to talk? You're nuts! It doesn't cost money to talk. Sit down," pointing at the chairs off to the side. "Are you tourists? Welcome to America. Do you like our country?"

Here was a member of a culture my mother hated and taught me to be afraid of—but I had to learn for myself. I asked question after question. I was curious. The man looked as confused as I was. Apparently, we weren't talking about the same thing. I thought he might be a lost tourist, while he thought I was a hooker. After this brief misunderstanding, the man left, making one more comment. "May you have an interesting life."

Seriously, I didn't need any encouragement.

Walking toward the elevators, I saw a group of reporters shouldering camera bags, curious where they were going I followed them. No one bothered to question me as I walked down the hall with them to a room where people were milling around the door. Ushered in with the reporters, I unintentionally met Donovan.

We shook left-handed because his right hand was injured while painting the billboard promoting his concert. Interesting life? You bet. Not long after this I met Luther, the drummer for the band Spooky Tooth, who was looking for "leapers"—Brit lingo for speed. The band was playing at the Whiskey, where all the new, upcoming acts were showcased, and a favorite hangout for me—and a few thousand other hippies digging the music scene.

How I ended up at so many parties with well-known musicians I don't have a clue, but I was there; dancing, drinking, and getting high. One night at a party in Benedict Canyon, I saw John Lennon sitting against a wall by himself, wearing a beatnik cap. I was bummed out over rumors the Beatles were breaking up. I really wanted to find out if it was true. Knowing I was too high, I walked away instead.

There were musicians sitting on sidewalks playing songs for coins, wrapped up in the movement of peace and love, many hoping to be discovered by some happenstance of fate, to be the next Jimi Hendrix or Joni Mitchell. Sunset Strip was alive with people from every walk of life looking for something… but not all had good intentions.

A guy who frequented the Eating Affair had been flirting with me for a couple of weeks, but something about him was off. I couldn't figure it out and kept my guard up, so I thought.

On my eighteenth birthday, I went to the Whiskey to meet up with some people after work. I ordered a Coke while watching the wide screen of images and trippy colors flash by, then left to use the bathroom with my cola on the table. Never leave a drink unattended, or someone will slip you a "mickey," a date-rape drug. I don't remember what happened after that.

The next morning I found myself in a strange place with the guy from the restaurant. Sore where I shouldn't be, clothes ripped, bruises on my arms and legs. Processing it all, I realized I was raped. The guy was passed out on the sofa. Pulling it together, I was out the door. I didn't know what to do. I went to work. Everybody noticed my quiet mood. I pretended it never happened.

By the time November rolled around, I was through with the Hollywood scene. My head was in a fog from too much partying, trying to forget. I was popping acid, doing speed, and drinking. Getting high on Acapulco Gold with either Bobby Hart or Tommy Boyce—I was too high to remember. Trying to light a joint on their stove, I kept asking, "Which one are you, again?" And broke the knob.

The whole scene struck me as funny and I started laughing, "Which one are you?" You're the writer? Right? Which one of you takes pictures?" In the middle of the living room was a tripod aimed at the view outside the window. As soon as he told me whose camera it was, I forgot.

## Sticks and Stones and Broken Bones

Somewhere in my foggy brain, I knew it was time to go back to Michigan. Life was moving too fast in the wrong direction. I didn't know what I was doing. I just wanted to keep life moving along until I found my way.

Within a week, I was back home at my parents' house, regrouping. "Well, did you find yourself?" Daddy asked. Reminding me of the day I left for California "to find myself."

"Linda, girl. You're standing in the middle of the living room. How can you be lost?" I was lost in my head. My father could hear it in my voice—I needed help. He suggested that I see a doctor but mom wouldn't hear of it.

"There's nothing wrong with her, Jimmy!" Mom said. "She has to get her head out of her ass. Everybody has problems. You suck it up and get on with it!"

No compassion, no understanding—just throw her to the wolves? My father expressed how disappointed he was. He couldn't believe as sensitive and caring she was to animals, that she lacked compassion and understanding for her own daughter.

"She's asking for help because she hasn't had it easy, Rusty." It was pointless: Mom had made up her mind. After a few days back in town, word got around that I was back. Tom Rousku called, saying he had something to ask me. When he picked me up at my parents' house, he looked different to me.

"You look very pretty," he said. "There's something different about you."

Tom drove me back to his place on Plum Street, showing me his latest art project and talking about God. He was looking for meaning, purpose and feeling guilty for being gay. Tom said he had to change his life around and wanted me to be part of it; he loved me.

"Will you marry me?"

In a heartbeat, I said "yes."

We had a few weeks to plan our wedding. We took part cooking the meals and decorated our own wedding cake. It was so impressive a guest remarked, "It looks presidential." This was the wildest event my family had ever seen. In fact, no one could forget the day we invited a black couple to our wedding. The ugly truth was harsh. Racism was embedded in my family. Despite how wonderful they could be, this was hard for me to believe. I wouldn't change my mind. Maybe I was pushing the race issue "too much," as they said—but maybe they needed to learn to get over it. Standing my ground, felt honorable. I was proud of myself.

Eventually, they came around. Who wants to pass up a party with free food and booze—and the guests? So very entertaining to look at. Not my family—they had a front-row seat.

On December 13, 1968, I became Mrs. Thomas Rousku. It was Friday the 13th. I refused to believe it was a bad-luck day and married Rousku anyway. During the wedding reception, Grandpa Beno thought he was having a heart attack, which turned out to be an anxiety attack from mixing his medication with a shot of whiskey.

Downstairs I ran to the payphone and called the operator to send an ambulance. Pushing superstitious thoughts out of my head. It wasn't my fault Grandpa mixed pills and booze together, but I still felt guilty. Grandpa was going to be fine. Rousku and I? That's a book in itself.

Religion taught it was a sin to be homosexual. Rousku married me hoping the gay will go away. He wanted to change because religion condemned the gay lifestyle. I still didn't get the whole gay thing. What I believed is what I was taught: Only men and women fall in love; that was the natural order. There was nothing normal about our relationship.

My sexual desires were subdued by the shame I carried from sexual assaults I had experienced. My sexual passion lay dormant from the trauma and the years of religious brainwashing. A very good reason to marry a gay man would be to avoid sexual intimacy and passion.

It didn't take long for Rousku to take control. He began telling me what clothes to wear, how to style my hair, and what makeup to wear for different looks. And then my housecleaning wasn't good enough. No matter how hard I tried to clean the outdated bathroom floor, it still looked "dingey" to him.

"I'll fix him." I grab a bucket of yellow enamel paint and giggled. "Problem solved."

Stunned by an illuminating glow bouncing off the bathroom floor, Rousku hesitated before saying, "You painted the floor?"

"Looks clean, doesn't it?!"

Our relationship was going downhill fast. One night, when we had a houseful of dinner guests, he picked a fight over dinner. At some point in the argument, Rousku tossed his plate of food on the floor. This was *familiar*, something my mother would do. I took the coffee pot and dumped the grinds on top of his mess. "You clean it up!"

By Spring of 1970, it was over. Rousku filed for divorce, claiming mental abuse. The fact is, gay people can't force themselves to be straight. And I can't fix gay. Tossed out, I had nowhere to go. I walked out the door, suitcase in hand, heading God knows where. I couldn't go home. Wild child on the run again.

For the next year and a half, I bounced around from one job to the next, one crash pad to the next, never settling too long in one spot. Getting high on LSD, doing coke, and black beauties (pharmaceutical speed). Self-medicating was normal. I, felt normal when high.

Dreams were forgotten. Nightmares, too. Living in an ambiguous world, you never let your guard down, but you will numb your senses.

For about a month I lived with a friend of a Johanna's in an apartment building on Delaware St. in Detroit. Across the street was a former frat house, home to a den of misfits. We would call ourselves "The Jones Family."

A group of displaced souls in limbo—that was us, the Jones Family. Trying to find our way through the drugs, the emotional scars of life, trying to escape our dark side. I was the first Jones girl to move in, then came Marilyn and Erica, two girls who were not afraid of their bodies. Empowered by their sexuality, they enjoyed being women.

I was a late bloomer to the sexual revolution, but they inspired me to embrace my womanhood and shake my booty.

"You need to find a real man, girl," Erica said. "Believe me. Sex with a real man is the best medicine for you."

At almost twenty, the world clawed at my memories, my childhood nightmares nearly forgotten by life's everyday distractions and the pill of the day. A few flings left an empty feeling in my heart, and I felt incomplete and lonely. My sexual scars were deep and painful. The cure was making a connection to one heart. One love, to heal the wounds that buried my latent sexual passion and desires.

A gypsy heart, living the bohemian life in search of meaning for life's journey: This was the mission. If I detoured, dreams would bring me back:

*A door opened and I walked in, greeted by a staff ready to assist me. Everyone was dressed in combat fatigues. Was this a military building? Standing on a steel staircase leading to the next level, I saw myself being reinvented, preparing for battle. My instructor said too many people were out to sabotage my goals. I needed another disguise before I could be sent back out to complete my mission. A new me, dressed in civilian clothes, a maternity dress. A flash of light—someone was watching in the distance.*

By August 1970, I was on the road to Charlevoix, Michigan, struggling to find another path with purpose. I was looking to experiment in other areas besides drug-induced fantasies.

My passion for music, writing, and the arts in general never faded. I dabbled in all of it. I even tried night school to get my diploma, but I had no patience with myself. That's when I started writing again. My knack of describing emotions on paper was improving.

In the back of my head, I could hear my high school English teacher's voice. "Write what you know," said Mr. Deku.

Underneath the smile I shared with the outside world was the sad truth: I knew about emotional pain, loneliness and disappointment. It was all I wrote about. Much too depressing for my happy facade. What can I say? Mom taught me to pretend and smile whenever feeling down, singing a line or two from some song.

"Smile though your heart is aching, and the whole world smiles with you," she sang.

Mr. Deku was right: writing was my path, but I kept taking detours looking for the ultimate experience life has to offer: love, "take me as I am," an unconditional love experience. There were a few guys I dated who were sweet and fun-loving, but something was still missing in the relationship. There was no passion. And, according to a few guys, I was *damaged* goods.

# THE DAYS OF LINDA JONES

## Run Amok

*"To be yourself in a world that is constantly trying to make you something else is the greatest accomplishment."*
- Ralph Waldo Emerson

Fucked up and nowhere to go… that's how I ended up here, there, and everywhere…

Between 1968 and 1972, my worldly experiences ran amok! In four years, I lived in more than twenty different places—sometimes crashing in an abandoned building, like the one in Windsor, Ontario. Already fucked up, I was loaded all the time, every day for a couple of years, on some kind of pill to block out what I didn't want to remember.

I still don't remember how I got there or what year it was but it was around the time I danced for the Metropole Supper Club in Windsor. Too high to be around strangers, I was looking for a place to be alone, to come down from an acid trip after having missed my ride back into Detroit.

Lying on the floor in the dark of some warehouse, I faced my boogeyman, proving to myself I could confront these unfounded fears trapped in my mind from years of institutional conditioning designed to conform my way of thinking to be like everybody else's. This was my problem: My life wasn't "typical in any sense.

My indoctrination to be afraid of sex, my body, the devil, and any other religion other than the Catholic version of God would not stifle my passion to unlearn the stereotyped opinions from growing up in a homogenized world, aimed at molding children to fit into society's narrow minded view of the past.

Until I was eighteen years old, I thought all black people were basically poor, lived in dirty places, were lazy, and to be feared. After less than a month of living on my own, I knew this simply was not the truth—but Mom didn't want to hear that one of my black neighbors had a house just as clean as hers. Many arguments took place in the family over this issue.

Emotionally desperate to determine what was good for me, often I crossed the line, breaking society's rules out of spite. Finally, I didn't care if people liked me or not. I had come to realize that I wasn't here to please anyone, but to learn, be happy,- be grateful for my life—be alive. But first, as I lay on that warehouse floor, I had to get back into my body.

I wasn't expecting a drug-induced out-of-body experience. What I recall was fighting hard to get back into my body—it felt like *something else* was out there besides me and my spiritual voice in the in-between world of spirit and flesh. When I awoke the next morning, the sunlight was shining through the broken and smudged windows. Looking around, reality sunk in, too close to death to ignore. No more doing hard drugs, drinking, and acid—at the same time.

Underage drinking wasn't addressed as a serious issue in the '60s. In fact, it was pretty damn easy for a girl to get served in most bars. I had been served alcohol since 1968, when I was seventeen and walked into the Red Foxx Club.

Alcoholism was hush-hush, a stigma to avoid. My parents didn't drink, so they felt no real need to talk about booze. My experience was limited to Uncle Charlie, who died when his "liver went bad" from drinking. My mother said he couldn't help himself; he was "weak-willed."

"You need a strong constitution to battle your demons," she explained.

I was consistent about one thing during my four-year insanity run: Leaving one job after another the moment I felt trapped or it no longer held my interest.

Major life-changing events and decisions I remember very well. Some things, however, I'm a little foggy about the exact time an incident occurred, which is the point: recognizing that the time for change is always *right now*.

Plum Street was dead and gone. Johanna was going through a divorce, and it was tough on her. She was dealing with the bills, the kids, and the pain of divorce while maintaining a good attitude. With the boutique closing, she was working as a secretary for a man in 1970 who refurbished homes.

While I was married to Tom Rousku, I was given an opportunity to use my typing skills working as a receptionist at his family's place of business, Rousku Electric. With Johanna's help, I was hired to answer phones and other tasks. Soon I would learn what a businessman's lunch was—and be introduced to Johnny Walker Red.

It was so grown-up: Like on TV, the owner kept a stocked bar in his office for lunch breaks. Johanna poured us a scotch while we ate our lunch. The limit was two drinks except on Friday, when we just went home early. It never dawned on me that Johanna had a problem. Since I was staying with her for a while, I noticed that every night on the way home she picked up a bottle of scotch. When we got home, she'd pour a drink for us and then start dinner for the kids. Most nights, we emptied the bottle.

One morning, I went to put a pot of coffee on. I wasn't feeling right. My hands were trembling, this had never happened before. Unaware it was the alcohol, I poured a cup of coffee, spilling a few drops due to the shakes. Johanna walked in the kitchen and poured herself a cup of coffee.

"Johanna ... something's wrong with me. My hands won't stop shaking!"

Johanna knew what to do, pouring a little Bailey's into my coffee, something I noticed she did, as well. I drank my remedy and was soon ready for work. But, like my mother, I put two and two together. No more drinking my lunches. No more – after-dinner drink, or one to unwind after work. I began restricting my alcohol intake to drinking on weekends and in social settings.

## Sticks and Stones and Broken Bones

A strong sense of self-preservation promoted my desire not to be an alcoholic or a junkie. Being in control was more about the vulnerabilities that I carried with me from childhood. I realized I was susceptible to danger if I was not in control. Booze made me talk, exposing my inner weaknesses. That had to stop.

The drugs I preferred kept me awake and on guard while the world slept, also allowing me a false sense of control. I battled back and forth with myself, removing every demon I found taunting my life force.

The following is a more accurate timeline of other significant events impacting my mental well-being after my dumb-ass decision to drop out of high school and leave home without an actual plan other than, a "feeling."

Late August 1968: A so-called "clean-cut" young man named Billy asked me out. I thought I was going out to dinner, but he took me to do a "job" with this older man named Sarge. They needed a lookout and put a gun in my hand, saying, "Shoot anyone coming in after us!"

My mother was wrong. I would have been a great actress, convincing enough to save my skin on more than one occasion, this being my first. As soon as they disappeared, so did I—but not before wiping my prints off the car and the gun with my dress.

In September 1968, while walking to work on Sunset Boulevard, a biker chick attacked me from behind, smashing my head on the curb, all because her asshole boyfriend said something that made her jealous. I had no clue what he said; my mind was on other things. My traumas were accumulating:

October 1968 – Date-raped on my birthday.

December 13, 1968 - Married a gay man.

Christmas Eve 1968 – My father-in-law attempted to molest me.

February 1969 - Nearly fell over a dead homeless man on the sidewalk in broad daylight one block from the Detroit Police Department.

Summer 1969 - Eyewitness in a stabbing of a 15-year-old girl in Detroit. My reaction saved her life, a cop said.

Around the same time, while going to the grocery store at 10 a.m., I was stopped by Detroit Police Department because my gay husband dressed me like Shirley MacLaine, who played a prostitute in the film Sweet Charity.

First wedding anniversary in 1969 - Rousku told me he slept with another man. I finally understood, the term *gay* after I walked in on him wearing my wig and antique 1930s robe.

Early winter 1970 - Uncle Johnny was home from Vietnam, "shell-shocked," on edge, drunk, in despair, and I understood his anger. I was angry, too.

Spring 1970- Marriage to Rousku was over.

Aug. 1970 - 10 days in jail for being a disorderly person; loitering in a place of illegal occupation. No. Not a brothel but I happened to be staying at a house full of hippies dealing pot and acid. While in custody, a ghostly visit.

Good Friday 1971 - Busted at the New York / Canada border for paraphernalia with a bolt in my pocket used by a guy in the front seat of my friend's car for a hash pipe. The judge was pulled from his cornfield, and we walked to his mini-courthouse, where he fined me $300, holding my driver's license hostage until I paid.

September 1971 - Rousku suggested we needed to work out the relationship that I thought was over. Since my head wasn't screwed on tight from dealing with my Catholic issues, I left with him for Hollywood, California.

Two weeks after we arrived in California, I had a dream about my sister and a bunny. The next morning, I received an early birthday card with a bunny on it from my sister. I began to believe in my dreams despite people's reaction that I was crazy.

Less than a month later, Rousku lost it, holding a knife to my throat, insisting he couldn't be straight. Tom Rousku was trying to cope with being gay—I was coping with life in general.

October 1971 - My twenty-first birthday didn't feel like a big deal. A few days later, I came home from work to find that Rousku moved out, leaving me to manage his job at the Yucca Motel, a dive on the corner of Yucca Street and Cahuenga Boulevard in Hollywood—either that, or be on the street.

Free rent in exchange for management was right up my alley. I was getting tired of being on the road. I was growing up, learning to cope with problems my way. Quietly, in control. No one would know what made me tick.

Thanksgiving 1971 - I tossed pot of turkey gravy on a hooker who came after me with a butcher knife after I evicted her from the Yucca Motel, which ironically was owned by a minister who preached at the First Presbyterian Church of Hollywood on Gower Street. I thought he was helping the poor and afflicted—naw—he was just interested in the rent. "Evict her!"

December 1971 - Back in Michigan, working as a governess in a dysfunctional household.

Spring 1972 I fell in love with life all over again when I met Thomas Eugene Holstin.

# MY MAN—MY LIFE

## Tommy, a ray of sunshine

**D**o you remember falling in love? I do. The only time in life that seems to make perfect sense. Discovering that love transports a damaged heart into a field of hearts and flowers is a worthwhile endeavor. Together, a force of one against the unjust world armed with the most effective weapon a mankind can attain: love.

After the fiasco with Rousku, I headed back to Michigan. I had to start over, again. Find a job and a place to live. In a few weeks, I had both. I was working as a governess in Grosse Pointe. I was not qualified but the father still, hired me. He was always out of town and the children's mother lived in France.

On the evening I met Tommy, there was something was in the air. A sense of urgency to go out nagged at my gut. I had had a strange dream the night before, *someone* was showing me how to fly. Calling up my only female friend to ask for advice, Johanna had recommended we go to Priem's, a bar on Mack Avenue.

Priem's was a local eastside hangout for the young crowd. I could hardly contain my words as I caught the bartender's reflection in the mirror, and gasped when he turned around to look at me.

Squeezing Johanna's arm, my witness to a dream come true, I blurted out, "Oh my God. I'm going to marry that man." I couldn't believe the words rolled off my tongue with such conviction.

"That's the man I told you about in my dreams when I was a kid." *The man with blood all around him.* Call it freaky, call it a figment of my imagination, it happened: The man in front of me was my future husband. My world was taking shape, I had a destiny to fulfill. I saw our future. He was the man holding me, loving me.

Tommy walked over to the corner of the bar where Johanna and I sat. He smiled, "What do you want to drink?"

Blushing, I smiled, briefly ignoring his question until Johanna ordered a drink. "I'll have the same thing," I answered. Tommy turned and walked over to shelving above the bar counter grabbing a bottle of scotch, then began pouring two drinks. "This is on the house ladies." Johanna noted, "He *is*, cute."

We stayed for a few hours and when it was time for Johanna to go home I decided I would stay a little while longer. I couldn't keep my mind or eyes off the man who was obviously flirting with me. I had to get home. It was a weeknight and I had to work the next morning, but I took every chance I could go down to the bar to see Tommy. We were almost obsessed with each other.

Three months our flirting continued before Tommy asked me out. Our little mating dance at the bar around the pool table amused his friends, because they never saw Tommy in this light: attentive, silly and head over heels in love. I couldn't help myself, either. This cosmic attraction was a first. I wanted no one else.

Laughter was good medicine for my ailing heart, and Tommy supplied me with a healthy dose every day of his life. Our life experiences had brought us together into each other's arms. All the horrible choices, mistakes and experiences we had before we met were unimportant. Who we were together, was everything. Tommy's teenage years was a lot harder than mine. His parents were divorced, his father worked long hours, too long to be a parent. His poor mother was certifiably, "nuts" and often hospitalized.

Money, jealousy, booze, drugs —not an issue. Tommy didn't even smoke pot anymore since his heroin recovery. We were past those chains of self-destruction. In fact, I pretty much only smoked pot at this point. I didn't drink much anymore, and it had been six months since my last acid trip. I was a pothead.

Love cleansed the stains of violence and emotional turmoil from the past, burning these chapters with its flames of passion. Without blame, no shame or angry tears, two phoenixes rising from ashes with tears of hope, our shared future focused on accomplishing goals and dreams.

Most times we played pool and talked about anything that popped into our heads. Tommy taught me how to make bank shots in the corner pocket, where to hit the ball and make the side pocket. The electricity between us was comically cosmic. When he leaned in to correct my posture, my body reacted, and I tripped over his foot onto the table, making an unintended shot.

The tingling sensation my body was experiencing was a latent reaction to my sexual desires. I wanted Tommy as if no other man in the world existed. My pool game improved, as did my appetite to learn what was it about him that made me feel funny inside.

For an amateur, Tommy was a pro. His friends and bar patrons would take bets every time he had the break shot. He'd call it. "Eight ball on the break." Rarely, he missed. It was a moneymaker for him.

"Game over. Tommy said. "Who's up next?"

Checking out for names waiting on the chalkboard, none. Quarters on table one, mine. After a few months of playing everyday, I wanted to beat Tommy at his game. He was *so damn cocky*, giving me the break shot. I was nowhere near his level, but a gut feeling said, "You got it."

"Eight ball on the break," I called. The cue stick slid through my fingers, hitting the cue ball dead on. The luck of a newbie. The eight ball rolled right into the corner pocket.

"I did it!" Very proud of it, too. I did what everyone was trying to do all night long, take the table from the hot shot. Tommy laughed at me doing my happy dance around the pool table and went over to sit with his buddies. It was getting late, and I was about to leave when Tommy walked over. He looked confused, as if he had a question on his mind.

After three months of playing the flirting game, I was hoping he was going to ask me out, I waited until his eyes met mine. "What's going on?"

## Sticks and Stones and Broken Bones

Almost too embarrassed, Tommy flushed when he said a five-dollar bet was going on between the guys—and he was picked to find out. Did I mention what I was wearing that night? An almost see-through black-knit lace top that fit snugly in the right places.

"Are you wearing a bra?"

Pausing long enough to watch him squirm, I said. "What did you bet?"

Blushing brighter he smiled, "You were."

Ha! "You lose." And I walked out.

A few weeks went by with the usual flirting going on, when everything changed one afternoon. It was early when I decided to play a few games of pool alone without a huge line of people waiting for the table. It so happened it was Tommy's day off. I wasn't expecting to see him.

I turned around to take a seat, and there he was, standing at the front door. My heart started beating wildly as he came through the door, and then I noticed that he had a bad limp. It was easy to tell from the expression on his face that it bothered him, but he played it off, acting like a tough guy.

Naturally, we wanted to hear how it happened. So Tommy took his usual corner seat at the bar and swung himself around like he was ready, on cue to tell his story, explaining in animated detail how he wiped out on his Honda 350 when he took the turn onto Cadieux Rd off of Mack Avenue.

"Did I tell you guys this was all during the storm?" No matter, Tommy said they were riding in the rain when he hit a rain-filled pothole.

"*They?* Who's *they*?" I thought. I certainly had no claim on his heart, but something felt like I was supposed to.

"W*h*o?" I asked. "W*h*o was with you?"

"W*h*at..?" "Careful, Tommy, of what you say" was written all over his face. "Just a friend; she wanted to go for a ride."

"Yeah, right," I'm thinking. "She wants the full tour." I laughed because he squirmed when the "friend" sat down next to him. She had suffered no injuries, wanting nothing more than to baby him.

"Your knee doesn't hurt that bad," I called out. "You're milking it. You want the sympathy."

The "lady" friend, with her batting eyelashes, looked annoyed with Tommy. He said something to her and she started talking to the guy next to her. Tommy limped over to me with a grin. "You want to go bowling?"

*Bowling!* Who goes bowling with a bum knee? A man after my own heart. The only means of transportation was to walk the mile to the bowling alley on Warren Ave. It was a slow walk, with plenty of time to share our life stories.

Tommy grew up in Grosse Pointe, Michigan. With divorced parents, it was a rough road. His mother, Sheila, had mental health issues to such a degree that at times she needed to be institutionalized. The family dynamics changed, leaving his father with custody of Tommy and his older sister.

Eugene Holstin was a practical man with a trucking business. Unlike many in the Pointes, the man labored for his wealth, which meant many hours away from home. Their grandmother cared for Tommy and his sister as much as she could, but teenagers in the 1960s were almost too much for any parent to understand or try to control, let alone a gentle-natured grandparent who submitted to her grandchildren's whims. Tommy got away with plenty.

Unattended teenagers have plenty of time to make mistakes—in Tommy's case, a pile of misdemeanors to infuriate a small town's police force. He told me about his heroin addiction. It was two years since he cleaned up at the Alexander House, a place where addicts did it the old-fashioned way, cold turkey.

Supporting a heroin habit in Grosse Pointe was "easy pickings," according to Tommy. These stately homes and mansions were no trouble to enter, since most of the doors were unlocked.

"I walked right in," he said. "There was no *breaking in*, I just *walked* in."

Some of the places he hit two or three times before they finally locked up. He robbed one house in particular four times before

## Sticks and Stones and Broken Bones

locking their back door. Tommy told me that he'd justified what he did at the time by telling himself their insurance would cover the loss.

"Most of the time I found cash stashed in the kitchen somewhere," he said. Explaining his routine, he said he would sit casually at the table and look around. One time he had to carry a poodle around the house to keep it quiet. The dog liked Tommy, and was happy to see him again.

"Sometimes I would get a beer and make something to eat." He chuckled. "I think the sandwich I made the last time I was there gave me away, but I still got in through the kitchen window—they didn't lock it."

Tommy's career in petty theft earned him a reputation in the Pointes as the "cat burglar." Yes, I married the cat burglar of Grosse Pointe. In all fairness, I met him after this drug-induced period in his life and other shenanigans. He was not the kid who got into trouble, but a young man with a dream and plans to see them through. Tommy was one of the lucky ones, too.

The one time he did get caught, it was because he was sloppy. He never carried tools of the trade. He got caught running down the street with a big-ass television at two in the morning—caught with the goods and drugs, too.

In our thirty-minute walk, we had already developed a bond of trust. Our past mistakes did not define who we were but what we would one day become, a family. It was the two-mile walk back to my house when we fell in love. A cosmic setup. Our night to fall in love.

We left the bowling alley still caught up in each other's stories and dreams, and with what was in our hearts. And there it was: The sound of love inspired. The illuminating glow of a full moon shone on Tommy's face as he got down on his bended and wounded knee to sing a medley of tunes. "There's a moon out tonight... woah, ooh, woah..ooh..."

"You say.. what makes me feel this way? My girl, my girl," grabbing my hand, "My girl..." From that moment on, we never left each other's side until 7/16/74.

Six months into my first pregnancy, Tommy and I were wondering if it was a boy or girl. With that thought in my mind, I fell asleep in Tommy's arms while I slipped into a dream...

*It was a boy! Sitting in a grocery cart, wearing a baby blue football helmet was the cutest little guy; he looked about six months old, and he was our son.*

As I patted the unborn child we would call Michael, Tommy said, "I saw a boy, too."

Always my prince charming, Tommy treated me like his future queen. Like all fairy tales, we fell in love. The smile on my face could light up any dark secret in the night. Love mended my damage heart. Tommy became the glue to hold me together. The past was behind us. Our little kingdom of love would soon have little clones.

Tommy loved me unconditionally, teaching me to trust. To follow my instincts. And he promised me a lifetime of friendship and laughter to comfort our tears. To feel free and speak my heart as well as my mind. Tommy encouraged me to write more than little notes of inspiration and poems that I would put in his lunch box.

Determined to reinvent himself, Tommy made a 180. Turning his life around wasn't easy. Past indiscretions kept coming back to haunt him. Cops with nothing better to do but follow him everywhere. This went on for years before I met him. Then I witnessed a few of those occasions myself.

Anytime they could find a reason, they would pull him over and give him a ticket for something or other, even a night when I ran out of gas. He was in such a hurry to get to me that he left his driver's license at home, just a few blocks away. But the cops arrested him anyway. It was then I called Tommy's father.

Eugene was pissed at the cops and at Tommy. I defended Tommy, explaining he did nothing wrong except forget his license on his way to help his pregnant wife. We moved out of his father's condo to avoid running into the cops. In a town that small, it was easy to be noticed and remembered.

Sometimes, keeping a roof over your head is more important than food for the week. In December of 1972, Tommy and I had such a

# Sticks and Stones and Broken Bones

week. We were living in an apartment on Van Dyke in Detroit. I was six months pregnant. Tommy worked at the Sunoco gas station on corner of Jefferson and Van Dyke. We paid the month's rent, but we had no food.

One evening, Tommy came home horrified to see I was eating an onion sandwich, and went to the bedroom to change into a bulky sweater and his oversized pea coat. When he walked back into the living it was obvious he was in a hurry.

"Where you going?" I questioned.

"Be back in a few," he said. "I forgot something."

Sure enough, Tommy found what he was looking for he walked in twenty minutes later with a shit-eating grin on his face. He couldn't bear to see me hungry, especially pregnant.

Tommy ran on foot a few blocks to the A&P. Having paid for the small can of peas with the change in his pocket, no one noticed he managed to "liberate" a few steaks to hold us over until he could get an advance on the following week's paycheck.

The cat strikes again! I ran to the bedroom to peek out the window to see if the cops were coming. Tommy laughed; he'd already circled a few times before coming home.

It was the only time Tommy had stolen since we were together. He adjusted his moral compass only to feed his wife and unborn child. What anyone else would do is not my concern because, despite the cognitive knowledge I gained through social institutions geared to conform our morality, one size does not fit all.

Sometime in June of 1974, Tommy came home very upset, looking pale. A policeman had threatened his life. He reported the incident to the Grosse Pointe Park Police Department, only to be told there was no such vehicle number. For the record, he also reported the incident to a friend and an attorney.

Tommy's birthday was Friday, July 12, it was also our "date night." Our second child was due. I was feeling heavy, with no desire to go anywhere. Like a good sport, Tommy stayed home to keep me company. We listened to music, talked about our new baby girl who would arrive soon. On top of the world, once upon a time.

Monday, July 15, rolled around like any other day. After putting our son Michael to bed, Tommy left to shoot pool to make a little extra cash, telling me if I needed him, to call the bar. I settled in with a book with the TV on in the background.

Life was perfectly wonderful. The baby was shifting her position—it wouldn't be long, I thought. Tired of being pregnant, I couldn't wait to be done with it. The quickest way for tomorrow to arrive is go to bed.

It was a beautiful midsummer evening, with an open window inviting the cool breeze in while I lay there naked, tossing and turning, the baby stirring.

Half asleep, I was waiting for Tommy to come home as I heard some sirens in the distance getting closer. Turning toward the window, I opened my eyes. Reflecting red lights flashed across the street along the bank of the Fox Creek canal. I turned to look for my glasses next to the alarm clock: 1:16 a.m. Suddenly, I heard a loud crash followed by a gunshot. My heart sank.

The front door flew open as I looked out the window to see our Jeep, a new CJ-5 parked in the driveway with a cop car up against the left rear end of the Jeep. Jumping out of bed, I ran to turn on the bedroom light just as Tommy came rushing in the bedroom. I went to reach for him, but he pushed me away.

"What the hell is going on, Tommy?" Panicking, I screamed, "What are the cops doing here?"

"Stand back, Linda! Stay away!" He never spoke like that to me. He was terrified.

It was coming to an end; he knew it too. But I tried to make it go away. I stepped in again as the cops entered the room, but he pushed me again towards the bed to safety.

Hands in the air, visible for all to see, Tommy had been drinking and was unarmed as he stood in his tank top screaming at the cops.

"Get out of my house! Get out of my house! Get the fuck out of my house!"

Instead, they came rushing in. Sergeant Charles Petrie ran behind Tommy, and another officer, Edward Serwach, ran in brandishing his weapon, yelling,

"Hold it right there, buddy. Hold it right there."

More screaming between the cops and Tommy. It was utter chaos. No one was listening to me as I screamed at the cops to leave us alone while keeping an eye on the weapon. Tommy's frustrated hands were still waving slightly over his head. He stood three and a half feet away from the barrel of the gun.

"You motherfuckers! Get out of my house, now!"

Clearly, it was our house. But it was too late.

Sudden flames exited the barrel of the .357 Magnum followed by a hollow-point bullet, which exploded in my husband's gut. He fell to the floor, squirming, the excruciating pain unbearable to watch. Collapsing at his side, helpless, a frozen moment in time, I looked up to see his murderer's coal black eyes looking down at me.

"You didn't have to shoot him!" I screamed, crying out, "It wasn't necessary."

Two big cops against a drunken man barely 5'9, weighing in at maybe 180 lbs. Easy to take him down. Petrie was positioned behind Tommy, and had every opportunity to grab him from behind—*if* they'd wanted him alive.

My painful words had no meaning to the cop. He was poisoned by his actions. He spoke, with words meant to shame me, and undermine my tragic sorrow.

"Get dressed… you're going to the hospital."

Realizing I had no clothes on was the turning point. He had no privilege to speak of my condition. It was my home he had invaded. Exposing my swollen belly was the least of my concerns. "You had no right coming in our house!"

Grabbing a full-length gown to cover up without underwear, I went back to Tommy. "I'm dying, Linda. I'm dying, I love you.."

I could hear our son crying in the next room. An old dream crept in the back of my mind. I saw it before. A man with cops all around, bleeding. I lifted Tommy's shirt, and saw a pool of blood was spilling down his side. It was a direct hit. There was a bleeding hole in the middle of his stomach. "I'm thirsty, Linda ... water —I need water."

Knowing it was the last thing I would ever do for him. I ran to the bathroom, grabbing a sponge to moisten his lips, holding on to the last thread of hope he could survive his wound. More cops were arriving on the scene. Grosse Pointe Police Department had crossed the Detroit line without alerting the Detroit Police Department.

Since Tommy was shot in Detroit's jurisdiction, it would be the DPD who would conduct an investigation into Tommy's shooting.

Cops swarmed all over the house. One entered our son's room and picked up the crying toddler from his crib. I'd left him there because his father was outside his door on the floor bleeding to death. I was angry: My baby didn't have to witness this cruel death scene. I lunged for my child. "Give me my son!"

The ambulance arrived, and I surrendered my toddler to a neighbor until my parents arrived. I needed to follow the ambulance. The loneliest night in the world was the ride to Bon Secours Hospital. The police did not allow me to ride with Tommy in the ambulance. Instead, they placed me in the front seat of a patrol car with a young cop to escort me to the hospital.

Bon Secours Hospital was less than four miles away, but it felt like forever. My last moments with Tommy were stolen from me. The deafening silence in the patrol car screamed at me. No fooling my brain into thinking "Linda, it's only a dream." The blood on the floor and my dress was Tommy's, not some man from a dream. Mumma, it was real.

Tommy's best man, Tommy Ireland, arrived. Emotionally torn apart and devastated by the news, he was also upset at the way the nurse delivered it.

"She says to me, 'I'm sorry,' he's expired," Tommy Ireland told me. "Do I need a dime for the meter?" He just lost his best friend after losing his brother suddenly a few months prior. The nurse's insensitivity struck him down into a pool of tears. Sobbing his heart out, this was more than he could bear.

"Why did they do that to you? They didn't have to shoot him," I said. Just two weeks before, Tommy had reported to the police department that a cop threatened him. I was no doubt suspicious about the connection.

"I don't know, Mrs. Holstin." Not wanting to comment, the young officer could only offer condolences. "I am sorry for your loss." Not as much as I was.

A nurse led me to the room where they had tried to revive Tommy, but he was DOA. Gently I caressed his face, touching his bare arms with the tips of my fingers. Looking for a miracle to say it didn't happen; that he was alive, and I was only dreaming. Touching his body, I lifted his shirt to look at the fatal wound, then leaned in to kiss him goodbye with a shred of hope my sleeping prince was waiting for my kiss to open his eyes, but he already was cool on my lips.

Dead is dead. He wasn't coming back. It was a goodbye kiss, after all.

Dehydrated from crying, I was getting a headache and feeling faint. Dr. Dwight Dutcher was notified of the situation and prescribed a mild tranquilizer to calm me down and delay a premature birth under this extreme duress, which could be harmful to the baby.

One more ride that night to set the wheels in motion: downtown to 1300 Beaubien Street, to be interviewed by a Detroit police detective. During the interview the detective said it all.

"The gun used to kill your husband could take down an elephant," he said. "The officer used hollow-point bullets. If you shoot someone with this gun, you want them dead."

The bullshit story the Grosse Pointe Police Department told the media was that the officers heard me screaming and believed Tommy was holding me hostage, etc.. This misinformation distracted people from hearing the truth of what really happened that night. Homicide charges were being considered by the District Attorney's office.

In the days to come, coverage by the *Detroit News* and the *Detroit Free Press* didn't slant the story, but the version I read in the *Grosse Pointe News* caused me to march right into Publisher and Editor Bob Edgar's office, demanding they print my version. This son-of-a-bitch dared to show me the concealed "piece" he carried on his person. What point he was trying to make I didn't get it at first. But it was an act of intimidation on his part to put holes in my story. He planned his strategy well, but the truth spoke for me.

The first question he asked was, "If Sgt. Petrie was standing behind Tommy, why would Serwach fire his weapon and take a chance of hitting his partner?

Without flinching, "It was a hollow-point bullet—any expert will tell you they explode upon impact. Serwach knew that." In the August 8 issue of the paper, a more accurate accounting was printed after my father-in-law and I demanded an interview.

Now I could not help but to piece together a few facts: Tommy's life had been threatened, but the cops denied having any patrol car with the number Tommy reported. The patrol car that crashed into the Jeep was a new car out supposedly for the first time—or was it?

The autopsy report supported my account of what really happened. Another false claim: Tommy was reaching for the gun when it "went off." Yeah, right. No gunpowder residue on his arms, just on the tips of his fingers, right where I had said his hands were at the time the gun was fired.

The report also stated that the victim was at least three and a half feet from the gun, just as I had said. There was one unresolved lie to expose: the officers' claim that they had thought I was a hostage.

"Who runs up to a strange house in the middle of the night and takes a chance a front door is unlocked while running away from the cops who are shooting at you?" Only a person who knows the front door was left unlocked just for them.

According to the court documents, the reason my husband died was over a traffic violation: *heavy acceleration from a stop sign.* Going to trial was about telling the truth for a man who could not speak for himself. For our permanent record, people would hear what happened to this man who had changed my life in a positive with his heart and soul.

One January night in 1973, Tommy had predicted that he would never make it to age thirty. I was very angry with him for saying it. The same night, I dreamed an incredible, detailed, sinister dream warning me that time was getting closer.

*A moment of peace and joy was all I had to be on top of the world before the sun faded away into nightfall. Now I am standing on a rooftop near the edge. The night air stirring up a wind of commotion. I didn't jump? I wasn't pushed? How did this happen? I was falling, descending at a great speed toward the ground. There was an object below me.*

*I was screaming, "What happened?" Beneath me, a police car. I was heading directly for it. The closer and closer I got, it became clear that there were numbers on the roof of the car: 716.*

July 16, 1974 was as *real* as it gets. I wished it had only been a dream. It is because of this night that I advocate that all law enforcement officers undergo extensive mental health evaluations before a gun is placed in their hands. The fact is, many are not emotionally qualified.

My desire to write intensified. I scribbled away at the emotions my heart was feeling, writing it all down in a wide-ruled notebook. How could I have survived and thrived through all that I had endured, only to be emotionally ripped to shreds? This was an unjust God.

"To forgive those who trespass against us," This quote is why I allowed the man who molested me to be my son's godfather, hoping my gesture of faith would remove this stain from the family and help me move on. This is how I am paid back? What sins should burden my children from these senseless acts? Some God you are... I lost faith in my Catholic God, but not in faith.

The day of the funeral my father-in-law took me to see an attorney, if the D.A's office wasn't going to do something about the shooting, then a civil suit must be filed. He was looking for justice, too.

# ANOTHER MAN—ANOTHER LIFE

## Leonard, my dark knight

**It** was the oddest conversation for a young couple to have. Prior to the shooting, Tommy wanted to find me a husband before he died. "I won't make it to thirty, Linda." What wife wants to hear that, or expects to have this type of conversation so early in a marriage? Tommy's first suggestion was his best man, Tommy Ireland. However, his buddy fell in love with a girl from the downriver area. Tommy had to rethink his choice and suggested a few different people. He wouldn't quit.

Sometime in May of 1974, Leonard Thomas King stopped by to see his friend, Tommy.

Tommy was curious what I thought of his friend, wondering if I thought Leonard was better looking than him. Did I like him? Not impressed with Tommy's game, I grumbled and walked away. He laughed at me, and I put raisins in his tuna casserole.

About a week before I met Leonard, Tommy Ireland's younger brother, a young man barely in his twenties, died suddenly. As we walked up to the coffin, I took my husband's hand in gratitude.

"This may sound horrible, honey, but I'm glad it's not you in there," I admitted. Two months later, those words burned into my soul the pang of regret only a widow could face, survivor's guilt.

In the moment of my greatest sorrow, a presence could be felt.

## Sticks and Stones and Broken Bones

Someone staring at me. Standing like a dark knight at Tommy's casket, I turned and saw Leonard, watching me with guarded eyes. My thoughts were playing tricks on me.

Was I burying one man to be with another? How can it be? My wandering mind remembered when Tommy introduced us; he said his name was Leonard, not *Leo…*

*"I prefer Leonard,"* he said. Where did I hear that before?

It would be six months before I saw Leonard again, at a New Year's Eve party. We spent the night talking about that night and "the incident." Leonard wondered how I was doing and cautioned me to wary of the local police. They didn't like bad publicity and had a good reason to come after me to make me look bad. Two months later, Leonard knocked on my door. Unaware this was a broken man with a tender heart, and a dark secret that took years to discover. Leonard was emotionally mistreated for not being his father's biological child.

I was still very much Catholic in the sense that couples remain loyal in sickness and in health. I didn't know how broken Leonard was when I invited him into my life. His mother cheated on her husband and became pregnant with another man's child. She kept it a secret until one day while in a fit of drunken anger she blurted it out to her husband who had been caught cheating on her. Leonard was four years old. Imagine how emotionally traumatic it was to no longer feel love and affection from the man you called daddy?

Clinical studies provide evidence of increased risk for those with a history of abuse as a child to fall prey to abusive relationships in adulthood. The state of my mental health was conditioned to accept abuse as means of penance, a Catholic tradition. Leonard's dark side was abusive but he kept it hidden from me for almost a year by then, it was too late to leave. I was pregnant with Nicole.

Leonard's first child and my third, Nicole was six weeks old, and I was going a little stir-crazy. Leonard and I had plans to go out with friends and celebrate the Fourth of July. A childhood friend of Leonard's had the hots for a recent widow friend of ours. A perfect babysitting couple. They both agreed, and I was free for the night.

Leonard would be right back, he told me, leaving with friends to pick up a few six-packs of Michelob. No problem. There were some things to do before the two love-birds (babysitters) arrived. An hour went by when Leonard called. He was at the bar, and wanted me to meet him at Diamond Lil's. Fine. He's already plowed. I could hear it in his voice.

I began regretting my decision to go out but I was committed to this night. I should have listened to my gut. Leonard had left the bar by time I got there. I waited for a bit then left around 11:15 p.m. that night, I left and went out the front door. Walking along the side of the building across from the parking lot where my car was, a vehicle was moving slowly west on Kirby. Suddenly, the driver swerved into the opposite lane pulling up to the curb next to me. I could see a stocky man with a full reddish-brown beard in the Kingswood station wagon was pointing a gun at me. "Get in the car."

Noticing the side door to Diamond Lil's was next to me, I grabbed the doorknob and turned. It was *locked*! The side door was never locked before? Why now?! It was a holiday, the place was packed. *He's going to shoot me in the back,* I thought. "I said, get in the car."

Out of viable options, I got in the car. The man then ordered me to put a ski mask over my face and get on the floor in front seat, holding a gun to my head for hours while he drove around the city looking for a place to do whatever with me. My glasses were removed, this was a trigger I was unaware of. I begged the man to be careful with them because they were badly scratched up and I didn't anymore 'chinese writing' on them.

"What are you talking about?" he said.

I was babbling. I wanted to get out of this situation alive. When the car pulled over. I knew this was it. He then ordered me to perform oral sex. I would have bit his dick off if the gun wasn't pressed against my head. I couldn't take a chance his reflex would pull the trigger. More than four hours passed before he dropped me off in front of a church about a block away from the bar (*Ironic* or what?). The car slowed down, though my face was covered I could tell we were pulling into a driveway when he turned. The car stopped. My abductor exited the car and walked around to my side, opening the car door. "Get out."

Quietly, I complied. Too many racing thoughts went through my mind. At the top, my children. It was not right they should be orphaned because of another man's actions. "Get on your knees," he said.

I thought, "this is it" you and me, Lord, whoever you are. I'm not ready to go, not yet. Not like this, too much sorrow for one family to endure. The cold steel barrel of the gun was pressed against the back of my head. "He's going to shoot me," then the unexpected. I was facing east and could see the grassy lawn in front of me, the night sky and the air..the air felt fresh, removing the stench of the ski mask. I could breathe but for how long?

"Don't move" he ordered, "and don't look back. Don't leave this spot for 15 minutes." The station wagon pulled out and sped off down Kirby in the direction of Mack Ave. The second I knew he was gone I got, shaking I didn't think I could walk much less run but I flew like the world was on fire, holding my blouse together, tears blurring my vision I made my way back to the bar, got into my car and locked the door.

This experience traumatized me. I needed to share but no one actively listened to me when I told the story except my father. He worried for my safety, he offered to ask a buddy of his, "Black Bart," to find me protection. "Lucky you weren't killed," he said.

My mother refused to believe things were that serious. My attorney, Joe Crehan had recently filed a wrongful death suit, advising me not to report it, stating the defense would use it to tarnish my reputation in court. No report was made for the sake of having no record to dredge up during my testimony. I felt victimized, again. I did tell Dr. Dwayne Dutcher, who prescribed me a little blue pill, Valium.

Despite my third husband's displaced emotions when he was drunk, I loved Leonard. It was hard for him to accept what happened that night, but he did. It wasn't Leonard's fault but he felt guilty because he kept ditching me all night. If he was at the bar as promised, it never would have happened. Right? Possibly.

Was it coincidence that this happened at a cop hangout (which I didn't know at the time)? Was this an opportunity for someone to get back at me for filing a wrongful death act suit against the City of Grosse Pointe Park and its officers? Was this planned?

This was the situation I faced. Doctor Dutcher said it sounded like a good idea to leave Michigan. My father and Leonard both agreed with Joe not to make a report. I never filed a report about my kidnapping and rape that occurred July 4, 1976 in front of Diamond Lil's in Grosse Pointe Farms.

Leonard was emotionally scarred as I. In the beginning of our relationship, there was no indication he would become abusive and hit me. He was honest about his inner feelings and if he was drunk or high they amplified, but no violence. I mistook this as passion for his beliefs. However, Leonard had secrets buried, like my mother. I never knew Arthur King was not Leonard's dad until after Leonard died. Ah, this is "need to know" information. Christ's sake, already…Anyone see something wrong keeping a secret hidden based on a lie? Is this going on in your family circle? Hiding from what? The truth to save face or escaping painful memories ironically tempts fate to call your bluff. My truth was covering the fact that Leonard was abusive when he drank.

Leonard turned into an alcoholic like his mother, Elaine. My parents warned me after meeting Leonard a few times, he had a problem with booze. I denied it, of course. In 1975, it was common for lunch to include cocktails. When I met Leonard, he didn't drink every day that I could tell. Like most young couples, in the beginning of our relationship, we went out to bars, had dinner, and drank socially.

It's easy to hide addictions when you have many places to go, to drink and party. It's even easier to hide it from someone whose parents didn't drink or go to bars. The only reference I had to go on was my own. Eventually, I quit drinking around Leonard—he took the fun right out of it. I had thought alcoholics were like my Uncle Charlie:Just big blubber babies who couldn't resist telling you what they were truthfully thinking. I never knew some alcoholics had personality disorders.

## Sticks and Stones and Broken Bones

As a young teen, accidentally on purpose I witnessed my Great-Uncle Charlie dying, in pain from psoriasis of the liver. Mumma and Auntie Gladys were changing Uncle Charlie's bedding and pajamas because he had lost control of his bladder. Mumma caught me spying on them, and gently closing the door, she said. "Uncle Charlie is very sick...go watch your movie."

The next time I saw a family member under the influence of booze was Uncle Johnny, a Vietnam Veteran recently redeployed to the States in 1969. He came to visit me and my first husband on Plum Street, drunk as a skunk and pissed off because our white-faced capuchin monkey wouldn't go to my mother.

What a traumatic scene for all of us. Within seconds, my uncle had his hand around the terrified monkey's throat because he didn't "follow orders."

My uncle was a tough son-of-a-bitch in his youth. No one could take him down. His Drill Instructor in the Army landed in a hospital for a few months after tangling with his new recruit from Detroit. "I'll show you how to make the little gook listen!" he yelled, lunging for the screaming monkey.

The poor monkey panicked, my mother was freaking out, and I was watching it all in slow motion. My father, bad back and all, pounced on his baby brother and pulled him off the monkey before he killed it. It was insane, watching my father punching my uncle in the face to bring him out of his flashback. In seconds, everybody piled on my father and uncle, trying to break it up.

"John! It's a fucking monkey! Daddy for the first time dropped the F-bomb in front of me. Unforgettably, Daddy said to me. "Your Uncle John is shell-shocked from the war."

Needless to say, Uncle Johnny was angry to begin with—his anger stemmed from childhood. The war intensified it. He drank abusively, but he wasn't an alcoholic. This limited experience with alcohol abuse and addiction could not prepare me to live with a loved one who drastically changed into a mad dog when he drank.

Before we met, Leonard served a short time in Jackson State Prison for drugs and transporting guns: another stupid kid growing up with too much money. Leonard said that his father shunned him and wouldn't help him when he was arrested. This emotional abandonment changed Leonard drastically, and he felt betrayed by those he trusted, just like me.

When we were first dating, Leonard worked full-time laying asphalt. It was a job he didn't care for, but I liked being around him more when he did manual labor, it gave his big brain a rest. He was the most intelligent man I ever met, and it was very sexy. He actually courted me for three months before making a move.

The early spring of 1975, I was working part-time for an auto body shop on Cadieux Road in Detroit when Leonard started driving by my house at night after work. I was unaware of this until my babysitter told me.

"Some guy keeps driving by your house every night around the same time," said Colleen "He slows down to look at the house and then drives over the bridge into Detroit."

This was a problem for three reasons: Me and my two children. Grosse Pointe cops were trying to intimidate me. Every route I traveled in the Pointes, I was met with a cop car tailing me, or one would turn and another car would be waiting at another corner. It was not coincidence. I reported this activity to my attorney and any family member or person who would listen. We could be in danger. I was going after the police department, and if anything happened to me, people would know where to look.

Perfect timing: The mystery car was driving by the house when Colleen was on the way out the door: "That's the car!" The '67 GTO made a right turn over the bridge. I closed the front door, wondering if I should get the ball-and-cap gun Tommy made. It was not very accurate, but effective. It was in a drawer next to the bayonet. Or should I get the .22 rifle?

A knock on the door set me jumping a foot off the ground. I looked out the living room window and recognized the guy at the front door, it was Leonard, doing his nightly drive-by check. He was concerned for our safety because he "heard things" and felt it necessary to keep an eye on us.

Leonard was shy. Tilting his head, he looked up, apologizing for disturbing me. That was all it took—I could see why Tommy had been a little jealous of him. Leonard was very handsome, shy, and loved his dog—he was a man's man who *preferred* to be called Leonard. I invited him in. "Can my dog come in, too?"

Everyone in the family was waiting for Leonard to find his niche in life. Whatever he wanted to do, I knew he would be great, but in the meantime he floated from one job to the next, fighting demons.

Leonard was not artistic like Tommy, but he could play the harmonica. I complimented him one night while listening to Bob Dylan's *Tangled Up in Blue*. He had learned to play in prison and enjoyed it, but was shy to play in front of others, which surprised me. He seemed so resilient.

Marriage was a lifetime commitment my parents honored with love. Tommy and Leonard both came from well-to-do but broken homes in Grosse Pointe City. Their family dynamics were completely opposite to my upbringing. What was the attraction?

One similarity in our combined family history is that each of us had a family member with roots dating back to the Revolution. Another side of our recent ancestral heritage was an overseas transplant from Europe. The main attraction? Both men were in the same dysfunctional dream I had as a child. What else can I say? It was a "twist of fate."

Leonard and Tommy were nothing alike; in fact, they were complete opposites. Leonard had a dry sense of humor. Both men were highly intelligent, but Leonard was closer to genius. Secrets concealed Leonard's troubled heart; he was more like my mother when it came to keeping things bottled up. In general, Tommy was cute, easy to love, and an open book. Leonard was tall, dark, and handsome: a bit of Clark Gable and Errol Flynn, combined. Mom said be careful, Linda - he's the silent type—they keep everything inside; then they go off, like a time-bomb.

The summer of 1977 was a turning point in our relationship. Leonard was drinking more and getting into more trouble with the local cops. He had outstanding warrants for his traffic violations. He loved to antagonize the cops. The stress of the situation was harming us. It was time for another change. A new start.

We planned to leave the state before another winter dragged us down. Leonard had nothing to do in winter but drink and get high. I got high now and then when the kids were in bed. I had no escape from my emotional pain. When Leonard drank, the fighting would begin. I ran out barefoot into the snow more than once to escape a beating. One night I couldn't take it anymore.

My plans for a romantic evening backfired the minute Leonard walked in the door. Candles were lit, Van Morrison playing *Moondance,* and I was dancing. I smiled at Leonard, but he acted offended. He sat in a chair, verbally abusive, demanding that I get him something to eat. I have no clue what possessed me, other than frustration, to walk over and "tapped" his knee but it started a brouhaha.

Leonard pounced as I ran toward the kitchen, hoping to make it out the back door, but he was at my heels and grabbed my hair, pulling me away from the door leading to the basement and the outside door. He knocked me down to the floor. I was leaning against the glass oven door and trying to pull his hands off me when his size-11 Fry boot was about to make contact with my face.

Quickly, I moved to my right while the pieces of shattered glass hit me and the floor. Leonard paused long enough for me to get away, but I had no time to make it out of the house and I ran to the bedroom to get a weapon. I was pissed! When insult is added to injury, I don't do well.

Next to my side of the bed in the nightstand, I had Tommy's bayonet. I pulled it out of its sheath, hiding it in the folds of my full-length dress. I needed a better position when he came in. I stood on the other side of the room with my back to the wall and the bed between us.

## Sticks and Stones and Broken Bones

Leonard attempted to come at me, but I wasn't drunk. I ran across the bed, turned around, and before he made a move, I flung the bayonet at him with perfect aim. The knife stuck in the wall a mere two inches from his face. I was sick of being tossed down stairs, with broken bones and bruises. Leonard did not know I had a thing for weapons.

While I was running amok around the country, I did learn the basics of hunting, fishing, gutting, plucking feathers, and tossing knives at rats in a quarry. I was a survivor. I also had an eye for shooting pool and hitting my target. Besides teaching me to shoot pool and take pictures, Tommy had taught me how to shoot a gun in the dark.

The look on Leonard's face said it all. He got the point. I should have left it at that but *nooooo*... I had to rub it in. Give him a taste how it feels.

"That's because I wanted to miss!" His facial expression changed—it was time to run.

I had the advantage and made my way down the stairs and out the front door, once again barefoot in the snow.

Domestic abuse was not addressed in the seventies. I held onto the hope that once we left Michigan, Leonard would be fine, everything would be fine. All I cared about was keeping Leonard out of jail. I believed he could change if given unconditional love.

We were staying a few weeks with Leonard's mother in Grosse Pointe City before leaving the state. We were waiting for the third of the month when my widow's benefits would arrive. On Labor Day Weekend, 1977, a knock at the front door disturbed our Sunday plans to say our goodbyes before heading to Florida.

Damned if I do, damned if I don't. Should I tell the truth, or a white lie? Looking straight at the Grosse Pointe City Police Officer, I replied. "No. He's not here."

"Look, Mrs. Holstin, I hope you're not lying to me, because I can go back and get a judge to sign a warrant then come back to search the house for..."

Cutting him off, I opened the door. "You can come in if you want to and see for yourself." The bluff worked, and the two officers walked away. I shut the door, locking it, wondering where Leonard was hiding in the attic, ready to crawl out the window. The look on his face was priceless. He almost crapped his pants when he heard me say, "Come in."

I looked at Leonard. "You need to trust my instincts more."

Embedded in old money, Grosse Pointe was a block away from Detroit, which was progressively becoming a ghost town of abandoned buildings filled with junkies, dealers, and the homeless. Grosse Pointe was, another world in comparison to the living conditions on the other side of the Detroit border.

As I said before, Grosse Pointe cops had nothing better to do than drive drunken old ladies home or follow me. It would be wise to move away until the case went to trial, and with the cops knocking on the door to arrest Leonard, it was time to go.

Without being seen, I packed the car with everything we intended to take, put the kids in the backseat with the dog, and stashed Leonard in the trunk of the GTO. It looked like I was taking a drive with the kids. I just had a few blocks to go.

"Mommy, why is Daddy in the trunk?" Wish I could explain to my son, but how do you tell a four-year-old we're smuggling his new daddy outta town? You don't. You tell a white lie.

"Mommy told Daddy to get in the trunk because he farts too much." Good thing four-year-olds think fart jokes are funny. We drove straight down Rivard Boulevard, heading for Mack Avenue.

The problem with anger is that most times, it outranks common sense to be afraid when you should be, and you become defiant. I should have been afraid but I was too mad at the cops. Leonard and the cops had their own cat-and-mouse game. He would drink and take the cops on a car chase. He was good at it, lost them a few times, once with me in the car. Now I was making the great escape at 25 mph out of Grosse Pointe to keep his dumbass out of jail for his own stupidity. I needed to get out of town and he was coming with me.

## Sticks and Stones and Broken Bones

After leaving Grosse Pointe City's jurisdiction, I drove a few more blocks into Detroit, pulling into the parking lot of the Cadieux Café, where I let Leonard out and put the TV in the trunk. My son looked at Leonard, still wondering.

Leonard started laughing and came up with something about Mommy playing a joke. In 24 hours, we reached Florida. For the next five years, I existed somewhere between a paranoia and limbo.

The first three years we didn't have a telephone in case I was being monitored. I lied about my children's last name when I registered them in school or took them to the doctor's so we couldn't be traced. Yes, that paranoid.

I drove down the street with my kids in the car, periodically yelling, "Duck!" as safety training in case someone was chasing us with a gun. This intense game of duck and cover was based on a previous experience in Detroit with my sister and babysitter while coming home from an Elton John concert in November 1974, when we were chased by a green car of black men for almost five miles on Jefferson Avenue.

"Where's a cop when you need one?"

As we drove, one of the men placed what looked like a shotgun up to their car's open window. I zig-zagged across the lanes, hoping to draw attention to a cop … no such luck. Not one cop around to stop the chase. Only when I headed straight for the fifth precinct and pulled in, horn blaring, did the car drive off. I stormed in, demanding action. "Get an APB out for a green Caprice with four-five black men with a shotgun!"

Startled by my entrance, the officer at the desk looked at me, "Ma'am?"

"We were being chased down Jefferson Avenue by a car of black men with a shotgun!"

He made a call to area patrol cars to be on the lookout, giving them my description. After about 20 minutes, we left and went home. The experience was just another chink in my mental armor. Now I was using the experience to teach my kids to be on the lookout. Bad parenting, for sure. If someone didn't listen, I'd turn around.

"Bang! You're dead!" I'd yell. "Listen, Sheila, you have got to pay attention! I am teaching you to save your life."

Conditioning my children to be safe was my primary objective. Explaining they needed to learn how to "follow orders" so they wouldn't get killed. Always stressing the importance to my children to watch out for others and help the less fortunate people. Protect your family, don't turn your back on your siblings, stick together. And for God's sake, never call the cops on family.

I did more harm than good, passing on my traumas to them, exactly like my mother had done with me. I just didn't see it.

From the moment we crossed the state line into Florida, I *felt* something… in the back of my mind, there was strange silence like something about to happen. I looked over to Leonard. "It's weird. I don't know why it bothers me but we haven't seen one accident or stranded driver the whole way down…"

Unconcerned, Leonard responded, "So?" His belief was to never believe in anything he could not see or touch for himself.

"I just feel weird about it," I said. It wasn't more than two breaths after I said that, "JESUS CHRIST LOOKOUT, LEONARD!"

Straight ahead, 300ft in front of us a camper flipped and rolled a half dozen times down three lanes on Interstate 75, southbound. About a dozen cars were involved in the pile up. Remarkably, we escaped and drove right through it. It was horrific. I could two dead bodies as we drove by the wreck. We were going to pull over when we noticed a state trooper coming up from behind. Noticing there were plenty of other vehicles pulled over to assist, with three kids of our own, it was best we kept going. Leonard, kept staring at me. He couldn't say the words to explain, what he experienced.

The road ahead of us was a journey that represented freedom. Florida, a place where my face wasn't recognized. I didn't worry about cops because I didn't lead a life of crime. I loved my renewed freedom in the Sunshine State. While Leonard and I waited to hear when the trial date would be set. Life went on.

Sticks and Stones and Broken Bones

We arrived in Fort Lauderdale late afternoon and took a cheap motel room next to the International House of Pancakes where the kids eat free. We stayed there until we found something permanent. My plan was to find work as a waitress, securing daily cash at the end of my shift to keep us afloat until my widow benefit's from Tommy's social security was transferred to Florida. I got the first job I applied for at a restaurant on Hallandale Beach Blvd.

It was foolish to think, Leonard would leave his demons behind. Instead, the next four years revealed just how damaged Leonard was. Often he had run ins with the law. Creating more stress on me and the kids. Sometimes, I popped a few pills the doctors gave me to numb my brain or smoke pot if I had it. By now, I discovered if I drank, I would start a fight with Leonard. It wasn't fun. Having drinks with friends, should be a fun occasion. It wasn't. Leonard almost, always created a violent scene when he was drunk. And, he was always remorseful the next day. Doing anything to make me happy but I wasn't. I loved life, living in the moment, and genuinely thankful, to be alive another day. *Why*, not Leonard? He loved us but it wasn't until my fourth child, Ryan, Leonard's son was born that he began to see a hopeful future, he found his niche' - cars.

For a while Leonard was working boiler room sales for a gas and oil lease company in Fort Lauderdale until it was time for me to be back in Michigan for the trial in spring of 1981. Leonard quit his job to stay home with the kids during the trial, he would come later on when it was time to parade Tommy's children in front of the jury, for impact.

After the trial, I no longer did I have to worry about someone over my shoulder trying to get me. No more lying about who I was or what happened to me. The freedom of taking my case to trial liberated my mind to think for myself.

Fall of 1981, we bought our home in Boca Raton, Leonard began realizing the potential we had for a better future. But the drugs dominated his thinking. Sometime later, before the holidays, Leonard's sister reintroduced her brother to someone he knew from high school, Dorian. At first it seemed like a perfect plan. Buy all the foreign cars up north that were being targeted by angry, American auto workers, and resell them for a profit in South Florida.

Jaguars, BMWs' and Porsches were selling cheap in the Motor City, it was an opportunity for Leonard to shine. He knew cars, he loved everything about them. Selling them was easy and fun for him. He was focused, but still, he was an addict. If he could not get a grip on this. I had too. I was going to leave him if he didn't clean up. The kids were getting older and would learn of his habit. I was serious and I had the money to do what I pleased.

Six months after we purchased the house in Boca, I found Leonard, dead in the front seat of the car.

# PART III
# Sticks & Stones

### Dedicated to Veronica -
### And the hits keep coming

Unexpected life events led me to question government and religion. Specifically, the Catholic Church and the way government conducted its business for the taxpayers. Over the course of time, I examined my own existence.

*What do I stand for? What do I believe in? What would I die for? What am I responsible for?*

I don't believe in government with career politicians. It limits new ideas and much needed change. I don't believe in a religion that pits soul against soul. I do believe that if God created us in his image, he is also part of us. I do believe in an invisible universe where spirit and flesh come into presence. Reincarnation is possible. I believe there's life on other planets. And, I know one person can change the world. At the very least, their own.

# A TRAIL OF SORROWS

## An angry woman

**P**ast traumatic experiences were spilling over into the present. My body and soul permanently tattooed with emotional scars. Leonard was dead for six weeks. Autopsy still listed cause of death as: "undetermined." My mind insanely twisted with a lack of faith in anything. Intolerant of the hand of fate. It was stacked deck.

Sorrow, depression, and chaos had become a learned lifestyle, though not by choice. Twice, someone put a handgun to my head and I lived through it, but on Christmas Eve 1981, I wasn't so sure I was going to make it out alive.

Leonard was drunk beyond reason when he came home late that night. We had flown my parents in for Christmas, which was tricky, knowing my mother's fear of flying, but I had managed guilt in my favor. The tickets were nonrefundable, and I knew that a woman who had very little of anything growing up could not stand to see money go down the drain. My siblings doubted she would use her ticket. Score one for me, I knew she would.

With my parents sleeping in the guest room next to ours, I hoped Leonard would attempt to keep his drinking to a minimum. Wishful thinking. Leonard entered the bedroom, and I pretended to be asleep, praying he would just pass out. I kept hoping he would not make a scene, or my father would step in.

Quietly, I lay there. Keeping my breathing at a regular pace, in the background I heard Leonard fooling with something in the closet. I peeked to see what he was doing. He had the gun. I closed my eyes he came back and sat at the foot of the bed.

"Click, click"—I heard the dry sound of an empty chamber. Then a cold snap, and Leonard had put a clip in the Browning 9mm. A moment later he placed the loaded handgun to my temple. Before I opened my eyes, I prayed to whatever God was listening to spare my life once again.

"Someone is going to die in this relationship... Please, God, it can't be me. You can't let the kids be left alone with him. I know it's fucked up... but I wish you'd take him out of his misery. This has to stop."

For once, the nuns were right. "Be careful what you pray for." I could hear my father in the other room. Leonard, did too, and placed the gun back on the top shelf in the closet. The worse part was over, for now. Leonard, had passed out on the floor. The next morning, Leonard, still laying where he fell, I then took a picture of him as an incentive for him to change. After showing him what he looked like to me, Leonard saw that I was at my breaking point. After the holidays, Leonard cut back on the drinking but kept self-medicating with street drugs. A vicious cycle with one outcome. Three months later, I found Leonard's cold, dead body in the front seat of a Navy blue Lincoln, just like the car in my dream a year earlier when I was in Michigan for the trial.

Finding Leonard dead was 'suspicious' for many reasons, but three in particular stood out.

First, Leonard *never* gave up the driver's seat regardless of how drunk he was. Second, his body was covered in fake hundred dollar bills—a fact that I left out of the police report during their investigation. A voice in my head told me it was a set-up—take the money." The way the money was spread over the body indicated to me it was intentional, to throw off investigators. I later discovered the money was counterfeit. We were wealthy and didn't need fake money. The third reason his death was suspicious? Leonard never drank alcohol when prescribed antibiotics.

## Sticks and Stones and Broken Bones

The Sunday before Leonard died, we were target shooting at a quarry off of State Road 84 near the Everglades. On the way home, upset with Leonard for shoving me in the back seat of the Lamborghini and doing 100+ mph, I began tossing one bottle at a time out the sunroof until the six-pack of Molson's was gone. Tired of fighting, I went straight to bed and fell asleep with my contact lens in. Monday morning, I awoke in excruciating pain, my eyes glued shut.

Leonard rushed me to Boca Raton Hospital. The doctor explained that gunpowder residue was underneath my contacts, causing the temporary blindness. While the doctor worked on me, Leonard checked himself into the ER. He had developed an infection from an injury to his big toe. He was prescribed antibiotics and began taking them immediately, which meant no booze.

Bedridden for a just day, I was lying on my right side in the dark when Leonard came in to see if I needed anything. Avoiding the light, I rolled over on my stomach, blind to the fact that the best man at our wedding was in the room with us. Leonard leaned over and kissed the back of my neck, apologizing.

Pulling up my nightgown with my ass exposed, I heard Leonard saying, "Now isn't that a nice-looking ass or what?" Gary said something to Leonard and walked out the room.

"What the hell are you doing?" Leonard was just being silly. He was sober and happy, and he kissed my bare ass. It was his last kiss. Leonard went out to get something for my pain, and I never saw him alive again.

The following morning he was dead, and I *felt* it before I discovered the body. My childhood home may have been free of alcohol and drugs, but not from our genes or our heritage.

Turns out, the Feds were keeping tabs on a few of Leonard's newly reacquainted associates from Michigan who were the last to see him alive. The Feds may have known that Leonard was dead before I did, speculated my attorney, Jack Musselman.

After Leonard's death, my stress continued surfacing as eccentricities in my lifestyle. Never knowing from one day to the next what would set me off, I was a ticking time bomb, self imploding. I regressed when Leonard died, my mind twisted by guilt and accountability. I was doing emotional time. Was it my fault Leonard was dead? Or was it his *time* to go?

Trauma triggers associated with PTSD include the date of an event, or a specific time, smell, sound—any trivial component of a bad experience can trigger a hyper-arousal state. I had a shitload. I feel it. I see it - the flames exiting the barrel of the .357 Magnum eliminating the first person I loved, heart and soul. Tick... tick.... tick...

Handguns, heated arguments, the sight of blue and red flashing lights, or any uniformed officer—all are triggers. My heart starts racing, I begin to pace, and my breathing is labored, or sometimes I realize I'm not breathing at all, but holding my breath.

With Leonard gone I was looking over my shoulder again. Tired being afraid of anyone bigger than me. I often carried the Browning 9mm around with me when I left the house. I wasn't trigger happy, just afraid. What happened to me - was happening to my kids. I was angry as hell, pissed off.

"This is not my destiny!" I shouted at my reflection in the mirror.

For weeks after Leonard died, I would sit on the floor and stare into the full-length mirror, lighting candles, hoping to catch a glimpse of his shadow, a ritual I maintained until I saw a dark window opening up inside my mind... I had to let go. I had another road to travel.

After putting the kids to bed, I went to my bedroom and sat on the floor in the candlelit darkness; searching for the ghost that haunted me in the mirror. A voice, I swear that wasn't mine commanded me to move my ass, take a shower, get dressed, and get out of the house. I called a babysitter and got ready.

Instead of taking the Lincoln Town Car, I grabbed the keys to the Lamborghini along with a couple of pillows and drove to the Wildflower, an upscale bar and restaurant in Boca Raton, a great place for distraction.

## Sticks and Stones and Broken Bones

Dancing upstairs, dining downstairs, I headed for the bar where solitary people go to sit among the lonely. Eat before you drink, a reasonable rule. I ordered the quiche and a cup of coffee with a shot of whiskey. It was a great distraction. People were lively, enjoying their lives, despite my own personal sorrows. It wasn't so bad, staring at the mirror behind the bar, watching people while I ate my dinner. It was better than staring at the mirror in my bedroom, looking for ghosts.

Dressed in black, my veiled hat covered swollen eyes, allowing me privacy to hide and to spy on people, imagining how their lives were going. Continuing my visual game of distortion, I wondered who was more fucked up in this bar than me? The answer walked up and sat down next to me. What a jerk.

As I sipped my spiked coffee, the man, an Englishman named Jack, claiming to be some kind of a race car driver, said he'd "noticed" that I'd pulled up in the Lamborghini—and he wanted to buy me a drink.

"No, thank you." I explained that I didn't want conversation, that I was in mourning and just needed to get out of the house, stating my wish to be alone. Jack kept trying to engage in conversation. He wasn't taking no for an answer. Lifting the laced veil that covered my eyes, I made eye contact.

"Look, I've buried two husbands," I stated plainly. "I'm not looking for a third." As the years went by, I would change it to: "You don't want to be the third."

Apparently, Jack thought he was "all that." Grabbing my hair at the back of my head, he pulled my face toward him and kissed me. I was overpowered, but before I could smack him off his stool, two very large bouncers wearing tuxedos pulled him off me and tossed his drunk ass out.

Though this wasn't a date. It reminded me to take a mental note; a rule to follow, Linda: Never date a man who couldn't hold his liquor or didn't know when to quit and switch to water. From now on, I would wait and see if the man changed into a demon or kept the same personality I was attracted to.

After finishing my drink and another cigarette, I left. One of the bouncers escorted to my car to assure my safety. Feeling extremely anxious after the kissing incident, I wasn't ready to go home.

The Rainforest Bar and Restaurant in Delray Beach was a spot where Leonard and I had gone to dinner a few times. It also had a Ms. Pacman game table. Here I could sit, drink my kamikazes, play the game, and be left alone. I wanted to be in public, but I wasn't ready to socialize.

Last call, it was time to go. Just as well. I was plastered and had developed two blisters at the top of my palm from the joystick. The kissing bandit triggered an angry emotion with his invasive kiss, reminding me of the past offensive sexual encounters I had to deal with.

Fishtailin out of the parking lot in the Lamborghini was not my intention but I was too short to drive the damn thing. The pillows propped me up enough to see over the steering wheel, but the car was designed with long-legged men in mind, not short women wearing spiked heels.

My foot slipped on the gas pedal, causing me to nearly stall out for the lack of speed as I attempted to shift gears, I overcompensated the pressure I applied when my foot found the pedal, and gunned it right in front of a Florida highway patrolman. Instead of grabbing two pillows when I left home, I should have grabbed the paperwork for the car.

The flashing lights were on before I could shift into third. I didn't care that I was being pulled over because I was pissed off at the world. Emotional triggers are dangerous because instead of being afraid when you should be, the sufferer is too angry to be fearful. When the officer approached the vehicle, I was ready for a confrontation. Angry tears began to fall. "What the fuck do you want?!"

The big black cop was stunned, his face had an expression that read, 'What the hell did I get myself into?' He maintained his composure despite my insult. "Driver's license and registration," said the officer.

## Sticks and Stones and Broken Bones

Taking my hat off, I reached for my purse, sobering up enough to remember my license was in my other purse. As I leaned toward the glove box, it hit me. No proof of registration or insurance. I was for sure going to jail.

"Well, hell... I don't have anything to prove who I am or if the car is legal."

Then those dreadful words: "Get out of the car."

The weight of the car door hindered my exit from the low-riding vehicle that I'd parked alongside the drainage ditch, and the dozen or so kamikazes didn't help either. My first and only sobriety test involved attempting to sing the alphabet—I was stopped before *C*. The officer then instructed me to repeat the alphabet backward. It took some doing, but I managed it, all the while bitching about how lying cops had ruined my life.

The next test required balance. One foot in front of the other, he asked. "Now, that's a problem," I replied, explaining that spiked heels were not designed for walking on rocks at the side of the road. "You seriously can't expect me to walk a straight line with these on do you?"

"Walk to the back of the car turn around and walk back to the front," he ordered.

Wobbling towards the back of the car, I turned around. "Ha!" I blurted. "I don't even have the license plate on the car."

The officer quickly stepped over to the rear of the Lamborghini to see for himself. He didn't know what to say other than "Get in your car."

After running my name, he came back to the car, saying that I had a clean record, adding that it was my lucky night. "Go home, lady," he said.

"I was having a lucky night until you pulled me over." What the hell was wrong with me? I was trying to cause trouble.

"Lady! Go straight home," he responded.

I did wonder why he let me go. I was grateful that this officer was somehow compelled to exercise the spirit of the law. Going by the book would have done more harm than good to me and my children. How did I get this privilege?

Saying I was lucky not to be in jail was an understatement. It hit me when I got home. Luck had nothing to do with it. The Browning 9mm was still under the seat of the car. Since Leonard's funeral, I carried the gun for protection when I traveled alone. This encounter must be a sign? The dead protected me. The next day, I put the car up for sale.

Time to quit challenging every officer for one cop's action. I needed to confront just 'one,' the man who started this emotional backlash. I didn't want anything except an answer. Did he think of Tommy, his children and who took away from us? In the meantime, I had other issues: keeping my sanity and my family safe.

Grief messes with your head. Decisions based on emotions usually are half-ass because most are hasty. I chose to start Kingsway Limousine while riding in the back of one on the way to Leonard's funeral.

No one could see my tears. I could cry alone. "I want one of these. Also, I was looking for something new to keep me occupied and distracted from my emotional situation. It made sense, since I was going to buy one anyway. May as well work a financial angle and run my own limousine service. Lucky for me, my father and brother John came down from Michigan to stay with me. Helping me through another life transition. I was not alone.

Regardless of my emotional decision to start a limo service, it wasn't a half-ass operation. I researched, crunched the numbers, talked to potential clients, hired an attorney, bought the car, and did everything required. I could have the car pay for itself. I would be the chauffeur until I made enough to cover another driver.

My father helped me study for my chauffeur's license, giving me pointers on how to drive a larger vehicle. I passed with no problem. "Ride the Kingsway" was my slogan.

I offered personal attention for the client's occasion, and something my competition did not have, a customized Lincoln

## Sticks and Stones and Broken Bones

Limousine Stretch. Lincoln Mercury vs. GM? The Lincoln also stood apart from the standard stretch Cadillac.

My opposition? The Boca Raton Hilton had a contract' with certain affiliates of the underworld. At the time, the hotel offered clients the standard Cadillac stretches—and they were the only limousine service in town. Certainly, there was room for competition? What can one little widow woman do against money and connections like that?

Confidently, I moved forward, filling out all the necessary applications required by the City of Boca Raton. My packet was filled with letters of recommendation that my service was needed because I offered an alternative to the only limousine service in town.

My biggest coup was an exclusive commitment from the newly built Holiday Inn at the Glades Road exit and I-95. I secured an agreement to provide a limo on standby. Then when a front-page story with a photo of Kingsway Limo company ran, trouble began.

In my father's words: "Linda, girl, you jump right out of the frying pan into the fire... I don't know how things could get any worse for you." But they did.

There were obvious break-in attempts over the course of three months. The family Doberman, Boozer, was having a nightly rampage: someone kept coming in the yard. I'd call the police; they checked it out. Someone tried to jimmy open the back door by the pool. Another time, it was a front room window.

My father had to get back home to mom after his two-month stay, leaving my brother behind to stay with me. Short time after, another story about Florida lawmakers deregulating the taxi service laws ran in the Palm Beach paper, and for some reason my name and company was used as an example.

The phone calls began. Answer the phone, it went dead, but sometimes we heard voices and music in the background. My youngest daughter answered the phone once to hear a man say, "Your family won't have much longer to live."

One evening in the late summer of 1982, my brother Johnny came running into my room whispering loudly, "Someone's outside the front window in the bushes."

On another night someone broke in the second garage where the limos were parked. A TV was stolen out of one limo, and gas was poured around the garage. The dog must have scared them off. But the final straw? Someone cut the screen out of my daughter's bedroom window. A warning that she could have been taken.

When I called the police again, I was advised that if I have to shoot the perpetrator, to make sure I take his hand and smash the window with it, then drag the body in. The officer said he would deny any and all accountability for this advice. That's the spirit of the law!

One night another disturbance in the yard set the dog off. I made the 911 call for help. When the police came to the door I had the gun with me, my paranoia was increasing. I stood away from the door in case someone wanted to shoot me. Boozer was barking, upset like I was. An officer who had been there before identified himself. I recognized his voice.

"OK. I'm going to open the door. I have my dog with me and a fully loaded Browning 9mm in my hand… I'm putting it down on the table next to the door."

I let them in, reporting a trespasser on the property, and another crime report was documented. It was tough enough living with unresolved issues but *strangers?* Threatening me through my children was the last straw—it was time to go ballistic. While the older kids were at school, I stormed through the house, talking to myself. "Threaten my kids, I will take you out!"

Repeated tragic acts of violence eventually change the way problems are resolved. For the next few nights, I hid in the bushes. Every sound, every suspect shadow was impending danger to my family and would be confronted with a 9-millimeter - including the rat that was trying to attack my parrot in the enclosed patio off the master bedroom.

## Sticks and Stones and Broken Bones

Ryan was sitting on the bed when I heard Mojo squawking as if his life were in danger. I got up and saw a huge rat attempting to bite his foot. I screamed through the glass, but the rat ignored me. I went for my gun, and loaded it, screaming for my brother to get Ryan. I opened the sliding glass door, *bam, bam, bam,* three shots to scare it off, but it didn't work. With one shot to the body, it flew across the floor, and out the door, dead. Meanwhile, Mojo's screeching, flying around the room and hs feathers were everywhere! I was hyper, ready for anyone—or anything—that night.

Completely under duress, dressed in black, including my face, smudged with coal, I sat waiting for the son of a bitch who was treading on the edge of my nerves, daring him to make a move toward my family. I was ready for him. But since I was waiting for the bastard to show up, naturally, no one did. Gotta love Murphy's law. Maybe the dead had something to do with it? What you don't know *can* hurt you.

According to Jack Musselman, my Palm Beach attorney, that was the problem, running a legal "taxi" service operation would set off red flags.

"You're money is clean, Linda," he said. "This is how some crooks launder their money."

In the meantime, he had hired a private investigator to camp out in his RV and patrol the property while my family slept. The investigator was the one who discovered footprints coming from over the wall behind the second garage where the limos were parked. This information was given to the police.

When the Boca Raton City Council voted my application down, I was through with Florida and its land sharks. "I'm selling the house," I told the kids. "We're going back to Michigan. It's time."

Michael, Sheila and Nicole were somewhat reluctant to leave, but excited to be seeing more of their grandparents and other relations. They had been cut off from family for many years. It was time to put their mark on Michigan. Ryan was still a toddler and didn't really care.

My father commended me for all the hard work and energy I put in to do the right thing as a businesswoman, not to mention the cash I spent. He was disappointed, but not with me.

"You did everything right, Linda. Those assholes (city council) weren't going to give you an operating license," he said. "You could tell they made up their minds before they voted."

What was I going to do now? The rest of my life seemed so far away. Moving back to Michigan was an emotional decision based on a feeling, "I just had to." I couldn't stay in Florida, besides my obvious legal and safety issues, an old friend of mine was toying with my sensibilities—*Boo!*

Less than a month after my father went back to Michigan, my angry tears woke the dead, and strange things began to happen around the house. The clocks would stop. Our dog Boozer would run from room to room, barking at empty space. Most times I attributed this behavior to something or someone outside, but then sometimes, I wondered... could it be... *Him?*

Tommy's daughter, Sheila was the first to encounter Leonard's spirit a few nights after the funeral. *Something* woke her up. She got up and went into the living room and, sitting on the sofa, she said to me the next morning, "I saw Daddy. He went into your room."

A couple of months after the funeral, while I was sleeping in bed with a light sheet on, I felt a chill in the air. When I opened my eyes and saw Leonard standing at the foot of the bed for a moment before he disappeared. I thought I was dreaming at the time. It occurred to me that Sheila had that special gift too. A few weeks later, a neighbor lady knocked on my door and confirmed it.

Sheila was at her friend's house playing while the neighbor was ironing in another room. The neighbor said she was thinking to herself about making cookies when Sheila answered her thoughts.

"Can I help you make the cookies?" It wasn't the first time something like that had happened, either, she said, which was why she had come to me. "This is the third time it's happened! She is reading my mind!"

A devout Christian, the lady was very worried about my daughter's unnatural talent. Life was getting stranger by the day.

One Thursday evening after Leonard died, my brother John came home to find all the gas burners on the stove were lit and the living room TV was airing *Hill Street Blues*. I was in my bedroom watching the show on another TV.

Johnny was very upset when I said for the tenth time, "It wasn't me." My brother had no idea that Thursdays had been our "dinner without the kids" night, our date night, the one night a week Leonard turned into our thing: Always steak and potatoes with a salad. After dinner, we would snuggle and watch our favorite show, *Hill Street Blues,* and talk; no booze, no drugs. Nights like this reminded me why I loved him. Leonard was watching us…

There was something Leonard was trying to tell me, I felt it. Then later, I had another dream:

*Leonard was alive, sitting in a hospital bed. He was telling me how sick he was and he was very sorry for everything he put me through. As I sat there in the dimly lit room, I could feel someone spying on us from behind the white curtain. I sensed my baby brother John. Ignoring the spy, I leaned in, kissing Leonard on the cheek.*

This dream was over.

The craziness going on at the Boca Raton house with attempted break-ins, paranormal activity, life threatening phone calls and now a weird dream was affecting my sixteen-year old brother's health. Johnny's blood pressure was dangerously high, so Mom wanted him to come home right away because my "lifestyle was too stressful." I wasn't trying to make things difficult for myself—shit happens.

From time to time, my parents argued over my mother's attitude towards her daughters. Considering everything seemed to go wrong when I did everything right to start a new business, daddy defended me, stating that I had managed to make a life for myself despite what happened in the past.

In the three months staying with us after Leonard died my dad did not see anything wrong with my lifestyle. I wasn't going out every night partying, taking in lovers, or ignoring my children. My only true vice? Pot. I didn't like to drink, but if I did, I got drunk, went to bed, and passed out.

Mom frequently said, "There is a time and place for everything." Using this as a daily guideline, I was up at the crack of dawn to start each new day clear-headed. I had to "maintain." I wasn't eighteen anymore. Quite frankly, *phew*! glad that's over.

Adjusting to another phase in life gets harder each time, but regardless what comes our way, the only way we adjust is to keep living. Logically, I knew I wasn't at fault for most of what happened throughout my life but it sure felt like it.

After John left Florida, I looked for a housekeeper, and found Hilda. As much as I need to be in control of things, I needed people who could think for themselves. I loved this girl. She was so good with the kids, and took care of the house without being told what to do. She was very spiritual, but facing spirits she never experienced until the morning we went to rent the U-Haul for the move back to Michigan [need some context here??].

When I had the kids with me, I drove my blue Lincoln Town Car, but around town I drove the Silver Bullet, our Mark IV with a four-barrel and a touchy carburetor that needed an extra splash of gas to help the engine get started. In other words, you had to gently pump the gas pedal twice before turning the key over. I knew that. But that morning, I forgot.

A typical spring morning, the kids were at school, and I had just placed my two-year old, Ryan, in the back seat of the Bullet. Hilda was closing the kitchen door as I sat behind the wheel. Just as Hilda opened the passenger door, I turned the ignition key over. No response other than a guttural groan from the engine.

"WELL, PUMP IT, GODDAMN IT!" I froze. Hilda froze. We both looked around to see where the voice, which sounded like Leonard's, came from.

Hilda was confused. "Did you say something to me?"

"No... I think that was Leonard's voice. I forgot to pump the pedal before I turned the key on."

"Linda, something won't let me get in the car!" Hilda was bug-eyed. She felt his invisible presence as I did. Leonard was sitting next to me.

"It's okay Hilda, watch—the car will start." I pumped the pedal, turned the key, the engine kicked in—and his presence was gone. Hilda sat down gingerly in the seat, worried that she might sit on him.

"He's gone, Hilda," I told her.

Hilda was a perfect fit for all of us. I offered Hilda a full-time job with pay and a place to live if she wanted to move to Michigan with us. I thrived with her around. I focus on creating a new life for the kids and me, whatever that was—maybe a book about Tommy and Leonard.

I wanted to do something creative in music too, and started writing lyrics, which proved to be pretty easy for me. My brother David challenged me to write a song before I left Florida. In less than twenty minutes, I had a country rock melody: *Another Man Crying*.

*I listened to man crying in his beer*
*He told me a story but it bored me to tears.*
*He said, "I loved her madly but she threw me out. I*
*tried to be honest and all she did was shout..."*
*"You take your dog, your cat, and bird. And*
*don't forget to take your toaster.*
*"But leave me the kids, the keys to the house, and*
*don't forget to shut the door on your way out!"*
*Three hours later and about fifteen beers, I'd had*
*all I could take; It'd been building for years.*
*It was just another man lying, another man dying.*
*Just another man crying in his beer.*
*You take your dog, your cat, and bird. And*
*don't forget to take your toaster.*
*But leave me the kids, the keys to the house, and*
*don't forget to shut the door on your way out!*

My brother David liked it. Like all my other poems, songs, and story ideas, I put it away for later.

I was leaving Florida without a plan except to write music and buy a house in the Pointes so my children could experience the area where their fathers grew up. A grieving widow with too much money can act out any unreasonable emotion that comes to mind. I was rushing my grief, trying to speed things up by moving away from the physical memories around our home. Dumb idea—one that cost me $40,000.

When I put the Boca Raton house up for sale, I was very specific. "I just want the $40,000 we put down on the house back." I wasn't interested in making a profit. The housing market was doing great. There was no excuse other than a slick, greedy agent who sold the house for less than we purchased it and mailed me a check for $4,000! I called her to say the check was a few zeros short.

"I thought you wanted to sell the house fast," She says to me, "And you only wanted $4,000." The lesson learned. Never make a money decision when you're emotional. But I had to learn the hard way.

# THE GHOSTS OF KENWOOD

## Can I get a witness?

> *There is never enough liquor to purge away*
> *the pain, but always enough to fuel the anger*
> *for a good fight... the truth within.*
> *- LLBK*

Leaving Florida was supposed to be a fresh start for me and the kids now that Leonard was gone I was looking for change. Life without Leonard meant geographically removing ourselves from the daily reminders. At least my children would have no time to dwell on the past. That was my problem, not theirs. I got what I wished for that night he held a gun to my head. Someone had to die. I got what I wished for on the summer day as a child. I was wealthy but I would take it back if I knew the price I had to pay.

In addition to my emotional state of abandonment and survivor's guilt, there was one issue following me around: the paranormal. Soon I would learn that this was something both sides of the Bodzsar-Bogard family had in common.

Wealthy enough to buy a big house, a "really big, big house," I went searching for something special, secretly hoping my parents would move in. Let mom and dad live free, go on trips, and be with each other. So, the real estate agent had a few homes lined up. None of them felt right. Driving from one house to another, I spotted the one I had to have.

"What about that house?" Pointing to the stately English Tudor with the slate roof and a pool in the back, without taking a tour, I said, "I want this one."

It had just been placed on the market and wasn't on the realtor's updated seller's list, but I wouldn't stop until I knew it was mine for sure. I was obsessed with 130 Kenwood. We went back to the real estate office while the realtor called to make arrangements to check out the property. "I gotta have it."

I accepted their full-price offer and wrote a check for the down payment for my new fortress. Then I made arrangements for my children to attend the Grosse Pointe Academy, a private school a block away from the house in one of the safest towns in the country.

Everybody loves a good ghost story, right? As long it is make-believe or it happened to someone else. To experience a ghost first-hand is not for the weak-minded, but the open-minded.

The first strange incident occurred in a matter of a few weeks after we moved in to Kenwood. I One afternoon it *appeared* to look like there was "a black bouncing ball, but it was a head going down the hallway." Hilda was the first to see it, and she quit the next day without a word. A few days later she called me to apologize but couldn't come back to the house because it was haunted.

Keeping in form with the Bogard way of dealing with life's curve balls, my cousin Sheri and I laughed our asses off. We were equally concerned the *head* may come back. I told my parents, friends, everybody. "Hilda says my house is haunted. So she quit." At least I knew I wasn't the only one who felt the spirits lurking around Kenwood.

After Hilda left, my cousin Sheri moved in to help. As we began to remodeled the 36-room mansion with the seven bathrooms, very strange and some scary things began to happen, without explanation. Way too many incidents were occurring to be denied. Our personal belongings would disappear, then reappear in another location. Bear and Mojo, our blue crown amazon parrot, were both reacting to things in the house as well. Dangerous things began to happen.

## Sticks and Stones and Broken Bones

Coming up from the basement stairs, my cousin Sheri felt someone push her, although no one was behind her. One evening *it* startled everyone at the same time, a table full of witnesses. We were eating dinner at the kitchen table when the *garbage disposal turned itself on.*

Each of us stared at the counter, trying to see who did it but no one was at the sink. No one wanted to turn it off, either. Everyone were frozen in their seats until I leaped up to flip the off switch. No one could finish eating, either—we were too excited. This was just the beginning.

One afternoon, Sheri went into the basement to do laundry. A circular saw was lying on the floor in the middle of the laundry room where the live-in handyman had left it earlier in the day when it turned itself on. Sheri left the laundry room, screaming for the handyman as she ran upstairs. "Wayne!"

Wayne ran downstairs and unplugged the saw.

In another incident, one winter's evening, Sheri and a few of her friends were hanging out with me in the sitting room of my bedroom. Bear was lying down next to the bed. As we were talking, a strange feeling came over me. Then Sheri exclaimed she felt "something weird," but it was the dog's reaction that captured everyone's attention.

Bear got up and stood next to me, growling toward the bedroom door. A cool breeze passed behind me. The hairs on my neck prickled, and Bear followed this chilly air right into the bathroom.

"Something's in this room!" I exclaimed I froze, it passed by me again. Bear was following *it*, chasing *it* out of the room, and then sat guard at the door, growling for a few more seconds. The dog went to lie down, but turned right around, running halfway down the staircase growling at *it* before coming back to the room.

"What the fuck was that about?" Sheri asked. "Did you guys see that? Bear saw something! What the fuck was it?"

"An angry man..." was all I felt. A man with a hat. But who? It can't be Leonard... or Tommy—They didn't wear hats. Needless to say, the rest of the evening was more a "show and tell" for all of us. It was apparent THAT spirits existed. I got what I came for: Validation and witnesses to boot!

Another time, a light fixture in the hallway next to the back stairs wouldn't turn off at either end— both switches. My daughter Sheila walked in from the kitchen when something said to me, "She can do it."

"Sheila, turn the switch off," I asked her, and you guessed it—the light went out.

The next day, my father came to do some work on the house and checked the wiring —there was nothing wrong with it. So many odd things were happening to everyone. Michael's glasses went missing and then, just *showed up* on the toilet seat in his bathroom. Sheila Marie was afraid to sleep in her room on the third floor because of a "ghost lady." Many mornings I found her sleeping in her sister, Nicole's room.

While doing dishes, something out of the corner of my eye got my attention. It looked like a black bouncing head-ball that my live-in help reported seeing. Now I saw it.

This freaked the hell out of me. I went to the hallway to see where it was going but it was gone. Mojo felt it, too: I heard him squawking and flapping his wings back in the kitchen. I turned and saw it: bounce through the doorway: a black head. I actually attempted to scream but it was more a yell.

"Holy shit!" I ran up the back stairs to the second floor, then up to the third to find my cousin and tell her what I saw. It was getting stranger by the day.

Besides costing a fortune to heat this fortress, when you walked in the furnace room, it looked we were running the Titanic—it was bigger than one of the bedrooms in my parents' house. Intimidating, to say the least if you didn't know what you were doing. Lucky for me, my father was a great teacher.

Since purchasing the house, the next person to check out the furnace was my father. Everything was running in "tip-top shape," reiterating the importance of one simple rule to follow with pilot lights: "Keep a window slightly open so it won't smother the pilot light."

The winter of 1984 was bitter cold, so close to Lake St. Clair, and I noticed aggravating old wounds and bones seem to hurt more

## Sticks and Stones and Broken Bones

in the damp and cold region of lower eastern Michigan. Kenwood had four fireplaces that I had prepped for the winter, and on a few nights, we had them all going to ease the fuel costs.

One evening the house felt a little chilly and I went to check all the radiators. On my way to the kitchen from the maid's quarters I went down the back staircase. *Odd*, I thought it was warmer in the staircase, which, usually was drafty. Instinctively, I felt the wall. *Hot as hell*. I ran and called the fire department. In minutes they were there. It was not the wiring as I thought, but a blown-out pilot light.

Somehow, the window that is never supposed to be shut was closed tight. Sheri, the kids and Wayne all swore they didn't do it. I believed them. Not one of them ever wanted to go into the furnace room, let alone close the window they all knew must stay open, or we'd die. Gotta love those old drafty houses—it's probably why we didn't notice the gas at first. It was a close call.

Leonard's sister was a spiritual ally when it came to anything paranormal. After telling her about our experiences, she informed me of a legend. "You know there's a curse on Windmill Pointe?" A great parlor story—but what about my house? I lived in the Farms, two Grosse Pointe cities away.

My curiosity was met with more questions than answers. My brother David, for some reason or another, was also curious about the property, taking it upon himself to research the history of the house. Incredible.

Our home switched more hands in its short 58-year history than I would have imagined. I was one of 15 owners, if you include the two banks that held title due to financial problems and a few same-day resales. I wasn't superstitious. After all, I did get married to a gay man on Friday the 13th—but this? It piqued my interest.

Over the years, there was also a lien placed on the Kenwood house, a civil action suit contesting the sale of the house, and another owner had to file bankruptcy. David wished me luck. Reading the property's history, I found it evident the land had a history of bad luck. Since moving to Kenwood, I had already lost $40,000 on the Florida house.

Kenwood, along with the Grosse Pointe Academy, was the former property of the Sacred Heart, an order of nuns who had built the convent house to school young ladies. In the 1920s, when the nuns needed money to expand their educational program, they sold the portion of their land where our home sat.

Adding to the home's romance and mystery were the eight magnificent full-grown silver maples in two rows planted on our front lawn. The story goes that the double row of trees were planted sometime in the late 1800s from the Convent to Grosse Pointe Boulevard along Kenwood Road, which became known as "The Nun's Walk."

A short time after discovering this, I had a dream:

*Looking out my bedroom window, facing the front of the house on the second floor, it was a clear day, looking below at the trees I saw eight nuns in coffins, one under each tree - they were turning over in their graves! Over and over.*

*Laughing in my dream, I woke. The probability of causing a few of the nuns from St. Tim's to do a few rollovers, if not, back pedal their way out of admitting any fault, was comical.*

"If they could see me now!" I chuckled.

Sharing my dream story with a few friends from Grosse Pointe had provided one rumor to find my ears. Some people believed that nuns were buried on the original property, though no evidence supports this tale - I did wonder, was it possible?

The history of Grosse Pointe legends dates back to the 1700s. A great story for children at the campfire, or entertaining guests on Halloween, was the legend about the sibling feud of Josette LeDuc and her brother, Jean Baptiste over family money and ownership of the grist mill. When Josette was on her deathbed, her brother was pressing her for information about his share of the mill.

Dying, with her last breath, she vowed he would never have the mill. "The devil can have it!" The people were real, but what of the curse? This was something Mom found curious as well.

## Sticks and Stones and Broken Bones

Like all legends, there is some truth behind them as goes the curse of Windmill Pointe. Tommy and I had lived on Alter Road, just a few blocks away. The home where Tommy was shot and killed was a part of the Windmill Pointe subdivision.

Fact: Thomas Eugene Holstin shot and killed 7/16/1974.

Fact: Josette LeDuc was a co-owner of the grist mill.

Fact: The Detroit War of 1712 between the French and the Indians at Windmill Pointe was brutal, and the dead warriors were buried where the battle was fought, along Lake St. Clair at Windmill Pointe. Relics can still be found if you look hard enough.

Fact: An English bomber carrying six crew members crashed on October 14, 1958, killing the crew. Strange thing about this? My father took me to see the wreckage from the plane, which could be found a few blocks over into the Pointes. The crash destroyed three houses on Ashland Street, the next block over the bridge where Leonard used to turn around to drive by my house— and the same name of the street I lived on with Tommy when Michael was born.

What I knew about factual GP history, I first learned from Tommy. The local Indians lived along Lake St. Clair before the French arrived. As a child, Tommy found an arrowhead at Windmill Park that he kept in a box. When he died, it disappeared.

By the time my children attended the Grosse Pointe Academy, I had given them a few experiences with various religious organizations. They attended service at a Jewish temple, a Baptist school, then to Sunday school with the Protestants in the summer.

Despite, the only time I went to church since '68 was for the occasional soul-searching moments of doubt, weddings, and funerals. My children would learn that people everywhere share a common ground, our human condition: we all bleed red, we all seek *something*.

# KENWOOD MANSION

## December 1983 Grosse Pointe, Michigan

It was too cold to think. The winter months had taken their toll. No way out of this miserable despair. Another restless night. No warmth or sleep, chilled to the bone by memories. Tommy had been dead for nine years. Leonard had been dead for 19 months, and it wasn't getting any easier. No sum of money could replace the men I loved or bring back my children's fathers. It was a cold day in hell.

Tossing another log on the bed of coals, no amount of wood could take the chill from my soul. Losing myself in a fire wind of thoughts, I had a shot of whiskey to ease the pain, to numb my senses. How far does one take loyalty?

After the trial in '81, I was prepared to write Tommy's story, but his sister couldn't see what good would come of it, asking me to let it go. I told her I would think about it. Two years I thought about it. "But it's my story, too," I realized, and started writing the facts down.

What do you do after being kidnapped, date-raped, sexually molested, mugged, then thrown in front of an oncoming car, held hostage with a gun to your head, a knife to your throat, a witness to the shooting death of a loved one and then finding the body of another?

I'll tell you what you do. You play out your hand the way you see fit. You learn to take the good with the bad. And do yourself a favor, see a shrink.

The winter of 1983-1984 in Southeastern Michigan was colder than normal. Ice storms, snow drifts, and ravaging winds crept

## Sticks and Stones and Broken Bones

through cracks of the master bedroom. My back and shoulders were stiff, my head too heavy to hold my neck up. The signs of aging attacked my compromised skeletal system. My bones hurt. Old broken bones, especially hurting from Osteoporosis.

The glowing fireplace radiated intense heat, warming the back of my legs. Ignoring the fire, I wandered back and sat down at the table, perplexed by the complexity of RAM and the world wide Web provided by CompuServe Network. My Macintosh was indicative of a new world changing rapidly, moving forward into the future—and I was stuck in the past.

I thought about Delray, Grandma Beno too, and what she said while holding her great-grandchild high above her: "If I could do it again, things would be different."

This gave me reason to believe Grandma may get her wish. and come back to do life, again. A do-over. I was having more déjà vu moments since meeting Tommy. For the time being, I could not see the point of changing anything if it meant never knowing Tommy or Leonard, I was the mother of their children. I did not want to change that, ever. This is who I am. A woman with an interesting history that isn't so pretty, but rich in lessons learned.

A computer setup worth $5,000 was useless to me. I had trouble following the instructions. It was like being in school except no one was yelling me because I didn't understand. I stared at the computer screen, lost in this new world of technology entering our lives. Technology could wait one more day.

Hoping to numb my distorted thoughts, I got up and poured another shot of whiskey, to make a toast.

"To the priest in the white convertible Cadillac and red-leather interior with a flask of whiskey hidden inside the pages of his Bible."

I'm remembering that mid-July, 1970, when I was hitchhiking to Charlevoix, Michigan. How ironic that a priest would pick me up and give me a ride. It was obvious to him I was having a hard time adjusting to my upcoming divorce from Rousku.

"Drink this, he said. "You need a shot of whiskey."

## Linda Lee King

I didn't drink a lot of alcohol—mostly whiskey sours. Beer just tasted awful. But this whiskey? WOW. I liked it. I found my poison. I had another shot as instructed, then placed it back in the book. Two shots of whiskey, and the next thing you know I'm confessing my life story to this priest. Alcohol, the original truth serum.

When I stopped blabbering about my confusing life, the priest said there was nothing wrong with me. He handed me another bible, without a flask in it. Told me to open it and read: 1 Corinthians 13: 4-13 and to pay particular attention to verses **8-10** and **13**. Whenever in doubt, this was my resolve:

*Love is patient, love is kind. It does not envy, it does not boast, it is not proud. It does not dishonor others, it is not self-seeking, it is not easily angered, it keeps no record of wrongs. Love does not delight in evil but rejoices with the truth. It always protects, always trusts, always hopes, always perseveres.*

*Love never fails. But where there are prophecies, they will cease; where there are tongues, they will be stilled; where there is knowledge, it will pass away. For we know in part and we prophesy in part, but when completeness comes, what is in part disappears.*

*When I was a child, I talked like a child, I thought like a child, I reasoned like a child. When I became a man, I put the ways of childhood behind me. For now we see only a reflection as in a mirror; then we shall see face to face. Now I know in part; then I shall know fully, even as I am fully known.*

*And now these three remain: faith, hope and love. But the greatest of these is love.*

The Church and religion in general had their flaws, the priest admitted, saying that I should use my experiences to help others and certainly, don't lose faith in myself. He lifted my spirit above the gray clouds of self-doubt with kind words of fortification to protect my heart with faith, hope, and love. Use my experiences to help others? Wondering how could I help others when I couldn't help myself?

But there I was, more than a decade later, back at square one. Another long night ahead. My bed empty... again, but not my life. It is full of adventure, mystery, and love.

## Sticks and Stones and Broken Bones

Sleeping alone where dreams should be shared—instead, I was in a house of madness, living in my Kenwood mansion with the kids and extended family. Walking in circles like a caged animal, hoping to understand the events in my life. My bedroom was a prison of haunting memories.

Driving me were extreme circumstances and a gut feeling to continue setting standards one situation at a time. Give myself an option because I learned nothing is set in stone and if one keeps chipping away the problem will be exposed.

Detroit was the same as it was when I left in 1977; another dreary and depressing day. "Why the hell did I come back?" I wondered. What was the point? Everyone I'd ever loved, gone, in a heartbeat. Sometimes, I would get drunk enough to sleep with someone, just so there would be a warm body next to me. One that breathed. Then one day. I just didn't care anymore. No one would get close to my heart again.

Haunted by Leonard's restless soul, I was angry for what might have been in a clean and sober world I had envisioned. My upbringing taught me to never give up the good fight. Ingrained, embedded...delusional. Sometimes, you have to walk away from all that is familiar to see where you need to be in life. I was right where I belonged, for now.

It is easy to love a dead man when the worst part of the relationship is over. It was disturbing, yet gratifying. The daily flight-or-fight routine with Leonard was over. This was taking a while to sink in. Writing songs, poetry, gathering the bits and pieces of my bittersweet world, I found myself staring at the spotted goose egg on the mantel, a hand-made ornament gift from Grandma Bogard, mocking me.

"Peace on earth, my ass." In the background, a song by the Doors was playing. "No one here gets out alive..."

I stood staring at the Christmas ornament on the mantel. "What do I do now?" My answer remained hollow as the nativity scene within the hollowed goose egg, while silently a voice sounding more like Grandma Bogard was in my head, scolding me because I wanted an answer that I already knew.

Shaking her head, often Grandma Bogard often told Mom, "That poor ol' soul, you should have let her go off to the convent like she wanted to—she wouldn't have had to go through all this."

"Poor old soul?" Why would she say that? It didn't matter that I felt old, but my soul was anything but poor. It was a vault filled with valuable information, but it was useless like the computer unless I learned how to use it. I asked a rhetorical question. "What do I do now?"

Ignoring the fire, I wandered away from the computer. Circling my room like a shark, trying to understand the events in my life that brought me to this prison of memories and tears. Commencing with the pen in my hand, unwilling words shared my thoughts, constrained by a cold shoulder of doubt.

Was I as strong as everyone seemed to believe? Did I really have faith or was I fooling myself? The fire was losing its strength. A battling flickr begged for attention. So did my heart and soul. I had to cope with my failures as a wife and mother. The phone rang.

In my mother's words, "You made your bed, now lie in it."

*"This was my doing?* I didn't pull the trigger, Ma." I hung up the phone.

All I wanted was for her to watch the kids for the weekend. How could she say this to me? Why did Mom resent me and my sister for not wanting to live her lifestyle? It was hard enough living our lives with the crap we went through as kids, but I couldn't be her.

Forgiveness came with a price—it had to come from the heart, and Mom wasn't willing to give it. Mom never forgave the Japanese for Pearl Harbor, or her father for being a drunk, and she would never forgive me for leaving home at seventeen.

Smoldering ashes gave way to these negative thoughts dangling in my head. Wondering if my deceased husbands' spirits met, like in the dream? Would they take turns watching out for me and the kids?

A signal to quit dwelling on the past broke my trance. Bear had his nose pressed against the window, barking at someone walking away from our house across the snow-covered lawn toward a parked police car in front of the neighbor's house directly across the street.

As the man walked in the outer light of the street lamp, I saw it was a Grosse Pointe Farms cop.

"What the hell do they want?" I didn't expect the dog to answer me, but I did need him to be quiet. "Shh, It's okay, boy." My new furry friend was very protective.

Together we watched the parked police car. The dog continued growling under his breath. The patrol car finally drove away into the night without the headlights on. I told my father, who wondered why I didn't move back to Trenton to be closer to them. But I couldn't do it. I wanted to be a constant reminder what happened to Tommy's children could not be forgotten.

"Just because I'm paranoid doesn't mean I'm crazy or someone isn't out to get me."

The facts were clear enough. Too many pieces of my life were scattered among the cremated ashes sitting in urns on the mantel next to the ornament, reminding me that every cop was a potential threat to my family's well-being.

It was impossible to make out the number on the patrol car to report the incident. Ever since I came back to the scene of the crime, my memory and paranoia were equally triggered. I thought I was behaving quite normally, considering my experiences. Twenty-five years later, my therapist explained the feeling to be "on guard" is called the hyperarousal state of PTSD.

Confined to the childhood visions playing in my head like an old movie, thoughts of an empty future faced me; a familiar chill forced the hairs on my arms to stand straight up. Then I heard that *damn voice* again. "Linda, how can you see a future if you haven't resolved the past?"

Surrounded with the souvenirs my dead lovers left behind, I rummaged through the boxes, collecting these memories; cards of affection, photos, and a tape-recorded message still in the answering machine that I kept. I pressed play:

"Linny? Are you there? Pick up... I'll be home in a little while... why don't you get a sitter for tonight?"

It was Leonard's last message taped a few days before he died. Not many people knew I had a nickname, but Linny-Lin Skins suited me. Leonard said because I was always changing, adapting to the environment like a chameleon.

Before Leonard died, I expressed my desire to have a career either writing, singing, or maybe do some acting, but something had to change for me. I wasn't doing all that I could to fulfill my childhood dreams. Lots of money and the time to do it, I dreamed big.

"Why shouldn't I tell our story?" I'm not ashamed of my life or the people I loved or the mistakes I made.

Leonard knew. When I made up my mind to follow through with an idea, nothing would stop me from accomplishing my desired goal. Any job I ever went after, I got it.

"Who's going to take care of me and the kids when you're on the road?"

It didn't matter what he thought now. Turning the recorder off, I remembered something Monti Rock III said after Leonard's funeral. "Widow weeds, that's your trademark. Go with that," he said.

I thought about it. Monti was right, I did handle death well—too well. I looked absolutely stunning in black. "Write something... anything."

The page remained blank, just like the computer screen. An empty soul searching for inspiration among the ruins of my past, I stared into space. Nearly a full year dressed in black, people were *forced* to deal with me. I made an entrance everywhere I went. Not flashy, but I found a more effective entry was one of subtly. My widow weeds said it all.

Sorting out the memorabilia was proof the men I loved existed. I opened their urns and tenderly sifted through the ashes, pretending to run my fingers through their hair. It was unfair. I could never choose between the two men if a choice had to be made. It was time to pry open the living tomb.

These tools chipped away every fact and plausible theory science taught and religion preached. They are both flawed, based on prejudice aimed at conditioning children to fit into society's conception of normality for that time period.

For too long science ignored anything supernatural. and the church ignored anything based on scientific facts. The only thing anyone can do is pick and choose what brings truth to your heart.

My life didn't take the conventional road, though I tried. The problem was after what I had been through, I didn't believe in a conventional world. My track record said it all. I was divorced once, widowed twice with four kids. What man could even come close to fill the gap in my heart with unconditional love? I needed a porter to carry the excess baggage I was lugging around.

Daddy was joking, but he was a tad serious. When Leonard and I married, he said. "Finally, now I don't have to worry about you." He spent most of my life worrying about me. He went out of his way to set me up on a blind date after Leonard died.

"Linda, girl, get yourself a man while all your body parts are still working. You're too young to be alone."

Marry another man? Why? He'll be dead within a year just like the other two. Besides, I didn't have any room for a relationship. I still grieved for Tommy. Out of respect for my worried father, I went out on that date to make him happy and to see what my father considered a "catch."

Honestly, not bad. If I had not been with Tommy or Leonard, this was a good match but in comparison, it was a step down. He reminded me of my California Angel on a Harley. Tommy was good-looking, smart, creative, fun-loving, and happy. Leonard, handsome, smarter and tougher than Tommy, but not so happy or creative. His talents worked the other side of the brain.

My blind date wasn't bad looking. Smart, too but I just couldn't see myself with someone who took a motorcycle apart in his living room while playing too much country for my taste. In another lifetime, maybe—not this one. He simply did not have enough life experiences to understand my quirky behavior.

Placing the urns back on the mantel, Mom's voice was in my head telling me "Don't cry too long. The dead can't rest," Mom always said. "Our tears keep them here."

So many nights without sleep lumped into days. Worn out. And a bottle of Wild Turkey. What more could a girl ask for? "You can't bring back the dead, Linda girl." But it didn't stop me from trying.

In the midst of my cluttered keepsakes, I found an untitled poem written after Tommy died:

> *Unwritten poetry filled with illusions*
> *Awareness a living matter of emotion*
> *Like a poem burning words on the pages*
> *Ignited by the touch of your fingers*
> *Romance and laughter is what I had here*
> *Covered in black I weep a silent tear*
> *The memory engages and a smile appears*

Tommy's sister could not ask of me what I could not give, my silence. It was safe loving dead men. I broke down and cried. With each sob, the wind scolded my negligence. The fire went out. Not my desire to be heard.

Mourning these unwelcomed losses, too young to be widowed twice. My young children subjected to my world of sorrow and obsessions induced by life-altering events. Past events evolved into chronic disorders. Self-medication numbed the senses. Another shot, another memory, another lifetime. It's been more than *an interesting life*.

Struck by Jack Frost, a chill emerged through my pores. The hairs on my arms stood up. A voice, so clear, spoke to me: "Linda, forgive the past." Function in the present.

It was obvious by my actions alone that I was chained to the emotional past. I has never spread Tommy's ashes; I had been carrying them around for eight years. Now? Two bodies to let go. "Ashen Lady, indeed," I thought.

## Sticks and Stones and Broken Bones

Still listening to the Doors, but instead of a beer, I had another shot of whiskey. It was going to be another long night...

A chill was running through my bones. It would remain until the spring thaw promised to announce summer's arrival, but it still wasn't warm enough to melt the ice around my heart. Asking myself countless times, "What else was I looking for in Detroit? What was the point?"

Craving a balance for my children was a primary goal, but in my mind, it always seemed impossible. I was sensitive to "things that went bump in the night." I came looking for the dead. Ignoring the cold shoulder of self-doubt, I began to write my way out of this wretched despair, with words to plead my case.

*Racing with time across the skies...*
*Medieval morning sunrise...*
*Time unlimited... exit unknown*
*Daybreak approaching*
*Steam off the burning earth elevates me to tears*
*Houses made from concrete fears*
*Time for a change*

Dancing around the room, I pretended my husbands would come calling. It was safe loving dead men. With each sob, the wind outside scolded my negligence. The fire had died, but never the love, the guilt, or the anger that burdened my life.

My parents were wholesome. Through thick and thin, they stuck it out. They were not alcoholics, violent people, or wanted by the FBI. In this light, I was a very lucky kid growing up, all the benefits of the American Dream. This was my parents' life, not mine.

Traumatic experiences such as rape, murder, and other atrocities of unkindness created a grave distance between the people I loved and me. The anger toward Leonard's uncontrollable drinking, the drugs, and the violence buried the love I had for him. My lack of sharing was a way to protect his children from my biased opinions.

Grief will not be deprived its right to properly mourn our dead. No matter how many years it takes or houses you move to, grief will follow you until it has been dealt with. Tommy's death was tragic. If I spoke about it, people claimed I was living in the past, but I never fully mourned this loss. No one knew the extent of my mental state, myself included.

Writing was my safety net I would cast out into my sea of doubts, dragging it along the bottom, reeling in anything in its path looking for the prize.

*Here comes the end of your world*
*No looking back*
*Living on the edge*
*Hear God's children cry at night.*

# A WIDOW'S REGRET

## Your wish is granted

Call it fate, bad luck, or the desperate wish of an abused wife, but what are the odds I would be wearing widow weeds, again? In less than a year after we were married, Leonard was dead. A bittersweet ending to a troubled life when death solves a problem.

The money from the court case may have eliminated the everyday stress of keeping my children well fed after many years of mac 'n' cheese. Money was freedom to shed the cloak of lies we hid behind so many years, but it's only money.

Too much drama living with an alcoholic/drug abuser: add lots of cash, and you get insanity. What do you do when the cash in your hand is cold as the dead you buried? You spend it when your head is in the wrong place. What did I do with the money? I spent. I lent it and gave it away.

Money fixes many problems, but it cannot repair a broken heart or save you from yourself. No amount of money can prevent mental health illness or the guilt that was eating at me from a desperate wish that came true.

It was a load off my mind to pay bills on time: no more coupon clipping, dented can sales, or reduced meats. Two, three times a week I was grocery shopping, coming home with $300 to $700 worth of supplies in case of an emergency. Two refrigerators full and two full pantries.

My disorders were well embedded in my habits. Grocery shopping was disguising some kind of disorder. Another habit developed. If

I didn't like someone, the moment they left the property, I would sweep away the bad vibes with a broom as they walked away. When I realized I was doing this, I fought to break the habit, but another took its place.

Blood money—hell of a term. The definition? Payment for the homicide (wrongful death) of a family member.

Expelling my self-pity, the next morning I woke up on the bathroom floor greeted by the porcelain goddess, wondering 'why' the hell the GPF cops wouldn't just leave me alone? What was that cop doing on my property last night? The case was over. Tired of being followed and spied upon, I wanted people to leave me alone to think and put my life into perspective. I called Hudson Meade, my attorney and told him what happened. He called me an hour later stating I would not have any more problems.

Clear-headed and relieved, I read the computer instructions again.

"I did it!" Proud of myself for figuring out how to operate my computer, I began to write:

*In our dreams we are told, coincidental history unfolds. Spirits too, heard screams in the night. Angel, angel take my message home. Tell the Father, things aren't right—it's an overload.*

How could any parent prepare a child for hardships they never experienced? My parents were at a loss.

So how did I get here on the floor, purging my anger into the pit of the porcelain goddess? Not a drop of booze in my parents' home growing up. We were safe and protected from things that happened to other kids.

Not once in all the years I knew my father, never did he place a hand on my mother in anger. Yet I had been abused by nuns, strangers, and lovers. These tears I shed are of anger... not pity!

Mental illness symptoms may not occur for months or even years following a traumatic experience but if you are living in a constant state of chaos, how do you know the difference between normal and abnormal behavior?

For a while, I avoided people and public places just in case of fear of a meltdown and that I would "lose it." No one in the family thought it strange to see a grown woman in her thirties growling at people. It was funny because I was normally eccentric. It wasn't until I caught myself growling at an inept Kmart cashier that I realized people were looking at me. I laughed it off.

"I'm trying not to cuss like a sailor," I said to the lady behind me. Not sure what she thought but I could see—I needed to pay more attention to tame my compulsive nature to be combative and defensive at the drop of a hat.

A life reduced to a cliché: *What doesn't kill you makes you stronger.* Or *Something good will come of this.* What a bunch of crap to convince ourselves *everything will work out for the best.*

Extreme ideas popped through my mind on that bathroom floor. Either I would go back to California again, or I was packing it up and heading for the Canadian wilderness.

"Yup, that's the ticket," I thought. "Get the fuck outta Dodge."

Life already proved to be a high stakes game; may as well place a bet and roll the dice. I was looking to replace my pain with new high-risk adventures. Try my luck elsewhere, since living among two-legged animals proved to be just as deadly as one on all four legs.

"I'd rather take my chances with the bears."

Everybody has their share of disappointments and heartaches; that's life but enough is enough. A battle began on that bathroom floor. Built-up aggression was being fueling by the meant-well condolences for the grieving widow. "Everything will work out for the best."

"Something good will come of this." Seriously, if one more person said, "time heals all wounds." I told Sheri, "I just might have to bop 'em one."

What good will come from my children being fatherless? No one could answer that truthfully except me. And I wouldn't say it. In fact, I didn't say much of anything about their fathers. What could I say without hurting someone's' feelings, because I still didn't understand the complexity of mental illness or addictions?

Money provided the means to stay busy with endless projects that kept me off the road of destruction despite my detours with booze and drugs. Money kept the kids busy trying out new things: Music lessons, karate classes—whatever they wanted to explore, I gave it to them.

Ready for a fight, I was looking to settle the score with a dead man for leaving us alone and damaged. It didn't matter now. Right before his death, I had been planning to leave Leonard if he didn't quit the drugs and drinking. Now, he was forever dead, and the option was no longer on the table, but a heavy dose of guilt was served.

Still feeling the whiskey, I was angry all over again. Pissed off at God, secretly hoping the relentless reaper would tell me *why*. I prayed aloud and cursed even louder. "Isn't this fucking over yet? Whatever it is? I have a few bones to pick!"

This was the pinnacle of my life. Fight or flight. "It's not fucking fair … I can't choose one over the other!"

That was the point. Love is not restricted to one soul mate. It depends on what the soul needs at the time you meet a soul mate. Washing my face, looking at my reflection, I reflected what my father said outside the courtroom.

"Linda girl, you hit the mother lode. What a shame it happened this way."

As the saying goes, "If Mohammed won't come to the mountain, then the mountain must come to Mohammed," or in this case, *me*.

Ghosts, the intense dreams I was having? There was *something* in my subconscious trying to get my attention, but dealing with the other daily issues while renovating more than 6,000 square feet of house kept me distracted me from this *feeling*.

To show my appreciation for all the work that went into the Kenwood house, I decided to have a pig-roast party for 300 on the Fourth of July. On the way to Kmart in St. Clair Shores, the strangest thing happened. I heard a paranormal voice give me an order. "Turn here!"

## Sticks and Stones and Broken Bones

It was the entrance to a car wash about a block away from Kmart. I had no reason to turn in because my car was washed the day before. I had people at home who took care of the cars, but I had to obey that voice. A Eureka moment.

In line ahead of me was Edward Serwach, the cop who had killed Tommy. I sat in my red Lincoln watching him, standing alone and staring at nothing but empty space. I froze, afraid to get out of my car. I waited until he got into his blue Cadillac. Often, I regretted not telling him in person, "I forgive you."

Coincidence? Ironic? No, this was my destiny. The hand of the universe guiding me to forgive this man who looked like a pale shell on some distant shore, alone with his regret. He too suffered from this tragic day. This is *why* I had to come back. Old business. 360 Alter Road? Altered my life and everyone else in its path that night.

Forgiveness is part of the healing cycle. Once realized, I began the grieving process for Leonard… nearly a decade for those issues to be resolved. In the interim of trying to heal old emotional wounds, my financial circumstances were causing stress and added trauma-drama.

The South Florida sunshine, with its warm, salty but buoyant ocean was a natural remedy for old broken bone injuries and aching joints, which went unnoticed until I moved back to Michigan. The last two winters I was constantly cold. My blood "thinned-out" apparently after living in Florida for seven years. Canada was out.

Sometime after the Fourth of July I went bike riding with Sheila and Nicole. We were just a few blocks from home. I hollered out to Sheila, "STOP!" Up ahead at the corner the stop light was about to change. Too late, she chose to ignore me and rode into the street just as the light changed.

A driver making a left turn hit Sheila Marie, she flew in the air and landed on the windshield, rolling down off the car onto the ground, landing in the car's path, luckily, the woman was driving 15 mph and stopped before running her over. The police arrived as I scooped up my child. I shouted out, "it's not her fault… my daughter rode into the street."

Needless to say, I was a wreck. The accident occurred right in front of Cottage Hospital. I scooped up my child, jumped over the hedges and ran into the emergency room. Minor cuts and bruises was all she suffered. Me? I had a flashback.

Crying, knowing what happened to another little girl decades ago, my rage exploded into life lesson lecture. Again, I reminded Sheila, "Duck when I say duck!"

"And for Christ's sake! STOP when someone tells you to. Listen. It might save your life! You could have been killed!"

Screaming at my wounded child, visibly she was afraid. I did not handle this well. I softened my voice. "I'm not kidding, Sheila I love you. It's a dangerous world. I'm trying to keep you alive so you can grow up."

It was an odd dream. One I should have paid more attention to:

*Through the darkness, a grand piano whizzed by me, its ivory keys playing out of tune—then it was gone. The next scene, I found myself in the bathroom, looking in the cabinet underneath the sink. Hidden there was $40,000 cash.*

The amount of the check I just wrote for studio time to record songs that I was working on.

One morning on my way to the airport, something was keeping me from making my flight to California. My bags were packed and ready. My glasses were missing from the bathroom counter where I left them. Sheri and two of my live-in housekeepers went from room to room. Nowhere to be found. I resolved this by wearing my contacts, but then, when I was about to put my boots on...

"Where the hell are my boots?!" Once again, we searched each room.

I went into Nicole's room, walked through the connecting bathroom into Michael's room - Sheri went to the third floor with Ann. Brad went to the kitchen. I was heading toward the staircase when I saw the missing boots standing together in the middle of the bedroom.

"Hey, guys?" I hollered. "Who found my boots?"

No one did, everyone looked as surprised as I was.

"We were looking for them with you," Sheri said.

No doubt we were all getting a little aggravated, looking for things that just seem to disappear, then reappear. I went into the bathroom to wash my hands. Sitting on the counter, where I left them: my glasses. Weird and unnerving—some spirit had a thing for glasses.

If I had missed my flight, the recording session would have been postponed, but not without added costs. I already booked and paid for the four-hour session. Much to my distress, when I did arrive, on time. tracks were already laid down. They were waiting on me to do vocals. I was not ready for this.

When I walked into Skip Saylor Studios, Davey Johnstone, a guitarist known for his work with Elton John, was standing next to the soundboard in the control booth. He came out to greet me.

"So, you're a mom?" He says, "and you rock and roll, too?"

"Yeah, if you want to call it that," I said. "How could you put the tracks down when I didn't get to work on any of the songs I wrote?"

That's when I discovered Johnstone had no idea what I was talking about. The man I hired as a manager to put the musicians together misled me as well. I knew I was going to do a remake, but I thought one song would be an original. "Yes, I expected one fucking original song."

I mean, I did pay cash upfront to the tune of $40,000! I made the best of it and recorded one picked out for me. *Supercool*, written by Elton John for Kiki Dee in the 70s, who happened to be Davey's girlfriend. Which is probably why I didn't need approval from Elton John to redo the song, that I struggled with for hours, but I finished it. I was surprised how many people liked the song.

The remake I picked out, *L.A. Woman*, was finished in no time. I knew that song —I felt that passion—it was more my style. It rocked! I knew it did. Johnstone, standing behind the soundproof glass in the control booth, had a big smile on his face, I could see he was excited about the mix. He picked up the phone and called Ray Manzarek, the original keyboardist for the Doors.

Davey raised the telephone receiver over his head and turned up the volume, shouting over the music. "Hear that? Now that's how it's done!"

Pretty much on my own, I was trying to earn what I had the hard way. Work my way up to success through my own efforts using the talents I had. Sharing fame and glory was never a problem, because I was afraid to be vain or egotistical. These were deadly sins or flaws in human character. What I wasn't prepared for? EGOMANIACS!

The music industry is full of self-proclaimed liberators—too many egos clashing among lead guitar players, lead singers, sound engineers, and writers too. I was not accustomed to working in a room full of people whose only goal is to be number one on the charts or among peers.

Granted, not all creative people are like that. Lucky for me, I met Vernon Bullock through another connection. Before meeting Vernon, I was more inclined to do *L.A. Woman*, but another producer suggested it wasn't a good remake for a woman to do. Yeah, right, I should have listened to my voice.

At the time I wanted to do *L.A Woman*, Manzarek was planning to direct a music video of the same song for MTV. I don't know but it does make me wonder—was this the reason for the phone call?

Vernon didn't mind helping someone else to shine because he wasn't an egomaniac. He also had a proven track record as a songwriter/producer from Motown Records since the 1960s. Knowing I was not qualified to put a music career together on my own, Vernon helped me to produce *Supercool*.

When I arrived in Los Angeles, arrangements were made for me to stay at the Sunset Marquis in West Hollywood. Much to my surprise, the hotel was booked as a hideaway for the rich and famous. Everywhere I looked, there was someone famous. The odd thing is, the day before I arrived, I was watching a Rush video on MTV, Early Distant Warning.

While packing my suitcase, I looked up, then blurted out to my cousin Sheri, "I have a feeling I'm going to see these guys."

## Sticks and Stones and Broken Bones

Sitting by the pool having breakfast was Geddy Lee from Rush. He was with his wife and son, the baby in the video. Polite smiles and nods was the best I could muster up when I had the opportunity to introduce myself.

In the pool was Rodney Dangerfield looking a little hungover, his face puffy with a red nose. Must have been a rough night, I thought. I sat there watching while a few were looking at me, wondering who this unknown could be. I fit in. I was just as strange as the rest of them.

Vernon came up to my room to pick me up to go out for a late lunch. When Vernon and I stepped in, a few people were in the elevator: a woman with her daughter, and an elderly man along with an inebriated roadie for Cory Hart's band.

As I was about to push the button, a feeling came over me I could not prevent if I tried. "Oh my God—we're going to get stuck." And still, I pushed the damn button, and turned to look at Vernon. The elevator stopped.

Let me tell you, I was freaked out. Then to turn around to see all eyes were all on me, as if I had done it, but I hadn't. It was an overwhelming feeling. I was getting my wish. Paranormal witnesses were piling up.

That night, I received a frightening phone call from home. Someone in a white van tried to kidnapped my daughter Nicole on her way home from school. She was two houses away from home, when the two men approached her, but before they could grab Nicole, she jumped off the bike and let go as she pushed it toward the men.

Running away and screaming, Nicole made it to the neighbor's house as they drove off. I was lucky to have a houseful of people to care for the kids when I was out of town, which wasn't often.

The police were called, but never found the guys in the van or her bike. I was assured of one thing. It doesn't matter what we do to keep our loved ones safe from physical or emotional harm if fate decides it's your turn to play.

With a good director, Jim Weiss, and with Vernon on board, *Supercool* ended up a quality video. But not without chaos. Starting with the day Marvin Gaye died.

We were heading out to an event in a classic 1967 Lincoln limo stretch with the suicide doors. Vernon sat up front in the passenger seat and Sheri directly behind him, while I sat behind the driver. t so happened that we were talking about Marvin Gaye.

Vernon knew Marvin and worked with him telling us a few recording stories—then we heard on the radio. Marvin Gaye was dead. "No, that can't be…"

It's got to be some kind of April Fool's Day joke? This is what we wanted to believe. We knew it was true. Vernon was a pale black man. He cared about this person. Then, for the life of me, I don't know how or what possessed me to open the suicide door while traveling at 60 mph, but I did.

It took everything to pull myself back into the vehicle before the car ahead would crash into me. Sheri just froze. Vernon was out of reach. I was speechless, but alive. Something made me do it like in the elevator—I could not stop myself. Was it some kind of reenactment before it happened?

"Why did you open the door!?!" Vernon was blown away. Sheri started apologizing and crying for not grabbing me. Breathing calmly was my objective, or my heart was going to jump out of my chest and explode. "I don't know *why.*"

One night, while filming at the Wyandotte Museum, a few of the extras and I were all feeling a little weird. One dancer thought someone pushed her, and I thought I saw a woman on the landing, but no one was there.

The night of our final videotaping of *Supercool* at Saint Andrews Hall in Detroit was another freaky night. It was an all-day affair, and next door, the employees of Blue Cross/Blue Shield could hear us and began wandering in during rehearsal.

By the end of the day people off the street came in, filling up the Hall nicely for the last taping. This was an opportunity to work with an audience—the energy in the air was intense. When we finished, the audience cheered and clapped. People were smiling, and that made me smile more.

Suddenly, a few guys grabbed me off the stage and carried me over to the bar, sitting me on top of it while people were clamoring over me, asking questions, having me sign autographs. I had a panic attack and bolted out the front door.

Mentally and physically, I was overpowered and traumatized. I flashed back. A few months earlier, a group of friends and I had gone to Cobo Hall to watch the July Fourth fireworks. Seconds before I was attacked, I said out loud, *"I'm not supposed to be here."*

A man came rushing behind me from the crowd, slightly knocking me off balance. Another man came charging through the crowd after the first man. The asshole raised his fist and punched me at the base of my spine with such force that I had no feelings in my legs. Luckily, Lewis Stockard, a longtime family friend caught me before I went down.

A Detroit police officer saw the incident and followed in pursuit into the crowd of thousands. I never knew if they caught the man or not. It made no difference. The damage was done. I was afraid to be in a crowd. s a result, I had herniated two discs. This added to my list of back injuries that have caused years of suffering.

The flashback was over. Gasping for air, I looked up. The full harvest moon, rising, shone its moonbeams down on me. "It's yours—you can do this." I was having a panic attack, but I thought I was just feeling a "little hyper—high-strung," as Ma put it.

Facing the crowd was more intense than my desire to succeed. so I would do all the right things to get where I needed to be and then sabotage each success with an excuse to hide my biblical –based fear that a rich man can't get into heaven.

I worked hard at going broke, but I had some professional help along the way from the crooks of Wall Street. Investing a sizeable chunk of money into the market is not for the fainthearted or anyone not willing to be a money-pawn in the game run by greedy corporations, crooked stockbrokers, and billionaires in power.

When I opened a money market account with Merrill Lynch, I had a decent portfolio and an account executive who did a fantastic job. However, something transpired that bothered me, causing me to change brokers when I moved to Michigan.

In the bathroom of the Fort Lauderdale office, my agent was doing a line of cocaine, which, of course, she offered to me. I liked the lady, she had a good background but doing coke with her during working hours was pause for concern, even though I tooted a line. I kept my thoughts to myself.

It was a plausible reason for moving my money to a local brokerage firm. In addition to investing my money, I read the business section intensively, following my investments like a hawk. One in particular, Great Bay Casino—this was a winner.

The day I hoped to be payday came and went below the value of my investment. This pissed me off because no attorney would help me or listen to how they ripped me off that day, the Feds had not yet discovered the shady practices these brokerage houses conducted and got away with, like the day I tried to sell my stock that jumped to 37 points. I called to place a stop-order should the stock go below 33 points…

Instead, I kept getting the receptionist who couldn't do anything for me and wouldn't put me through to the broker who wouldn't call me back. How many people went through this crap before the feds didn't anything about is a shame. Two days of this, and I lost over $50,000.

It's one thing for me to blow the money, but to have people steal it, knowing what they know, well… shame on you. Shame on me for being so damn trusting in spite of the hard lessons.

One afternoon my father and I were talking about my projects, my goal to work in the entertainment world, but at what capacity I still wasn't sure of so I wanted to try it all, especially writing "the book."

"Linda girl, you ought to sell it as fiction," joked my father. "No one would believe all the shit you have been through but the family. Hell, it's a wonder you haven't put a gun to your head. I don't know if I could have handled all you been through."

It hit me. Another point—live for another chance to dream.

Somewhere from the past, my father's voice stirred a vision in my soul, and I saw time go back in my mind with pictures in my head similar to the experiences I had in Chicago back in 1968, like the kind I had when Tommy was alive. A strangeness was around me. My father, dressed as a Roman soldier, pleading with me to go with him, but I pulled away—and I died.

The next picture in my head was a woman in front of an altar, bending over, with blood coming from a self-inflicted knife wound to the abdomen. Maybe there was something to that "old soul" theory after all. wasn't sure of anything except everything changes.

My stability issues kept me moving around the country, never staying too long in one place. I continued to go with my gut feeling, and it was telling me, "Time to move." California dreaming again, I put Kenwood up for sale and made plans to buy an elegant home in need of great repair, my new project: 2340 Laurel Canyon Boulevard.

Working on original material in the recording studios with talented people was everything I wanted to do, but it didn't feel right. I was not as committed to music as I was to my spiritual path of dreams. Writing down lyrics inspired by dreams eventually transpired into a database of information for "the book."

*This isn't the way it's going to end*
*Running with a hit list, a trail of dead men*
*Too many ships have passed from sight*
*They too heard screams in the middle of the night*

# ROLL THE DICE

## Rolling in Crap

*Vehemently speaking*
*The tongue twists he cursed you*
*Tell me now – has he stoned you too*
*Here comes the end of your world no looking back*
*Can you hear God's children cry at night*
*It's time for change*

**B**ack to the West Coast to a better climate, one that suited my all-around interests. In addition to working in the recording studio, I was also attempting to write a screenplay and decided to work as an extra in a couple of movies to see if I even wanted to do this line of work.

Curious about the film industry for reasons to cultivate my writing skills, I also discovered a fond interest in the food they served to the crew and cast. I was told the quality of the food is a good indicator what kind of budget they have to produce the movie.

Leonard was working in Miami near the set of *Absence of Malice* when he and his co-workers had an opportunity to meet Paul Newman, followed by an invitation to have lunch. Everyone working on the set was fed a quality meal: Roast beef, crab, shrimp, and a variety of cheeses with plenty of fruit and vegetables.

During the span working on the set of *Number One With the Bullet*, we were served a quality, healthy meal. The next set I worked,

*Scenes from the Goldmine*, twice in one day we stood in line for the same cold boxed lunch. A happy meal would have been more nutritious.

It was exciting meeting many different people on the sets with a host of talents to offer, though some had a talent to stand out more than others, like Harry Perry. Known as the singing, roller-skating musician of Venice Beach with a turban on his head, Perry had made his way up to the club, where they were shooting the outdoor scenes on Sunset Strip and Vine.

Perry was an extra in a few teen movies in the '80s. We spoke a few minutes while we waited around to be part of a crowd scene. Standing across from me was a punk rocker with a foot-high Mohawk. He kept eyeing the birthmark on my right shoulder. I felt a little uncomfortable, but I waited for it having heard it often. And then he said it.

"You know they would have killed you at birth for being a witch with that mark, it's the devil's mark." A few polite exchanges, he then turned and walked away. Having heard the "devil's mark" before, I was accustomed to this insensitive comment, but unsettling was his "kill me at birth" remark.

"Well, that's a nice how-do-you-do!"

While trying to find a career direction, I made arrangements for the three older children to broaden their academic curiosity, training, and independence. It was essential they learned how to care for themselves, be independent of me, and learn to live with others. I secured their well-being to the Ojai Valley Boarding School.

Tutors and counselors were available on the premises, easing the burden of guilt I carried for my lack of knowledge to help them with homework. I didn't feel too alone, since many parents discover what we learned in school was either outdated or not true. Columbus didn't not discover America, and Pluto is not a planet.

My intention was to give my kids a well-rounded view of the world. Kids from all over the world attended this facility. My children were being prep to enter the world with an open mind, unlike the one-minded world from which I came from. They did very well there.

I saw happiness in their faces when I made my weekly journey to have dinner with them or to pick them up for the weekend.

Nicole was often opting to stay at school and tend to the horses. Michael was a social magnet, and Sheila? Getting *stranger* by the year. The first call came from her teacher, a sweet and kind woman from England, who, by all appearances, was a normal person with an education, who believed paranormal activity was indeed, possible.

"Mrs. King... I'm not quite sure how to say this, but I must ask you. Do you ever get the feeling Sheila can read your mind? When she looks at me I feel like she knows what I'm thinking?"

What do I do? Laugh. I apologized for laughing and explained I had a nervous laugh when something true comes to light. "Yes. I have heard it before."

Living in the country with farm animals is great for a child's emotional well-being. Connecting with nature is a calming experience. Unless you happen to be a fly. Above her bed on the wall, Sheila scotch-taped all the flies she killed in her room.

"I'm warning the other flies leave me alone when I'm sleeping." It made sense to me and I let it go, but I would keep an eye on her... something else was going on with her.

While working on a list of ideas for a book/movie script I found it was easier to write fiction than trying to weave pieces of my life into something legible, believable; above all, into something worthwhile I could share with others with the same concerns or interests.

California in the 80s would be my last attempt at a career in the entertainment industry, but not before suffering another financial fiasco in the commodities market. I took a big hit. I was pretty much cash-flow broke.

And let's not forget shady building contractors, like the one who took my money and went on vacation in Hawaii, leaving the second floor balcony unfinished with no barricade to warn anyone not to step outside. Luckily, I was the one who almost walked off a two-story drop, not my kids. I was pretty ticked off. The contractor said he would return to finish the job in about a week.

A week goes by and I'm fuming. No contractor. I went to check on my five-year old son, who was playing in the yard at the end of the driveway with his truck when a man walked up to him. Everything I experienced came rushing through my mind. Without my glasses on, I didn't recognize who it was. I thought it was the delinquent contractor coming back to finish his job. Boy! He's going to get a piece of my mind!

"I hope you don't think I'm giving you any more money!" Shouting like a madwoman that I was. I ran toward the man when I noticed.

"You're not my contractor!? Shit! I'm so sorry!" I couldn't apologize enough to one of my favorite actors, Robert Hayes. Hayes was visiting a neighbor of mine a few doors up the hill when he noticed Ryan was playing alone, and just wanted to say, *hello*.

Hayes thought my son was a nice kid. I walked back to the house thinking, "that poor bastard." Even if he wanted to ... how could he forget being chased by a crazy woman? The contractor never did show up. More money down the drain.

Then the strangest dream:

*Flying, my body moving fast across the hilly landscape. Below me in a clearing, there was a crowd of people and a priest around a few of the children with long wires attached to their heads. The sun began to shine down on them. Behind them were people in white coats and clipboards. A sense of peace as I flew over them. I wanted to stay and watch but something important pulled me to the cliff's edge over the gray sea below. I landed on my tip-toes at the very edge.*

*Standing tall, looking out ahead of me I raised my arms out for balance and bending my waist, I leaned over the cliff. Embedded in rock, a grotto with the Virgin Mary looking me in the eye. "They have forgotten me... you have forgotten me."* And I woke up.

What the hell was that all about? I wondered. This dream was strange enough to share with my house guests and with Bradley my butler, nanny, chef in-charge. Everyone was clearing the cobwebs out of their heads when I came downstairs to get my coffee. After sharing this dream, I looked down and saw the *National Enquirer* sitting on the dining room table.

"Obviously, Brad made his morning run to the store for his paper." We were all laughing at this routine, it was predictable. Randomly I opened the magazine, thinking how my mom loved to read this rag…

"This is what I dreamed!"

Tossing the magazine on the table, opened to the page I just described in a dream. Everyone saw it for themselves. I never read the magazine. Brad purchased the latest edition while I was still asleep. It was impossible for me to know what was going to be printed. More disturbing was another article in the same edition.

The front cover had a picture of Andy Gibb, claiming he was going broke. Apparently, I was listed among his debtors: Linda Lee King, Esq., $4,000 for limousine rental.

Losing more money than what was coming in, I had leased my limo to a company who chauffeured Gibb around. Mom was laughing her ass off when she read my name in the Enquirer. "Enquiring minds want to know," she teased.

It was a running joke: "Linda made the papers again!"

It was harder to make payments on Laurel Canyon, so I rented it out while I listed it for sale. Then I moved us to the flats of Beverly Hills before heading back to Michigan. It went downhill from there but hey, it's only money.

# IN SPITE OF T ALL

## Adjusting my moral compass

Money, money, money. What can I say, except you can't take it with you—might as well spend it or become a slave to it. Accumulating debt was not a great concern if it involved the well-being of my kids. I learned to adjust my moral compass: *What can I live with? A lot!* I adjusted my moral compass long before I went broke.

During the interim of mapping out a future I could live with, my spiritual road crossed paths with the reality of making decisions in the material world. This quandary proposed situations to test my moral compass, as it does; with every *conscientious* living being.

Keep in mind, rules are for guidance—it doesn't mean they are always appropriate or necessary to follow— even if it is a law. I have broken agreements, laws, and rules on many occasions without feeling remorse or shame, but justified.

When the money was fluid, a few people from the past sought me out for a handout. Many were turned down. I showered relatives and friends with dinners, parties, tires, cash in hand, and I gave a lot of money away. I had to, to honor the promise I made as a child to my God on that swing to give it away and help others.

Most people worried about the money more than I did. And when it was gone, many people were quick to point out my inability to adequately manage the funds and live within my means. But I didn't care what my critics said; still don't.

Granted, I'm not above living beyond my means if necessary. Suppose your child needs to see a doctor and you have no insurance? No money for the office visit or for the prescription you need filled? What would you do?

Some parents will do anything; like me, write a bad check and ask forgiveness later. Robbing Peter to pay Paul pretty much sums it up for most families raising children. No parent can bear the thought of a child going hungry, in pain, or living on the streets.

Society will shun a prostitute or stripper who, instead of accepting welfare, works her body to feed her children. While the same moral majority expects its society to work their bodies for less than a living wage. This is morality, not freedom of choice.

Isaac Asimov, the science fiction author, once said, "Never let your sense of morals get in the way of doing what's right." This quandary is one that eventually all humans will face. Sooner or later, time will test our moral beliefs with a moral dilemma. The question is do you adjust your moral compass to do the right thing?

Over the decades I have made such choices when a few fated circumstances presented themselves. To understand my point of view, I will expose a few of these so-called moral dilemmas I have never regretted adjusting to.

In 1979, I worked as a waitress at the Whale and Porpoise, a private club in Fort Lauderdale. It was before Christmas and we were broke. No presents, no Xmas tree, barely enough food. My best wish was to earn enough money to make it home after work—the gas tank was on empty.

It was a slow night. After three hours, not one dollar in my pocket. Luckily, a few of my regulars sat down in my section. Meanwhile, a man came in acting twitchy. He sat down on a corner stool at the downstairs bar next to the kitchen, where all the waitresses had to pass by.

It didn't take too long to figure out this guy was trouble. Coked up, drinking hard liquor, he made us nervous when he began flashing his money bag around. Asking questions about another girl bartender who worked there. Lucky for her, she had the night off.

# Sticks and Stones and Broken Bones

One of the waitresses spotted Mr. Moneybags at the bar and kept flirting with him, pretending to be interested in his questions, offering to find out when she will be back at work. The guy was high but not stupid. He grabbed a few hundreds and tossed it on her tray.

"That's to go away," he said. "Now stop talking to me." Not another word did she speak. In her hands, four one hundred dollar bills.

A couple of girls tried the same tactic but he had other plans. Every so often he went into the bathroom. Clearly by the powder on his nose, he was doing more coke. His mouth wouldn't stop. His rudeness was getting to me but I kept my composure.

The two young men sitting in my section decided to order food, and as I walked back to the kitchen I noticed that a five-dollar bill had fallen on the ground underneath Money-bags' seat. As much as I needed the money, it wasn't mine and I knew it belonged to Money-bags.

"Excuse me sir," I handed him the money. "You dropped this." Does he say *thank you*? No.

"This is what I think of five bucks!" He crumbles the bill into a ball and tossed it at the bartender. I was pissed. He could have at least said *thank you*. You can push a person so far. So, never be surprised if one day, they just don't give a damn!

Towards the end of the night, Mr. Moneybags started talking about his guns and bringing some of the girls back to his place to do some coke. I warned them to avoid him. He was ready to explode.

Heading toward the kitchen to pick up the food order for my two regulars, I had to pass by the coke-headed freak. As I walked by, he grabbed my hand and put it on his cock. I yanked my hand away. Forget about being pissed, I was livid. Insult to injury sets me off.

Under my breath I kept mumbling, "You're going to pay for that!" I didn't know *how* or have a clue what I was going to do about it but I was through with being nice. The universe was listening.

The bartenders announced "last call." I went to my only table to collect on the bill when I noticed the man at the bar was giving our night manager a hard time. The only male working that night was the cook and he was long gone. Recognizing this situation, I asked the two young men to hang around until this guy left the building.

Some of us girls suspected he was either a drug dealer, a hit man or both—South Florida is notorious for harboring people who live this type of lifestyle. Aware of this made it especially crucial to get him out of the club without a commotion.

Moneybags resisted. He wasn't leaving until he was good and ready, he wanted information on the bartender who ripped him off for 5Gs. That was his story and certainly not the ending he had hoped for.

It was obvious. We had a problem. The man with the bulging moneybag became combative when the two younger men politely asked him to leave so we could all go home. Typical male-macho crap mixed with a lot of coke and liquor set the wheels in motion.

Feeling challenged by the younger man's request to leave without a hassle, macho-man went into fight mode. Jumping to his feet he tossed the money bag across the room and went after the taller guy.

All eyes were on the men rolling around on the dance floor, except mine—I kept them on the prize. The moment the money bag hit the floor, my little brain formulated a plan to teach this asshole a lesson with the universe's blessing. And I had to be quick to pull it off.

"Payback's a bitch named Linda."

Nonchalantly I walked over where the black money bag lay back in the shadows under the upstairs bar. Allowing my full-length skirt to conceal my intentions, standing over the bank deposit bag I dropped a pen and picked it up while my other hand grabbed the bag and stuffed it underneath the waistband of my skirt.

"I'm going to call the police."

Turning, I ran to the front lobby and grabbed the phone to call the cops while I was on the phone I unzipped the deposit bag, at least 10G's. All hundreds. I grabbed a handful of cash and shoved it in my pantyhose. No reason to be greedy.

While I informed everyone the cops were on the way, I kept walking toward the money drop. I had to put the bag back. I needed a distraction. The side door was a few feet away from the brawl.

"Push him out the side door!" I shouted.

That was a good idea. The manager and a few other girls began pushing the two men out the door. Everyone's attention was focused on the action at side door when I let go of the bag, dropping it between my feet. Quickly I nudged it back into the shadows and left to be found by the manager after the cops arrived.

Once the door was slammed shut, the scuffling sounds quieted down to a silent knock on the door.

"It's over," a voice on the other side of the door said. "You can open the door now."

The manager was considering this, when I said,

"How do we know he doesn't have a gun to your head? The guy told us he had guns with him."

No one wanted to open the door. We waited for the police in the corner of the kitchen. Officers arrived shortly after and placed the man in custody. An officer knocked on the side door, it was safe for us to go home and they would wait for us to lock up before leaving.

"That's OK," I said. "I'd rather you leave now so the guy doesn't see us walking to our cars."

We were pumped up with adrenaline and running on high-strung speed when it was over. Either we were crying from relief or uncontrollably laughing. No one suspected my tearful act was anything but our mutually shared emotions from the incident, when in fact, it was an act.

To keep up appearances, I went with the girls to Big Daddy's to unwind and slipped into the bathroom to count the money - $100 bills - trapped between my nylons. My legs were covered in money. I counted $1,000. It was going to be a good Christmas after all. I had two shots of whiskey and went home.

Leonard waited up sober and worried; I was never late before. I explained what happened, playfully throwing money at him. "He didn't even get a hand job," I laughed.

Leonard's face was worth every bill I tossed at him. He didn't know what to say; he had never seen this side to me. Neither had I, and I was loving it. Something about feeling justified was liberating and empowering.

"Don't tell anyone what you did," warned Leonard. "This guy sounds like he could be trouble."

I did tell my father who gave the same advice as Leonard. "Don't advertise it."

In the morning I woke up congested, with a fever and nausea. A few days later the lab confirmed I didn't just have the flu—I was pregnant. A perfect excuse to quit. my job without raising flags. My children were well-fed and had a memorable Christmas. I have never regretted my actions.

At the time the jury awarded me (interest included) $2.2 mil to compensate for Tommy's loss of life, Nicole and Ryan were not included because they were Leonard's children. My children were never raised as half-siblings. The money set aside for the two oldest was also spent on their younger siblings, which I wasn't supposed to do legally, but morally? As a mother? It wasn't fair to give one child more than another child due to their last name.

When money was tight, the kids learned to adjust with a little nudge from me showing them other people had it far worse than they could imagine.

Listening to a radio show one summer morning in 1987, a news story reported a woman in a nursing home had her battery-operated wheelchair repossessed. This pissed me off. Though I couldn't afford to pay the bill, I had to. It took almost a year, but I paid the balance off. However, not before introducing my children to the bedridden Mary Ellen Smith.

The woman's tears of appreciation brought tears to my eyes, and my children learned a valuable lesson in compassion. One person can make a difference in someone's life, and money can never give what the heart needs: love.

The next five years were the same as the last 35 years. Dreams, gut feelings and the occasional paranormal hocus-pocus dominated my immediate world. In 1988, I had an overpowering urge to go to Mexico.

## Sticks and Stones and Broken Bones

After months of planning, the Lincoln broke down, and our journey was detained by a few weeks while I helped my dad and brother put in a new engine. Ironically, the day I arrived in Mazatlan, an elderly man from the State of Washington approached me while I was having breakfast with my daughters by the pool. "Are you the mother of Michael King?"

Naturally, my first thought was, *"What the hell did he do?"*

"Yes, I am?"

"You should know this... Your son saved my life." The chill that ran over me. My spirit voice said, "You can go home now." But did I listen? No. I wanted to stay there for other reasons but it was time to go. If I don't listen to my voice, then so be it. That night, I had a serious warning in a dream:

*My young blonde and blue-eyed daughter, Nicole, had been kidnapped. I saw her terrified face. She was in a type of prison or dungeon being held down by three men who were about to assault her.*

I jumped up in a cold sweat and stayed awake the rest of the night. The next morning, I took Michael in confidence. I could trust him to keep his mouth shut and help me pack our things without anyone, including his siblings, knowing what we were up to.

A woman alone with four kids in Mexico needs to be extra careful. That day I gassed up the car and bought a few things for the road, including some pills the local pharmacist recommended for my upset stomach.

That night the kids went to bed as usual. Sometime after 11 p.m., Michael and I packed up the car, keeping an eye out for anyone who might be watching. I didn't want anyone to see us leave Mazatlan. Once the car was packed, I woke up the three other kids and told them about my dream.

"We're getting out of here, now. Let's go." Without questioning me, the kids piled in the car, and we were heading for Brownstown, Texas. When we crossed the border, Michael took a good look at the cows grazing out in the open fields The experience had a lasting impression.

"Our cows eat better than the people of Mexico," he said. "That's messed up."

The next five years living back in Grosse Pointe, I juggled between jobs, keeping a roof over our heads and the creditors on the hunt. Meanwhile, I continued writing "the book," along with every other brainstorm idea that popped into my head.

Using my personal experiences as a baseline; I was on a quest encouraging people to change their perspective to modern-day problems with positive solutions.

Motivated by statistics released in the late eighties showing the national average dropout rate hadn't changed in twenty years. Since I had dropped out, I was hoping to *fix* the problem at a national level by making it impossible for kids to drop out of school; have them graduate high school at sixteen. Implementing year-round education could be a solution to the dropout problem and certainly realistic in accordance to the working world of everyday business.

My questions led me to do more research. In 1992, I contacted Dr. Charles Ballinger, the executive director for the National Association for Year-Round Education. He informed me the dropout rate still was a problem in their program, but not nearly as high as the national average. One major factor contributed to this problem: self-esteem.

Ballinger recommend reading John Goodlad's "A Place Called School." Goodlad's study indicated that for each year a child spent in school, the lower their self-esteem becomes. Looking at my school experience, I thought, "Wow, that makes sense."

The conversation fueled a cause for improving our educational system and to encourage young minds to believe in themselves. I spoke to many students and parents about the plan to improve the system. After explaining a very detailed *how-to* vision, I gained support but I didn't know *how-to* execute this plan into action without the aid of a politician and money.

Like many ideas, I put this plan on the back burner too, along with the other unfinished projects. But I did manage to write the first draft of one book, titled, *In Spite of I All*. I gave it to Peter Spivak, an attorney and a judge in Grosse Pointe, who tried to find a market for it, to no avail. He ran into a few problems.

First, I wrote the story in third person. *Why?* I couldn't believe I was writing about a person who, in fact, was me. Another problem? I was an unknown, unpublished writer. No experience. *Who is she?*

I had quite a few books started but all lacked that special *something*. I had many chapters written for five different books based on experiences as a single parent, abusive relationships, widowhood, and the Catholic religion—many topics I was familiar with, but I had new problems that needed my focus. Rebellious teenagers. *You can lead a horse to water...*

Yes, I lived beyond means just to keep my kids in the Grosse Pointe School District. At the time, it was rated one of the best districts in the country. Over the years I emphasized the importance of education to my children. I read to them and made them read, too. I didn't want them to struggle as I did. Expressing the importance of an education to get that piece of paper that I lacked, a high school diploma and a college education.

It was a struggle, but in 1993, the two oldest finally graduated high school—two more to go. Michael wasn't ready to be in another classroom—he had other plans and college wasn't on the list. Sheila had plans too, though I'm sure a baby wasn't one of them. Life goes on, in spite of it all.

# STICKS & STONES

## Broken people

In March 1993, my first grandchild was born. Unlike my mother, I didn't tell Sheila "I'm too young to be a grandmother." At the time Maria was born, I was planning a move back to the south Florida area. My plans were coming off the back burner: I would pursue a writing career.

No more relying on chance alone to take me where I needed to be. It was time to make an *active choice* to gain experience and name recognition needed to work my gift of storytelling. Though writing my whole life, this announcement was met with genuine skepticism. I wasn't getting any younger.

Some family members thought I was "too old" (42) to start a career. Plus, I didn't finish high school and I lacked a journalism degree. Why would I let that stop me from trying? I believed in myself, I believed in fairy tales… dreams do come true if you work at them.

The one thing I could do was communicate on paper better than the spoken word. When the world threw sticks and stones at me, I armed myself with pen and paper. Linda Tucker was a friend of mine who introduced me to goal manifestation. Everyday I told myself, "It's time to get paid for writing."

To keep track of my goals, I posted notes along with a weekly bestsellers list on the refrigerator door, next to news articles I had other ideas about. Watching Superman as a kid, I wanted to be like

Lois Lane, news reporter. I saw myself going after the bad guy—without a gun, but with the mighty force of a pen.

"When I get to Florida, I'm finding a job as a writer."

The universe is like a magnetic Puppet Master, pulling its invisible strings to aid in our requests. Within six months of arriving in Coral Springs, Florida, I was employed by *Bachelor Book* magazine. It was the first writing position I applied for.

Sharing personal history with an interviewee often enabled me to hear intimate details that were off-the-record, but essential information for an effective bio. Listening to people tell their life story, I recognize the broken hearted. I was one of them.

Sheila decided to move out a year later, because she didn't want to help pay any of the bills for her child. I had to go on welfare to make ends meet, and I was working, too. By now, maintaining a job that didn't pay the bills wasn't making much sense.

Eventually, I quit due to the unusual circumstances developing at work and home: my sanity was at stake. I got what I needed, more experience, but I was broken again.

My so-called *adult* children were giving me more problems than they did as children. They lacked understanding of the burdens I carried, leaving me to foot all the bills and pick up the mess they were creating for us all. I quit more than my job. I stopped paying the rent and moved to Tennessee for a few months, looking for a positive change.

Without all the details, it was worse. Within 5-minutes after I went inside the store to buy a gallon of milk, a family 'friend' molested my 4-year-old granddaughter. I made my way back to Florida, but not before my name made the news again due to an act of revenge by the family of the accused. Once again I had to exonerate myself in a courtroom, the truth prevailed, and exposed that it was a vengeful act toward my family in retaliation for making a report.

Down and out, I counted on friends to help me when I got back. For a while, Maria and I lived with the Lucchesi family. Pam Lucchesi and I met through our children. One conversation between us created a lifelong bond of understanding and friendship we maintain today.

Pam had a cleaning service, and to show my appreciation for her kindness, I would go along to help. My Motor City roots were deep in motor oil, and sometimes I went to work with her husband Steve at Kelly's auto body shop. He enjoyed having company and taught me to wet-sand, dismantle a front end, and pull off fenders.

At night we would sit around, brainstorming ideas to make money, help the homeless, and especially troubled youth. Steve wanted a unique program to combine counseling and teaching kids in a more natural setting. The goal would be to give children hands-on experiences to reconnect with nature, to learn respect for all living things; a balance lacking in the modern world of education.

Meanwhile, Nicole and her live-in boyfriend, Greg had their first child. Sheila was still living with them when she decided to move east, inviting Nicole's family to join her in Pennsylvania.

Sheila didn't have a mothering bone in her body. She gave me custody of Maria when the baby was five months old. *Why?* After four years caring for Maria, why did Sheila want her daughter back? She rarely saw her in the four years I cared for her. Against my better judgment, I let Maria go. I was sick of it. I had every family member fighting me. I knew *one day*, Sheila would send her back to me damaged and broken but I had to keep moving on my journey.

Still working on "the book," I had other plans to help my professional writing career take off. There was a Chili Cook-off Contest in Fort Lauderdale being promoted by AOL and the local media. In conjunction with the cook-off, there was a lyrics contest. I submitted the first song I ever wrote for my brother David, *Another Man Crying*.

Apparently, I won, but I never showed up. My son Michael and several of his co-workers heard my name over the loudspeaker being repeated several times. "Would Linda King please come up to the stage?" I didn't care anymore about winning. I just wanted to see if the universe was still listening. It was. My dues were paid in experience.

In early Spring of 1998 I left for Hollister, California, in search of another dream as a journalist. Secretly, the goal was to have my own opinion column. "Why not?" I have plenty to say.

# READY OR NOT

## Here I come

California, ready or not, here I come, hanging on a dream. On the way out of Florida, I made a stop to see my cousin Dean. We talked about the years gone by, what the family in general had endured, and what I was hoping to do.

My oldest son's escalating problems with drugs were creating legal issues for him. At the time I was relocating to the West Coast, he was on probation and wanted to get out of Florida. Hoping this fresh start would help him recreate a new life for himself, I made arrangements to transfer his probation to Northern California.

Since I had absolutely nothing holding me back, I was focusing on my career, no excuses or issues to distract me. Dean suggested looking up another cousin, Jeannine, in San Benito County, to help me until I was settled in. It was better than the plan I had, which was the usual live day by day in motel rooms until I was established.

For once, I listened to a family member. Perhaps it was easier accepting my cousin's recommendations because he was my peer and not an authority figure. My issues with authority usually surface when the power robs and abuses the innocent.

It didn't take long. In less than a month, I had my first assignment as a stringer with the *Hollister Free Lance*. Lucky for me, it caught the attention of the editor from the *Pinnacle*. I got a break. Hands-on experience! Marvin Snow taught me how to write as a reporter. I owe my writing career to Marvin.

My time was filled with meetings, interviews, and deadlines, exactly what I wanted but there is more to life than a career. One night, with a passionate desire to end my self-imposed retreat that rejected intimate relations; I called out to the heavens loud and clear.

"Grant me another wish." I had not done that since I was a child.

Expressing my needs to the universe, I dared to ask for affection and attention; someone to love and grow with during this transition in a new town, my new job with another chapter to "live and tell" about. A week later after a planning commission meeting, I met my future fiancé.

Aside from writing assigned articles, I looked for more interesting stories to write about. The human interest story. Mental health, the homeless, unwanted children and animals, too. It was the only way I knew how to help—with words.

In 2000, the *Free Lance* offered me a full-time position, which I accepted. In a few months I convinced the editor and publisher I could write a weekly column based on my experiences: "Tales From Linda's Last Chance Ranch."

My professional life was a safe haven from my family. Between the time differences and my job, I could avoid hearing most of the petty crap my adult kids were causing each other. I had enough problems of my own with Michael and his trouble with drugs.

In July 2003, I broke my ankle. Two weeks later, I was fired. However, my column would still run. One by one, nearly 80 percent of the staff was let go for one reason or another, all over the age of forty. We filed an age discrimination lawsuit that was settled out of court. That's all I can say.

After many heated debates with editors, I knew I wanted to be a publisher. My fiancé supported this idea and backed me up. My philosophy was "just because it 'bleeds doesn't mean the story has to lead.' I wanted a newspaper a kid could pick up without a parent being concerned they were reading something negative.

Meanwhile, I was still writing "the book." Far more complicated than planned. I wanted to write about Tommy's trial, but it was more than that. I wanted to write about being in love or widowhood, but it still wasn't enough.

My terrible parenting skills would make for a good read, but the truth is I could not write "the book" without including the paranormal world I lived in, including my crazy-ass dreams, since they were linked together. I had witnesses to validate my spooky stories. Including my fiancé, a man who claimed he did not believe in God or anything paranormal, until…

Around 4 a.m. on a rainy night, he and I awoke from a dead sleep to a male voice calling my name. *(LINDA!)*

"What?" Uncertain that I even heard my name. "Did you just say my name?"

Just as dumbfounded, my fiancé said to me, "No… I thought you called out?"

"Now," I asked. "Why would I call myself in the middle of the night?" I never heard this voice before. I didn't recognize it. Still, in an eerily and familiar manner, it disturbed me. The next morning, when my fiancé was leaving for work, he found Spats dead below the window above our bed. My special kitty was calling out to me as he was passing.

My fiancé had confusion written all over his face. He heard the same voice as I but his logical brain said, "it's impossible" testifying, "Spats was saying goodbye to you. He wanted to let you know he was passing."

Another critter attached to my heart. Another idea popped in my head: Our life story through the eyes of my animal friends. My Eureka moment caught up in somber awareness that Spats was gone.

I had been telling my fiancé for years that I never accepted the fairy tale that animals have no soul. Also, equally convinced all humans have a sixth-sense ability. Call me crazy, but why should I care if anyone accepts my uneducated theories or anecdotal answers? Does it make a difference? Does it change the facts? No.

How we actually learn, remember things, and solve problems is a collective cognitive process. The paranormal cognitive process is thought to be the consequences of our collective, normal cognitive process that obtains information through our dreams or mental images. One day, my fiancé and I happened to be driving by the home of a young couple expecting their first child. An image popped in my head, and I blurted out, "She had the baby sometime after eight this morning! - it's a boy."

My fiancé didn't care to hear this kind of talk. It went against everything he believed, but he had to consider the facts. A few hours later, word got to us that the couple had had their baby, it was a boy, born around eight a.m. that very morning.

# LINDA'S LAST CHANCE RANCH

## Aromas, California - 2005

All the money and houses were gone. I was back on the road again like a damn gypsy, remembering the little nomad child I was in 1959, going to Grandma's house, leaving behind the soft rolling golden hills of California and a community I had come to love.

Leaving Linda's Last Chance Ranch was my only option. On March 17, 2005, I packed up the last of my belongings crammed into every square inch of my '76 Cadillac Eldorado Classic, then rolled out the driveway heading east to Newfoundland, Pennsylvania, heartbroken.

Looking out the rear window of the classic El Dorado, I said goodbye to Linda's Last Chance Ranch: my home, my animals, an established career in the news industry, and the last man I would allow to break my heart.

Fate, cheated. It was dealing from the bottom of the deck. A full house in my hand, I lost by an underhanded royal flush. Just another bad experience to deal with. Unaware an emotional trigger put a gun to my head, firing another round of post-traumatic stress disorder.

Every success, every failure, well-earned the hard way. Engaged to be married, my fiancé called it quits two weeks later. His political aspirations and financial reputation were far more important than me—time to go. From what he told my youngest son, Ryan, it sounded like his ego was threatened. The closer I got to the Pennsylvania state line, the realization punched me in the gut. I was tossed out like yesterday's news so *he* could be a star in his own universe.

"There could only be one star in *his* life's story, Mom." Ryan laughed, adding a little dig, "He may be the star but he's a very bad actor in his own story."

What a cool thing for a son to say to cheer up his mother. The man I was living with for nearly seven years questioned me after he discovered the credit card payment I sent in was not posted. It happened a *second* time. From where I stood? This was sabotage caused by the gods of fate. I recognized their pattern. In his mind, I broke a promise to keep his credit untarnished.

"I don't know why the payment wasn't posted on time." Maybe someone was lazy or it was the intentional billing practices credit card companies are known for, which he didn't believe they would do. Oh, well. I tossed in the losing hand. Time for a new dealer, a new deck of cards.

Ironically, a year later a documentary, *Maxed Out*, proved credit card companies intentionally held payments past their due dates. I wonder how many relationships were ruined because of this intended practice?

Eventually I realized that the man was looking for an excuse to end the relationship for political intentions. Indicative of a strip miner, wouldn't you say? Marrying me would have been a political disaster, considering my history and our relationship—it made for great gossip in a small community.

Another transition I hadn't planned on and the best I could do? Fake it. At least long enough to *fix* it. Whatever *it* was preventing me from taking the next step down the road ahead. Another state line to cross before I reached the coal mining regions of Northeast Pennsylvania.

Now I was stuck in the frigging cold-ass Poconos a.k.a. the Honeymoon Capital of the World since 1963. Life magazine ran photos of the heart-shape tubs designed for lovers. Great place to mend a broken heart. Better yet, how about a meltdown?

Blurred by the emotional storm in my path, I didn't see it coming: An emotional crisis building. Crash and burn. Night after night, all day long, the tears would fall into a fitful sea of depression, anger, and restlessness. Seeping from my subconscious mind was every emotional drama hidden behind daily distractions. Nothing now to distract the screams in the middle of the night, waking a sleeping household, scaring the grandchildren.

Widowed, alone for nearly seventeen years, I decided to let someone special back into my life. Another relationship ending badly, and I was crying over commercials showing happy families at a table, sharing a meal. All that was me, stripped to create an image acceptable for a news woman dating a political consultant. The gypsy died. It was time to wake the dead.

Driving my adult kids to the edge of their patience, I could not get a grip and shut the waterworks off. They could not understand what they didn't know. How could they? It slipped by the experts my entire adult life. This meltdown went on for two years.

# THE ROAD TO CHAOS

## Welcome back

No longer a publisher of a friendly, weekly newspaper, I had to figure out what I was going to do with the rest of my life. Despite attempts to get back into a career in journalism, my heart wasn't in it anymore. I just didn't know it. I tried to convince myself the lack of interest was a temporary pause.

Looking for work ain't easy when you're 54 years old. One ad caught my eye.

Penn Hills Pocono Resort, Analomink, Pennsylvania was hiring at the Reflections Nightclub. They needed a Master of Ceremonies slash Hostess and Entertainment Director to open up for nightly acts. "Hell, I could do that," I told my daughter. Yeah, I got the job.

The job suited me. It was a break from my depressed routine. I was forced to smile, get dressed, do my hair and makeup. Shedding the old me included changing my style.

Adding a bit of show biz flair, I traded in the drab reporter look and pulled out my gypsy wardrobe, thinking of my Hungarian mother, our past, wondering what will the future bring. "Que sera, sera."

A few impromptu jokes to break the ice while the honeymooners waited for the couples' games to begin. My job as MC was to make everybody participate. "How well you know your spouse?" Keep them happy, laughing, and dancing while the band played.

No matter how small the club or unknown the entertainers are, show biz people smile in public even if it hurts. A lesson my mother taught me in a song. "Smile when your heart is aching." What irony? My opening monologue summed it up.

"So, here I am. stuck in the Poconos with a broken heart, no job, and what do I do? I land a gig at a honeymoon resort club in the honeymoon capital of the world. What the hell was I thinking? I must be a glutton for punishment or raised Catholic, right?"

A few more pokes at my romantic history generated laughter among the couples who obviously were having a good time. It was an opportunity to be creative and spontaneous and to control my mood because the audience counted on someone cheerful and personable. Improving my outlook by default.

A month into the job, Hurricane Katrina hit the Gulf Coast. Every TV news station aired the catastrophic event with 24/7 updates. The real-life drama of mass devastation distracted any singular problems I had. I was engulfed.

Whatever these people were going through was the level of pain and loss I understood. In survival mode, people change their usual behavior when life is threatened. Understandably, but it's no excuse to take advantage of others.

People extended their humanity, helping strangers—a sign of hope, a vicarious thrill—mankind at its best. For all the good being done, another side of the human race exposed the ugly truth. Not everyone cares about their fellow man.

Greedy store owners gouging prices, thieves using the chaos to steal whatever they wanted. Cops deserting their duties. Nurses, doctors, and other professionals abandoning their patients. It was a mess.

Displaced, hungry people. angry beyond reasoning. People trapped in the SuperDome with no food, feces on the floor, everyone humanly reduced to a number in line. What would happen to humanity if the entire world was altered, destroyed by the forces of nature? Would we unite? Or, every man for himself? Katrina proved most people do whatever it takes to stay alive.

Hurricane Rita reminded us all that no one is safe from natural disasters and the inhumanity that follows in its wake.

In a million dreams, despite the weather predictions-no one would imagine the Gulf Coast would get hit again so soon after Katrina. In less than a month, Hurricane Rita bitch-slapped the coast, causing more devastation and trauma. My desire to write was inspired. I was going to Texas, but first stop was New Orleans. I had to see this drama for myself. I gave my two weeks notice.

My oldest son, Michael saw an opportunity to find steady work rebuilding these communities. In two separate vehicles we headed out, Michael, drinking all the way. He was begging for trouble, so I called him on his cell phone. "Speeding, drinking—why draw attention?" It was the worst road trip ever.

All I had was a ghost of prayer he would not crash and kill someone, or get arrested. "Oh my God, Tommy, I don't know how to help our son—please keep him safe—he couldn't take the guilt if he hurt anyone."

The stench of death reeked for miles as we approached the City of New Orleans. Arriving at night, it appeared the road was leading us to the end of the world. For many people, it was. We drove around, avoiding debris in the road, staring at a few boats that had washed up miles from where they were docked. We headed west on I-10 toward Texas.

# FALLING APART

## A monstrous life

Living with my daughter's family was stressful enough, but I was also living with my son, Michael which was harmful to my mental health. He was getting worse, with pills and drinking, badgering and blaming me for his current situation. It was then I made a decision to leave Texas, looking to escape from my family because after living between two households, they were driving me crazy with their constant badgering to *get over* my problems. Michael was looking for steady work in Pennsylvania, when the hurricanes hit. He saw an opportunity to make money and followed me to Texas. I hoped for the best, that he would stop using drugs if he was away from familiar surroundings.

Beaumont, Texas, was a dirty little city covered in oil by-products coming from the refinery factories located in Port Arthur. It had the smell of Hunkeytown—the only thing missing were the Hunkies. Instead it had cowboys and oilmen. I was informed that the two don't mix well.

My son found employment almost immediately. Hard-working young men were needed to help reconstruct the City of Houston and surrounding communities. For me, at fifty-four, finding work was not so easy.

I had made a mistake based on a gut feeling. Texas was where I needed to be. I told my daughter, I believed I would find work as a reporter there. How could I be so wrong? I always follow my instincts. Months, went by with no success. Desperate, I went to social services.

My bags were packed, in the car, my cell phone rang. It was the editor at the Examiner, the first place I dropped off my resume. The interview went well, and I was hired. If everything else in my life would give me an emotional break, I could jumpstart my career in Texas, and find a place of my own. That would have been too easy. It wasn't in the cards.

As fate would have it, a puppy I recently acquired caught parvo, usually a death sentence, though I always have hope beyond reason or financial means. No one tells me medical attention is denied due to lack of funds. I will lie to save a life, even for a dog.

The vet wanted an advance payment to treat the puppy, I wrote a check, knowing it would bounce if I didn't cover it in time. The plan was to pawn my computer, but I didn't make it in time. No big deal, I took care of the bill, but I lost Dylan, the first dog I owned since my beloved Bear mysteriously disappeared from our home in Laurel Canyon nearly twenty years ago.

This was another personal loss, setting me back further into depression. Faking a normal life was getting harder to do. My mind was not focused on work. I struggled with the simplest task. Making phone calls, following up leads to a story; I would break into a cold sweat. I could not pick up the telephone.

It was just a phone, but it may as well been a venomous snake. I felt as if I had made another mistake. I wasn't ready to come back and work as a reporter. I hung up the phone without dialing. My mind was stuck. I had more serious issues with my son, who was losing it. I had to keep it together.

Lighting campfires in the back yard, hollering obscenities at the world was my son's nightly routine, and it was wearing out my last nerve. One night after I went to bed, he was having an episode that included tossing a propane tank in the middle of the blazing fire. I found him kneeling in front of it. Waiting for it to blow. It did.

By some miraculous stroke of luck, the half-filled tank flew in the opposite direction from where my son knelt with his arms stretched

# Sticks and Stones and Broken Bones

out, waiting for the hit that didn't come. In the background, sirens could be heard getting closer to the house, Someone had called the fire department.

At this point, my son was on his own. Avoiding any contact, I slipped unnoticed into the dark house. Maybe they would notice his mental condition and call for medical help. A warning was all he got. The *second* time this happened, another warning, with the threat of charges.

Naturally, the news desk editor saw the fire department's press release with my son's name and address. It was one thing after another in one month. I made the mistake of sharing my personal situation. It was more than the paper was willing to tackle. Don Dodd, the editor in chief had to let me go. I wasn't producing the work required, and my life was "chaotic."

Tell me something I don't know. It was just one more setback before crawling out from the ashes to rise once again, as a Phoenix of change.

Extreme trauma changes a person's neurology and physiology, affecting not just the mind, but our physical brain and body. If you spend a lifetime learning to survive by gut instincts, the immediate flight-or-fight response system built into our brain stays on stand-by. My system was shorting out from an overload—based on the number of traumas I've faced, my brain is fried.

Desperate to leave Beaumont, Texas, to get away from my son for both our sakes, I sold the Caddy and bought a train ticket to back to Pennsylvania. What was behind this compulsive nature to keep moving, without staying too long at one destination?

It was like trying to stop the past from catching up to the present. I was emotionally traumatized.

No distractions but my own erratic thoughts and flashbacks to keep me awake until Philly. Along the way, I began writing a new chapter out of this nightmare until I found another direction. I knew I was a mental case. I heard it all my life. And I was sick of it!

Tired of being a scapegoat for all that is wrong in my family's life or anyone else's while in the same breath telling me how to live my life. As if! I have never allowed any government, religion, or person keep me from living my life as I see fit. So, why now? Why was I shying away from confrontation? I wouldn't defend myself, emotionally retreating into the past.

What I couldn't say out loud screamed at my subconscious mind. This time, it was worse. The more my family attacked my moods and fits of tears as a sign of weakness, the angrier I became. They believed I was "feeling sorry" for myself. I was pissed off! These were toxic tears I needed to purged or be poisoned by doubt.

Certainly, I am not above feeling sorry for myself after a major loss, but after it runs its course, I move on to the next level of recovery. A new me. But not this time. The woman everyone called "strong, resilient, one tough cookie and a bulldog" was a blubbering mess. The accumulation of years dealing with emotional pain caught up with me again.

One dead puppy tripped the trigger. Lost my job, and I was losing my son to his addictions. What the hell am I supposed to feel? Happy?

"Linda, you're the strong one. You have been through this before." The problem is sometimes the "strong" ones need a shoulder to cry on without feeling shame or having to explain their life story. Give me a break, already. How much can a person endure without cracking? My overall health was suffering. About a month later, Michael left Texas and returned to Pennsylvania.

Countless doctors and therapists in four decades never put two and two together, except for one, Doctor Dashael Patel in 2006. It was not anxiety, bad dreams or a case of the blues. It was post traumatic stress disorder.

Tolerating physical and emotional pain is something I'm very good at. Living with back problems most of my life, I got used to it. Unfortunately, it can be harmful to your overall well-being.

A pain level chart was given to me to describe my discomfort from 1 to 10. The number I picked didn't match my facial expression.

"You selected 3, but your face says 8," said the physical therapist.

Osteoporosis, rheumatoid arthritis, a cracked tailbone, a few crushed vertebrae, and more— I was falling apart. Pacing, crying, I was a desperate woman pleading for help.

"Everything hurts, Dr. Patel." For more than 30 minutes, he listened and watched my body language as I explained my living situation, including my insomnia, not getting more than three to four hours a night of sleep. Always tired. Always waking up and crying.

"I'm pissed off!" I said. "My whole life it's been this way! I never get a break. One damn thing after another."

Patel asked me, "When do you first, wake up at night, how long after you fall asleep?"

"Sometime after one, usually," I said. "I get up... lie back down a few times before I can sleep, most times between four and five in the morning I'll fall back to sleep. I've been this way it seems like forever."

Like clockwork, I wake up after 1 a.m. and sometimes exactly at 1:16 a.m. Leonard died around the same hour Tommy did. When I finally calmed down, Dr. Patel said, "Linda, hasn't anyone ever told you before that you have post-traumatic stress disorder?"

Patel said the trauma I experienced in the past was probably triggered by the recent events. The breakup, my trauma history, the job loss —all major life events. My aches and pains were compounded by PTSD.

My issues were seriously affecting my health and my ability to work. Years of being untreated for previous traumas made it difficult in my present situation to cope, which was about to get worse now that my son was back.

Michael left Texas shortly after I did and returned to Pennsylvania. Once again, I was living with an alcoholic and drug user who was self-medicating to hide from his demons. It's a war zone.

"Well, I feel like I have been through one battle after another, just trying to stay alive," I said.

One October night in 2008, the sound of glass hitting the wall above my head woke me up. Shattering slivers of glass covering my hair. The bed, pricking my skin as I quickly got up to defend myself.

The battle had begun. Michael was on a rampage, drunk and high, too high... Sometimes the knives came out. "More knives, that's all I need."

When you've had a knife to your throat on three separate occasions, it does not get any more personal than that. "I'd rather be shot."

Michael was wielding a knife, making threatening gestures at his girlfriend. Rambling on about his soul, the government, and how evil men were, it was insanity. Chasing after my son as he ran after his girlfriend with a butcher knife, I ran up behind him.

Remembering a trick Leonard taught me, I flicked the reflex nerve on his wrist. As always, it worked. The knife dropped to the floor, and I grabbed it, running out of the house to hide it along with the other knives. It was a long night.

Unfortunately, Michael and two of his siblings suffer from a range of disorders based around my PTSD experiences and their own traumas—and it shows. One night it almost went too far for both of us.

It was January 2009, the dead of winter in Scranton, Pennsylvania—bone chilly. Michael again was too high. With the covers over my head, I could hear him open the front door, mumbling how "hot" it was. Aware of his condition I pretended to be asleep.

We had no heat except for an electric heater, and it was 20 BELOW! A few moments later, there was an unusual silence, and I *felt* it: the angels were coming for him. I leaped out of bed, running out the wide open door, to find my son with no coat on, sitting too still in a chair: He was stiff, passing on before my eyes.

"MICHAEL, NO, NO, NO! You can't do this to me." I shouted in the dead of night for help, but no one heard... no one came running to help me. I grabbed him out of the chair and began CPR, pumping his heart, breathing air into him.

"Maybe I should let him go. Get it over with," I thought. Put him out of his misery. A horrible thought for a mother to have. It only made me want him back more. I slapped him, shook him, and screamed for help while I pumped his heart. No one came. He gurgled. I ran to the bedroom and screamed for his girlfriend to help me drag him in. He had come back.

Two days later, I cracked. Michael was drinking as usual, being obnoxious and arrogant.

"Thanks for saving my life, *mother!*" Too glib for my taste, and I was consumed with raging anguish. I grabbed the screen door, beating it, kicking, knocking it off its hinges. I turned to my son.

"I know dead when I see it!" No mother should ever have to do what I did. Crying, I was beating his chest with my fist. "If I were a man, I would knock you out!"

No wonder I don't sleep—bad things happen. I can't be caught off guard. Lives depend on it. Living in this hell, staying guarded saved my son's life.

It was during this period I discovered I had a rare hereditary blood disease known as Hemochromatosis. aka the Celtic Curse. "I guess I was cursed all along," I laughed.

My therapist listened to my life story, including the recent near-death episode with my son.

"Monstrous," she said. "Your life is monstrous."

She was right. I never went back.

However, I did follow my therapist's advice and physically removed myself from the life-threatening problem. I got as far away as possible and moved back to California. I wasn't running away from anything. Leaving a stressful situation is self-preservation. I had been doing it all my life since 1968, changing course whenever I'm drowning in a sea of doubt setting sail toward a new horizon.

# THE UNIVERSE IS LISTENING

## Invisible ears

Since 1968 I have relocated to California five times, slowly working my way up the Coast. This time I would try my luck in northern Cali. In Spring of 2009, I moved to Shasta County, California, "This is where I belonged." At least for now.

Heading north on I-5 toward Shasta County, I vowed to finish "the book." This was it. Do or die trying. Nothing would distract me this time. Chaos, PTSD, dreams and every other drama that played out would not deter me.

Many conversations with my grown children have come full circle: My trauma created issues for them, but their adult issues are exactly that, *their* issues. I did not fail teaching my children basic human kindness, manners, and respect. I did fail to understand the impact of PTSD on their young lives.

The emotional hurt they endured as children was visibly apparent years later when my daughter Nicole recalled that as a child, all she knew was her mother cried every day. That was painful to hear. When my son Michael was in his teens, his demons were beginning to surface. They haven't let go of him yet. My life is still *monstrous*.

In December of 2009, when my granddaughter and I were terrorized by that lunatic I noticed, while yelling at me, he was chewing tobacco like a pig in slop, slurping his drip after he spat in a cup. I was repulsed by his sickness in general, but his evil presence along with the tobacco drool on an empty stomach made me vomit.

After this traumatic experience, I couldn't stand looking at anyone who chewed tobacco without a flashback of our ten-hour ordeal. I told my friend Lisa that I would never even consider kissing a man who chewed "that crap." Me and my big mouth—the universe with its invisible ears heard that.

My bed: no man smell... too sterile, too alone. No need to change the sheets. Evidence of a heavy heart in tow. March 17, 2010, on my wedding anniversary I was reflecting.

Every man I loved died on a *Tuesday*, my father too. Today is one of those bad days. Where was a man of quality, like my dad, like Tommy and Leonard (without the drugs)? Probably dead, married, or hiding in a cave like me. It didn't matter. I had better things to do between dealing with Maria and writing a book.

A good man isn't hard to find. That isn't the problem. Finding a partner who admits having similar experiences of the paranormal nature is a rare bird to find.

But when we're not looking, love comes a knocking on the front door, literally. No matter how old we are. The heart may know what the heart wants, but I believe the soul finds what it needs.

If necessary, the universe will test our misguided social boundaries and beliefs just to prove how willing people change and adapt for love. Six months later, a new man appeared in my life—with the habit of chewing tobacco. At least he didn't drool and wasn't a lunatic.

My son Ryan served in Iraq with Marc F. Dougherty, who had left Colorado looking for a change. After their service, Marc stayed with my son and his family for a short while until it was decided he could move in with Maria and me since we had more living space. A relationship with this man was not even considered—it was the furthest thing from my mind.

My goal was to make sure my granddaughter graduated high school. Also, I needed to finish at least one book, and Marc was younger than I was. Why would a younger man be interested in me? A universal bond pulling the strings? We would spend hours talking, laughing and learning new things about each other. I told Lisa he was smarter than any man I knew.

No drug or alcohol issues. A kind, generous man—the best man to walk into my life, who happened to be extremely handsome and desired by many women. Charming, witty, a diversified thinker, and not a conceited bone about his looks.

"Eye candy, and he's so buff," said Lisa. "That's a bonus. You should jump his bones."

Too wrapped up in my plans to consider an intimate relationship with anyone, let alone a younger man who's never been married or has any children, I laughed my ass off. "Yeah, right."

Marc had one advantage. He knew something about me through stories my son told. It also surprised me that he knew my brother John. I found it curious to learn that while Marc was cleaning out his jeep, he had the same print I did: Van Gogh's *Café Terrace at Night*. I had bought the exact print a few months before because I'd wanted it as part of my goal manifestation exercise. One day I planned to visit France.

After many months forming a friendship, Marc and I became very close. We talked openly about the worst mistakes we'd ever made without feeling self-conscious or passing judgment on each other. Marc wanted to learn French, travel to France, and the world. It was his childhood that struck a familiar chord.

Marc had PTSD, too; not just from Iraq. We had a common history. He too, was four years old when he saw a man tragically die. The rest of his youth was spent in violence, fighting bullies but that's his story to tell.

Marc left for a few months because he was being sent to the Veterans Hospital in Menlo Park for PTSD treatment. Meanwhile, my name was on a waiting list for therapy. While in treatment, Marc called nearly every day to give me an update, describing what he'd learned. In turn, I was learning more about my own issues.

When Marc came home, our relationship grew beyond friendship. Now, we have been living together going on four years. I'm not concerned about creating a future together with Marc. The only guarantee is the present moment we have that matters.

Marc recognized the hordes of triggers that my granddaughter set off. She was impossible to deal with. She had no respect for herself let alone anyone else. Throwing things at us, stealing my meds, and lying. Then she dared to raise her hand at me. Hell no. This is elder abuse.

It was time for a take-down. I used one of those tricks my father had taught me when I was fourteen, and she was flat on her ass. PTSD triggered my response. I felt threatened because I was. If I choose to be afraid, I remain a victim. I have been the victim of many misdeeds, but I don't live like a victim—I do something about it.

Not everyone likes my methods, but it's the madness I don't have to live with. I made arrangements for my granddaughter to go back to Pennsylvania after high school graduation. This is what she wanted all along. She never wanted to live with me. Her issues were her mother's emotional abandonment and neglect.

Graduation day wasn't far off. My granddaughter needed to find a dress. She wasn't happy with anything she found in Redding. I agreed to take her to Chico, dreading the two-hour drive with her nasty mouth. I warned her, if she acted up in public it would trigger the dictator in me.

It was a pleasant day after all. We were heading back home when for no reason at all, I felt *something* calling for me to turn right... to take the long way home. I turned the wheel and began driving into the Lassen National Forest, heading toward snow-covered terrain and isolation.

"We're going to do some sight-seeing."

Maria wanted to go straight home. She wasn't planning on a side trip, she had made plans to meet up with friends. "This is boring," she said. "It's taking too long."

I wanted to be alone with Maria and talk about things without distractions to keep us from having a heart-to-heart conversation. She could be anything she wanted to be, she didn't need her mother's approval. I encouraged her to fight the negative energy—be herself. "Listen to the voice in your head, not your mother's words of doubt."

Maria, upset we weren't home yet, began to complain. "I told you we shouldn't go this way." I explained if someone is doing you a favor, you don't order them around.

"Besides, I listen to my inner voice and it wanted to go this way."

Maria didn't understand why we didn't go back home the normal way. "We know what's down that road," I said.

"There's something about this (Mt. Lassen) area I wanted to explore ever since I moved up here. I don't know why but I felt had to go this way."

Having a spiritual conversation with Maria was important. I spent most of my life unaware how negative thoughts begat negative results. I couldn't let her go into the world without sharing that, even if she didn't believe me. I advised her to pay attention to the energy coming out of her mouth. Not a kind word she uttered.

"The universe can hear you, Maria." Be positive with that energy or all the negative crap will come back at you." But this was mumbo-jumbo to her. I was "crazy" and didn't know what I was talking about.'

"It doesn't work like that, Grandma," Miss-know-it-all snidely replied. "And it's stupid."

Was it stupid of me to turn down this road? Or was it the universal chord in my head playing a tune? The scenery was magnificent... a Eureka moment for both of us. A song began softly playing in my head, then it crescendoed into a booming revelation.

We drove past a sign marked, "Bogard Campground." We were traveling on the same road our Bogard ancestors had over a hundred years ago. I wasn't surprised, I was elated. I had listened to my spirit voice.

"Maria! Look, Bogard Camp. That's our family name! Now, tell me—was it stupid I listened to my voice? Something has been pulling me to come up here. Now I know why."

This tempered Maria's mood, and she accepted what had happened as "weird" while I explained further. "This is what I'm talking about... that voice inside your head, Maria, it can save your life. Learn to listen for it—don't block it out. There was a reason the universe brought me here."

Maria needed to know her spirit voice. A valuable lesson she would come to learn in a short time but not before the hard lessons of bad choices. Her self-hatred had nearly cost her life. In less than two years, she faced death's door., twice overdosing on drugs. Then a major car accident nearly burned her and a friend alive, but that inner voice screamed at her, "Kick out the window." Maria did, and pulled herself and her friend from the inferno. It was a wake-up call.

Maria knew it was just short of a miracle that she and her friend survived. It opened her eyes to see that the path she was traveling would claim her life. My hope is that she will always hear her spirit voice and not rely on others for happiness.

All the girl ever wanted was her mother's love and affection, not her resentment. But you can't get blood out of a stone. My daughter is very much like my mother was at keeping an emotional distance, but unlike my mother, my child downright abandoned her daughter. My siblings and I knew our mother loved us, but never Maria... even when she was close to death, her mother could not show her child compassion.

How could my child be so cold to her daughter? Regardless how unbalanced I felt, I was never cold or distant with my children. If I had a bad day, it was especially important to talk it over with their subconscious. I told them how much I loved them even while they were sleeping. I would whisper in their ear how wonderful they were, kissing their foreheads and playing with their hair.

The relationship between mothers and daughters in the last four generations of our family had my wheels turning. Was there a pattern in our family history for this behavior? I wanted my mother's attention. Maria wanted hers.

As a child, Sheila had rejected my attention, just as did my mother did with me when I was small. However, it didn't make sense that even with Mom's thing for "boys are better than girls," she favored Sheila for some reason over the other kids. Here is the kicker: My grandmother and mother were exceptionally close.

When my grandmother died, my mother was lost. She had called Grandma every day as part of her morning routine. Then she started calling me. We talked about our issues, how often I was accused of things I didn't do, but what I also discovered was that the more I learned about the woman I had feared as a child, the more I understood that she was in fact, *still* a child.

An innocent victim of violence, a witness to life-and-death events at an early age, mom had memories (flashbacks) just like me. Our mutual pain brought us closer together. When it was too much for her, she would say, "Today's a bad day."

In time, I learned how to read between the lines. A silent pause between words meant it was a horrible day. Painful memories ruled her heart, and emotional distance was her way to "toughen us (girls) up."

Listening to Mom throughout the years, I filled in the blanks with the information provided to me when I was younger. "You have to put up with more crap… men can walk away from their problems."

I remember thinking, "This is nuts!" My father never walked away from anything. What was she talking about? Mom was talking about *her* father.

It took many years and plenty of tears to understand the extent of damage from parental and spousal abandonment, but I suspected my children had been affected as well. Sheila was displaying the same pattern with Maria.

Emotionally neglected and abandoned, Maria was shipped off to another family member every time there was a problem. Would you feel wanted? Loved? Deserving? How do you *fix it*?

My concern was that future generations born from this dysfunctional pattern will suffer the same hurtful behavior learned in the last four generations. This was a good enough reason to finish "the book." A guide for my dysfunctional family. How to get over it in forty years or less.

# "THE BOOK"

## A piece of work

Most of my life has been devoted to writing "the book." A piece of work. It was simple: "Write what I know." Sometimes, it wasn't that simple. I knew plenty: Something was missing. Often, running into a mental roadblock, I was forced to take detours, researching what troubled me. If permitted, the soul finds what it needs.

When I had my meltdown in Pennsylvania, the PTSD factor needed to be addressed. Armed with new information revealed, I wasn't "just a little hyper," as Ma kept saying. I was in a "hyperarousal" state of mind as the result of life-altering traumas.

PTSD explained a lot about my behavior. It didn't answer the mystery of paranormal activity or the great traumatic sorrows our family endured. My ancestors, it appears, had an unwilling penchant for witnessing tragedy.

If I shared my offbeat views, strange dreams, or the weird experiences outside the family circle, many people laughed. Family members just describe this as "kooky." To many who value money, I am a financial joke. I have no mansion, but I do have debt collectors on my back. Yet, here I am. Like a bad penny, I'm back. And I'll keep coming back every time, looking for the Eureka moment. I get it.

It would be physically impossible to prove a paranormal universe working behind the scenes of our life. Yet if I neglected to include this important piece, what is the point of writing this book at all? At least I had another family witness when I allowed my soul to take me down Highway 36 to discover that our family's history is well documented in Northern California.

Maria and I discovered the Bogard Ranger Station Camp on a "coincidental whim," some might say, but that's not true. Laugh all you want, but a spirit voice whispered in my ear, "Turn here." No other information was provided to me. I had no idea that our Bogard bloodline had extended this far from home. I wondered if some unknown ancestor's spirit was influencing me to discover my history in Northern California.

My moment of Aha! Eureka! "I get it... History is in the blood."

I wasn't quite sure what I meant by that blanket statement when I said it, but I was going to find evidence to back it up. I did: A first cousin four times removed, John Jasper Bogard lived in Red Bluff, California with his wife, Annie (Gibb) Bogard, whom he married in 1880 in Shasta County.

Not only had my ancestors lived in the area, but J.J. Bogard was a local hero and had served as the sheriff of Tehama County. He was shot and killed on the Southern Pacific during a famous train robbery on March 30, 1895, in Sutter, California. Bogard blood split in violence. He was forty-three years old.

J.J. killed the robber Jack Brady, but Browning, Brady's accomplice, was outside the car. He shot the sheriff and escaped, leaving three children fatherless. He was caught two years later and imprisoned until paroled in 1940.

The more research into our family's history I did, the more questions surfaced. Did our family have a violent history? There may be some truth about the sins of the father passed onto the next generation. It's genetic, in the DNA, not the sins of the father.

Nagging questions persisted in the back of my mind, genuinely concerned for my family's future. How to change a dysfunctional pattern? What else did the dead pass on from one generation to the next? I found a trail of violence dating back to the Revolution.

Several generations of Bogards died young, tragic deaths, leaving young widows and children orphaned throughout the family history. I found a few shady Bogards, who were violent, political and religious zealots. A multi generational problem? Reflecting on this, I went down another path.

While researching information about the long-term effects of trauma within a family's history, I found a study was conducted on mice by geneticist Professor Marcus Pembrey and researchers at Emory University School of Medicine in Atlanta.

Pembrey discovered traumatic experiences could be passed down to the next generation of mice, suggesting that an experience of our ancestors might be a transgenerational response passed on through DNA, and the cause for an individual's irrational fears and phobias.

Does history repeat itself within families through a transgenerational reaction? What about memories of another lifetime? Is it reincarnation or a manifestation from an ancestor whispering in your ear? I don't know, but I do know this: In the early 1990s, I had a vision that felt like a past memory.

*In our dreams we are told*
*Coincidental history unfolds*

It was somewhere out west in California. A warm, sunny afternoon. It looked like me, standing on a modest wooden porch looking out towards the east, a wagon was approaching. I was excited to see my friend coming to visit. That friend was Linda Tucker but it was the wrong century—this was the late 1800s. The zinger?

As I described the scene to my friend, Linda could see my vision like she was there, then began describing the dress I was wearing, while waving to her. It was the same dress I made thirty years earlier when I lived with the Jones family, a gingham print like women wore on a ranch. It was the only dress I ever made.

How could this memory effect both of us? How could Linda Tucker describe a dress she never knew I made? This was all philosophical fodder to feed my head.

Analyzing and philosophizing about life in general is something we all do. I could share my wacky ideas with my father. Though my tendency to debate any philosophical view is based on personal knowledge, my father advised to remember a very important rule.

"Don't over-analyze or you'll miss the obvious answer under your nose." Dad also commented that philosophers didn't make a lot of money, adding, "It's a great hobby."

In recent decades, the paranormal began gaining scientific interest emerging from the dark ages of the 50s, 60s, and 70s, when people absolutely denied the supernatural with an exception to the rule: angels, the Devil, and God, all acceptable paranormal beings.

From the second, I caught a whiff of "onions melding in wax," permeating my nostrils one mysterious night in 1955, I have known our ancestors' spirit roamed. They speak to us in our dreams, whisper in our ears, helping us along our earthly journey.

My first paranormal experience was sixty years ago. Edgar Cayce and Sigmund Freud, though long gone, have cleared the way for reputable research into the paranormal and dreams. In light of recent discoveries I decided to do my own research. "The book" took another turn.

First of all, an uneducated theory I had for years is that all humans are capable of a sixth sense. Second, did certain anxiety disorders trigger this dormant portion in the brain?

Curious to see if a life-threatening experience can spark a heightened sixth sense as opposed to the hyperarousal symptom of PTSD and other disorders, I presented one question to fellow members on a PTSD forum.

**Has PTSD increased any psychic abilities?**

At the time, of the 111 people who participated in the poll at ptsdforum.org, 67.9 percent said "Yes." When comparing the national average that three in four Americans believe in psychic phenomena or have had an experience with the paranormal. PTSD did not make a difference for many people.

A few respondents had tricky answers, voting "no" while claiming a "sixth sense" experience. Yet for various reasons they were reluctant to post *yes*. A few people also noted experiencing paranormal activity before PTSD. The point is, keep an open mind.

Albert Einstein once said, "Science without religion is lame; religion without science is blind."

Most people have a religious belief or a feeling that something greater created the universe. Science aims to understand how it works and our role in this amazing space and time. Religion and science are catching up.

After decades, dodging the dubious questions of life after death, and the paranormal, some scientific researchers decided to take another look into the arena of the supernatural. Universities around the world are conducting extensive research of the human brain. In the last decade, remarkable findings how the brain functions while performing telepathic or experiencing paranormal activity has caused some scientists to search for proof to the spiritual experience. Looking for the "God" link.

More people are brought back to life today because of modern technology, many reported near-death experiences. It was the increased number of people reporting these experiences that could no longer be dismissed by scientists.

Today's technology can test our brains and monitor our sleep, the following studies show there may be more to that *gut feeling* when something tells you "turn left." Standing in front of you: the man who killed your husband.

More than thirty-three years ago, Dr. Moody opened a door, and not a window to the other side. Many reputable names have followed down this path. Among them neuropsychiatrist Dr. Peter Fenwick, also a senior lecturer at the Institute of Psychiatry, Kings College, London, UK.

Fenwick's scientific findings on NDE were released in 2003. A number of the experiments supported the theory of a human "sixth sense" that may be linked to the past when the ability to sense a predator was a matter of life and death.

Dr. Fenwick has suggested the human mind may very well exist outside the body as an invisible magnetic field. The idea people are capable of paranormal experiences such as telepathy and out-of-body experiences is supported by research with NDE patients.

With this information floating around in my head, the magnetic field theory was pulling me in. What do I find? Butterflies.

In an unrelated study, it was discovered proteins in the human retina can, in fact, detect magnetic fields, as they (proteins) do for all living things. Even if we cannot see a magnetic field in front of us, our brain still can: A possible, physical connection to the "sixth sense" theories.

Dr. Steven M. Reppert is an expert on navigational skills of the Monarch butterfly and a neurobiologist at the University of Massachusetts Medical School. Reppert, with his colleagues Lauren E. Foley and Robert J. Gegear, has been studying the human cryptochromes (proteins) in the retina.

Their research found that protein in the human retina reacted to electromagnetic waves and is particularly sensitive to blue light. This raises the possibility that the magnetic field may act like a visual warning system after all. Just because we can't see something doesn't mean it isn't there.

In a separate study, researchers at Washington University in St. Louis have identified an area of the brain called the anterior cingulate cortex, that checks out our environment for signals that indicate danger. Joshua Brown, Ph.D., a research associate in psychology, authored these findings, suggesting that science needs to explore sensory biology in people.

To make things more interesting, scientists elsewhere have discovered and identified areas of the brain that, if damaged, can develop increased spirituality. One spot in particular, is the right side of the head.

*"Whack?"* Another Eureka moment. The right side of my head has taken quite a few blows, by a 2x4, for one. Was this the cause for my intense spiritual quest? A whack upside the head? Hell, I hope not.

With a Ph.D. in health psychology at the University of Missouri, Dr. Brick Johnstone conducted a survey among patients with brain injuries. He concluded that spirituality is a complicated phenomenon, proposing that many areas in the brain are responsible for the types of spiritual experiences we have.

Meanwhile, on the other side of the planet, Dr. Cosimo Urgesi at Italy's University of Udine searches for mystical answers by using the neural basis for spirituality through neuroimaging..

A neuroscientist, Cosimo and his colleagues Salvatore M. Aglioti, Miran Skrap and Franco Fabbro, authored *The Spiritual Brain: Selective Cortical Lesions Modulate Human Self-Transcendence*, a study of patients before and after surgery to remove a brain tumor.

After examining the neuroimaging of these brain injuries, a network of activity was discovered within the brain connecting the frontal, parietal, and temporal cortex to spiritual experiences, with more activity happening on the right side of the brain.

What causes this link from injury to spirituality is yet to be determined, but any life-threatening event will awaken a person's sensibility to appreciate the life they have, no matter how horrible things are.

Imagine, all these scientific minds from around the world extensively researching the capabilities of the human mind. Each researcher on a separate path, yet despite different perspectives and goals, concluding there was a connection—but what is the link?

Perhaps determining the causative link to spirituality or a sixth sense would be easier to solve if more scientists collaborated on research. And certainly, a multigenerational approach to solving genetic physical and mental health issues is a preventative measure that would benefit all mankind; no more sociopathic leaders dictating the lives of others.

If society knew in advance the mental health status of a potential political candidate, we could eliminate the wackos who use the rest of mankind as pawns in their power struggle to control the world with their fanatic ideals. Hey? *I can dream about changes.*

Give all political candidates CT (CAT) scans, MRIs, DNA, and psychological analysis. Why not? Let's avoid finding reasons not-to do things, as in the Affordable Health Care Act (Obamacare).

Wasting time and money trying to stop health care instead of figuring out how-to make it happen. A healthy society is a productive one. A mentally healthy society promotes positive change for humanity's future. Stop speculating and over-analyzing problems. Start fixing the issues with positive actions. And use your words wisely—the universe responds to all energy.

If you say, "I can't," "you won't." Say "I will," and "you do."

Eventually, our human improvements could impact society as a whole. We must change or be doomed to repeating the same painful pattern that leads to war and violence. It is evident that the cruel aftermath of such atrocities is transmitted through generations to come.

Science and religion have crossed paths for centuries. It's time they joined forces and realize they seek the same answers, but have selected different paths to follow in their quest for truth.

Attorney Tom Robillard pointed out to me during an emotional transition, "It's not where you start out in life, Linda, but where you end up."

The world began in chaos. It will end in the same manner. I'm not concerned about the earth coming to an end. I have a feeling humans will be relocating to another world. It's our humanity that concerns me.

According to WHO (the World Health Organization), violence is becoming a worldwide public health problem. It's escalating with each generation born into a violent culture.

"Many who live with violence day in and day out assume that it is an intrinsic part of the human condition. But this is not so. Violence can be prevented." Nelson Mandela, 2002.

# PTSD

## The next sleeping giant

*Remember men in need do dirty deeds*
*Masses of nations paralyzed in fright*
*They too heard screams in the middle of the night*
*This isn't the way love is going to end*

No one is safe from inhumanity. Every second of the day, good people around the world are subjected to the cruel, sick intentions of others. Often, I'm in the wrong place at the wrong time. I'm lucky in that way.

I am a functional human being with a few flaws like obsessive compulsive disorders, depression, and PTSD. This little malfunction in the brain is like waiting for the other shoe to drop, but it never does.

Countless times, my good-natured spirit was violated by bullies, abusers, and sexual predators. Despite attempts to destroy my life and take my humanity, it's still intact. Damn lucky, too, for the rest of the world. It doesn't need another bitter victim.

Violent crimes has affected millions of innocent people worldwide. Today our world is becoming more desensitized to the pain and suffering of others. The stress of materialism, the insanity of religious fanatics, and the political games behind a veil of secrecy all add weight to existing problems. Hateful, cruel acts of intentional violence are plaguing society, creating a perfect breeding ground for PTSD, the next sleeping giant.

Not everyone wants to rule the world or be rich and famous. Most people want to enjoy the wonders of life, find a purpose, and not worry about having enough food on the table or being afraid of other people. Who are we fighting? Ourselves? Who is the real enemy of mankind?

Personally, I have had more guns and knives pointed at me than I can count. I have been mugged and thrown in front of a moving car. I have jumped from moving cars and witnessed the shooting death of my husband.

With all this on my plate, not once have I considered suicide as an option. *Why should I?* Again and again, someone else was willing to put a gun to my head or slit my throat. Sure, I was afraid, but deeply angry, too. Nothing had the right to crush my spirit, not even PTSD.

Up until the 1980s, post-traumatic stress disorder was unfamiliar to most civilians because this mental health problem was a combat soldier's issue, when men who were traumatized in war were commonly labeled *shell shocked*.

You may know that shell-shocked guy, the one sitting at a bar, alone. Maybe, a beer bottle drops, but the guy hits the floor, covering his shell-shocked head from imaginary debris. He's having a flashback. It's a common reaction when hearing any loud, unexpected sound to duck and take cover.

The younger patrons laugh at this war reenactment. A few older ones understand. They lend a hand, helping the veteran to his feet while lecturing the "ignorant bastards" on the lasting effects of combat. "It isn't funny to see your buddy blown to bits..."

PTSD among civilians was never considered until it reached a level that could no longer be ignored by health officials. So, in 1989, the National Center for PTSD was created to extend information to civilians who survived violent traumas such as rape, aggravated assault, child and spousal abuse, or any other severe accidental trauma.

The National Center for PTSD is managed by the United States Department of Veterans Affairs (DVA). The DVA recently reported that PTSD is a major public health and behavioral health problem, affecting more than 10 million Americans at some point in their lives.

Imagine what it must be like for the rest of the world? Countries where civil war is constant, women are often treated worse than dogs, and children forced to kill other children. Is this our past or our future? A worldwide succession of broken people.

Millions of people are brutally treated across the globe. Society accepts these atrocities, in part because war is expected to happen. The next generation of children who are raised under these suspect conditions are profoundly influenced by the unhealthy mind of the parent(s) and their traumatic experiences in an insecure, dangerous world.

Recently, Save the Children reported, more than two million children in Syria were affected by the Syrian civil war. Children and teens who suffer severe traumas tend to have the highest levels of PTSD symptoms.

Sadly, too many children of Syria have lost their families. How will they recover, if no one is there to comfort them when the flashbacks strike? An answer I can only wish for: It will take more than a village to help these victims.

Polluting our minds is mainstream media, the vehicle used to change public opinion with its subtle messages that create a false sense of security and happiness, followed by a word from our sponsor advertising products we don't need. In the meantime, those orphans will still need help, not a sound byte.

We are overrun with ads showing "happy people" using the right toothpaste or shampoo to "get the girl or guy." These expectations are impossible to live up to. For starters, happy people don't count on someone else for their happiness. Happiness is not possible if you count on everyone else for it.

If anything, "happy" ads send a hopeless message that promotes self-destructive behavior. Not skinny enough according to the ad? A bulimic is born. Self-absorbed ads. "It's all about me." Unimportant crap to keep us believing everything will work out just fine if you buy this product or some "ideal" to keep the sheep in line. Desensitizing humanity one sound byte at a time. "It's the real deal."

The world is revolving around materialism and greed instead of evolving spiritually. In the last century the desensitization of mankind rapidly progressed with the visual aid of main street media. Images of the Twin Towers crumbling with all those people inside, have affected millions. Before Iraq and Afghanistan, there was Vietnam.

Civilians watched the drama of war take the stage on the nightly news. At times, live coverage of soldiers running for cover. Then the bodies, frozen at the time of death. Civilians, visibly aware the casualties of war were women and children, too.

Most of America did this nightly ritual while they ate dinner. Parents, wives and children straining to see if the soldier running pass the news reporter was a loved one. How surreal is that?

Media needs to rethink its job as messenger. When television was invented, no one could foresee the long-term effects it would have on society. No one ever thought sitting at the dinner table could cause a mental health problem. Yet it happened. Mankind is traumatized. The world, an eyewitness to murder, war, and every ugly side of the human condition.

Social media is a tool that should be used more to correct the atrocities damaging the heart and soul of mankind. Quit giving the politicians air time. Let the voice of the victims be heard over and over until something is done about it.

The National Center for PTSD reported that one in three women in the U.S., will be sexually assaulted in their lifetime. For many, the sexual and physical abuse began in childhood, as it had with me. However, what I went through is nothing compared to 150 million women and young girls forced to undergo female genital mutilation. My point is more than 80% suffer from PTSD. That is the data collected by WHO's Global Program on Evidence for Health Policy.

The World Health Organization began collecting worldwide information on PTSD in the 1990s. The majority of the countries participating reported more than 50% of the victims who had experienced extreme violence suffered from PTSD. The truth is, this is much higher, but many victims feared retaliation and would not participate.

Society is left to contend with the emotional casualties suffering from PTSD because of the inhumane actions of others who violate our personal beliefs, our bodies, and our lives. There is a sleeping giant among us, and if mankind's future relies on the next generation, we are in trouble.

In between a series of violent crimes are the victims, a family of emotional misfits harboring more drama than a Shakespearean play. The aftereffects of extreme trauma can follow families into the next generation, as they have with my family, which brings me to the bigger picture.

What are we breeding as a society but perversion, violence, and fanaticism sewn in with our inter-generational brainwashing. Have we become so desensitized that no one can realize this? Or don't we care anymore? It's personal. It's global. Crimes against mankind are destroying humanity.

The circumstances of a moment in time may have robbed me of happiness, but no one can keep me or anyone else from being happy, it's a choice. I don't have God-given answers. All I have are the anecdotal observations from living through experiences that mar the heart, but not my soul or the will to live vigorously with a big fat smile on my face.

It would be prudent to ensure that society's mental view of the world is a healthy one. Healthy thinking will help disable the destructive behavior that follows a person and their family after a tragedy strikes.

The way people treat each other is heartbreaking. More and more people lack basic simple manners, the cornerstone of civility. No one ever came up to me asking, "May please put a gun to your head?" Let's face it: violence is uncivilized.

When you hear the sad truth, feel free to cry until you laugh at blind ignorance. Whatever emotion it takes to feel something; anything, to help understand that to those suffering from PTSD, it isn't funny. The sleeping giant awakens from its slumber, hungry for truth - not the spoon-fed gruel of conformity.

Soon enough, millions of PTSD children will become adults. Many will suffer a lifetime of anguish without receiving any mental health treatment, ending up homeless or in prison. I am one in a million of casualties, alive but not so well, just lucky enough to figure out what to do for myself before it destroyed me. I have lived with PTSD and the paranormal since early childhood. Today is a good day.

# EPILOGUE

Another summer has slipped into fall. My internal clock is counting down the seasons of my life, another birthday reminding me that this mission isn't over until the last breath. What I will do today to improve the quality of living for all life around me? For starters? Turn the radio up.

The world is not black and white; it bleeds red with violence. A sleeping giant lies dormant in the aftermath of violence. One moment in time changed my life forever, but it never changed my spirit's quest; only my determination to live this life the way I see fit.

Worn out from the latest news, tweets, blogs, and Facebook posts, I opted for a little music to start the day. "How does your light shine in the halls of Shambahalla?" An upbeat tune by Three Dog Night to put anyone in check.

Shambahalla, a mystical place, just as Atlantis is said to be, but maybe not? It's all perspective, isn't it? If you believe in a heaven and hell, why not Atlantis, or Shambahalla? The point isn't a place, but *how* the soul shines.

I still have panic attacks and other PTSD episodes I live with. Using PTSD as a productive tool can be helpful whenever the "Rainwoman" in me is stuck on one way track. If, I cannot see past my issue... I pick up a rake, a shovel or a paint brush and I start to work on "fixing" what I know I can, while the other problem works itself out in my subconscious, where the root of the problem exists.

The challenge the human race faces is finding the common ground between religion and science, politics and humanity. Not to believe everything we are taught but to question its validity in relationship to our current issues. Outdated views will always be championed by the next generation if it doesn't ring true for them. As it should be.

If you are looking for answers, this is not the book for you. However, if you believe one person can change the world, imagine what we all can do with one goal in mind, to repair our world of broken people with the power of universal love.

I have lived life with the understanding that there is an invisible world where the spirit and flesh meet before we are born, a paranormal belief. Religious and government institutions set rules for us to rigorously live by without consideration—life has many exceptions to the rules that challenge our moral compass.

In spite of all my pain, I find joy waking up every day with the possibility of learning something new. Also, not to resist when the winds of change are taking me in another direction to challenge conformity with common sense.

Most of all, I've learned to be happy in my world because no one is responsible for my happiness. The dead are gone but some will hang around if you need them. As for my men, I have spiritually evolved from the woman they married. I'm more than OK with that. I've learned that my spirit is capable of loving more than one soul. Besides, I don't want to pick up where I left off in the next life because I can't move forward in this one.

Every ugly hand that fate dealt, forcing me to reinvent myself, has only strengthened my cause for the sake of humanity's next generation of children Intervention and preventative measures must be implemented if mankind is to survive this cycle of insanity.

It is true that "what doesn't kill you does make you stronger." But it doesn't magically happen; it takes effort and the faith to carry on despite our fears. Courage comes later.

Who I am and what I have become boils down to a simple testimony of my personal beliefs I held as a child, regardless what the Catholic Church had to say about it.

As human beings, our purpose is to help each other grow with our experiences, no matter the cruel or embarrassing manner with which we acquired the knowledge of this experience.

A *monstrous life*? Yet I desire to wake up every morning curious to what the day will bring, with or without my interaction. Craving the sun and a cup of coffee, life is everything I hoped for and more. I have lived gigantic dreams with monstrous results, but a monstrous life? Hardly, but an interesting one.

In an unusual way, I did become a missionary like the ones I met as a child. I have surrounded myself with damaged people in need of kindness. Knowing what it feels like to be hungry, I feed anyone in need. Knowing what I do about the idiots running the planet, we're all lucky to be alive.

An interesting life, yes it is. A monstrous life, indeed. A charmed life, most certainly. No one knows the half of it, but I have escaped death more times than what is written. I consider myself the luckiest woman alive. This book is just the beginning of my story. Imagine, what I haven't said.

Since the first homeless man I had found one cold winter day, dead on the streets of Detroit, I have actively championed for the less fortunate. A meager attempt to show appreciation for my *charmed life*.

What readers experience from this piece of work is unknown. My human condition is meant to inspire a desire in others to rediscover the child that once explored everyday as a mystery. Everything I don't know about life, I am grateful for another day to discover something phenomenal about this planet and still be as amazed as a child of four.

Fate alone or aimless luck aren't the only forces that change our life: Destiny requires participation. Visualize a goal and work toward it. Every road leading me here, a learned lesson to fulfill this mission and write what I know is true. This book is to lift the veil of sorrow from the eyes of my children, may they see how much my world means to me, with them in it, though separated by miles, of land and differences; in my heart- you are nearer to me, than ever before.

My written request to the universe: *Please* show my children the way back to the children they once were, to see life with the eyes of child, and listen to the spirit voice from within—it begs to live.